## About the author

David Henley is Professor of Contemporary
Indonesia Studies at Leiden University. He
obtained his doctorate from the Australian
National University and has worked as lecturer
at Griffith University, as researcher at the Royal
Netherlands Institute of Southeast Asian and
Caribbean Studies (KITLV), and as research
fellow at the National University of Singapore.
His fields of interest are the politics, history
and geography of South-East Asia, particularly
Indonesia. From 2006 to 2012 he was a coordinator of Tracking Development, an international
research project designed to compare Asian and
African development trajectories with a view to
identifying practical policy lessons for development and development cooperation in Africa.

# ASIA–AFRICA DEVELOPMENT DIVERGENCE

## A QUESTION OF INTENT

*David Henley*

Seattle, 14 Nov. 2017

Zed Books
LONDON

*Asia–Africa Development Divergence: A question of intent* was first published in 2015 by Zed Books Ltd, 7 Cynthia Street, London N1 9JF, UK

www.zedbooks.co.uk

Set in Monotype Plantin and FFKievit by Ewan Smith, London
Index: ed.emery@thefreeuniversity.net
Cover designed by www.roguefour.co.uk

A catalogue record for this book is available from the British Library

ISBN 978-1-78360-278-0 hb
ISBN 978-1-78360-277-3 pb
ISBN 978-1-78360-279-7 pdf
ISBN 978-1-78360-280-3 epub
ISBN 978-1-78360-281-0 mobi

# CONTENTS

# FIGURES AND TABLES

## Figures

## Tables

# ACKNOWLEDGEMENTS

This book grew out of Tracking Development, a research project with the ambitious aim of comparing the development trajectories of South-East Asia and sub-Saharan Africa over the last half-century. Running from 2006 to 2012, Tracking Development was financed by the Netherlands Ministry of Foreign Affairs with a view to obtaining practical policy advice regarding the conduct of development cooperation in Africa. My book remains true to the aims of Tracking Development, both in its methodology and in its aspiration to provide results that are relevant for development planning in Africa. However, it concentrates mainly on three pairwise country comparisons (Indonesia/Nigeria, Malaysia/Kenya and Vietnam/Tanzania) and presents a concise, relatively consistent, but necessarily simplified overview of some of the patterns emerging from the comparative data. The central thesis is that the great divergence between African and South-East Asian development performance since 1960 results not from differences in geographical or institutional endowments, but simply from the absence in most parts of Africa, and the presence in most parts of South-East Asia, of a serious developmental intent on the part of national political leaders.

Tracking Development remained throughout its existence a facilitative rather than a prescriptive undertaking, based on a common methodology rather than a common set of interpretations and explanations. Accordingly, it generated diverse and sometimes contradictory views on the causes of the Asia–Africa development divergence (Fuady 2012; Berendsen et al. 2013; Van Donge et al. 2012; Kilama 2013; Kinuthia 2013; Un Leang 2012). Although my conclusions in this book owe something to almost all of the researchers and research components involved in the original project, they are in the final analysis my own conclusions, based on my own reading of the data. I would like to stress, however, that they were not preconceived conclusions. The key arguments regarding the importance of developmental turning points, of correct macroeconomic policy choices, of pro-poor public spending and of the 'developmental mindset' were not conceived a priori, but emerged from consideration of the data itself, and were refined through a process of iterative confrontation with further statistical and historical material from the countries in question.

Some words of explanation are perhaps in order regarding my own experience and its relation to this work. A geographer and a South-East Asianist – more particularly, an Indonesianist – by training, I conceived Tracking Development in 2005 (together with Deborah Bryceson, then of the African Studies Centre in Leiden) in the hope of putting what I had learned over the years about South-East Asia to a worthier and more practical use than I had previously been able to. At a time when despair about Africa's development prospects was still at its height, the idea that the key to an escape from the African impasse could be found in South-East Asia's spectacular – and, until it happened, largely unanticipated – development success was a captivating one. At a personal level, however, my greatest inspiration here was the memory of my own surprise, twenty years earlier, not on realizing how much faster development was taking place in Asia than in Africa, but on realizing how much faster it was taking place in Asia than in Europe.

Although Tracking Development was a new direction for me, it also harked back in some ways to my own earliest experiences in Asia. Like many others I became fascinated with South-East Asia essentially by accident, as the result of a backpacking holiday I spent in that region while an undergraduate student. Among the things that most struck me about the countries I visited were their unexpected modernity, their rapid development and the sense of optimism and progress which pervaded them. The economies of Indonesia and Malaysia were growing at the unprecedented rate of 7 per cent each year, and it showed. Almost from day to day, new skyscrapers, motorways, factories, hospitals and schools were springing up from the rice fields.

I was impressed, and surprised. At school and even at university, I suddenly realized, I had been told a great deal more about the problems of the developing countries than about their achievements. I was not blind to the negative aspects of the changes I saw, or of the political regimes which directed them, and I was disturbed by the juxtapositions of wealth and poverty. But unlike many visitors I felt no aesthetic revulsion for the South-East Asian idealization of progress. I admired the high modernism of Singapore and Malaysia and the optimistic aspirations of Indonesia and Thailand. Their orientation towards the future and their acceptance of rapid change made my own country, Britain, where in many places even the cracks in the pavement had not changed for generations, seem a tired, slow old place, weighed down by the past. In South-East Asia I thought I saw something of the confidence and excitement, as well as the problems and confusion, which Britain had known in its own great era of progress and transformation in the nineteenth century. Two decades on, it was partly the memory of this insight which inspired my conviction that the study of South-East Asian development history could also throw light on the contemporary African predicament.

Between 2005, when Tracking Development was conceived, and the present (2014), public perceptions of Africa's development prospects have changed considerably, with almost universal pessimism giving way in some quarters to unbridled confidence that a new cohort of 'African lions' or 'African cheetahs' is being born to match the 'Asian tigers' of the late twentieth century. In this book, I suggest that such optimism is for the time being exaggerated. African economies may be growing fast, but poverty in Africa is not falling nearly so fast, and certainly not as fast as it did in South-East Asia during that region's transition to sustained growth in the 1960s and 1970s. Still less does any part of Africa appear close to the kind of industrial transformation which the leading South-East Asian countries underwent in the 1970s and 1980s. The reasons for this, I believe, have to do with contrasting policy choices, and ultimately with underlying differences between African and South-East Asian ways of conceiving, or imagining, the whole development process. These differences, in turn, have their roots in the cultural history of the two regions' encounters with modernity, the world economy and the West.

Writing this now, I am struck once again by a possible analogy from British history. Cultural historian Martin Wiener's inspiring 1981 analysis of British economic retardation, *English Culture and the Decline of the Industrial Spirit*, opens with an apt quotation from British politician Enoch Powell: 'The life of nations no less than that of men is lived largely in the imagination'. National imaginations, of course, do not operate in a political or historical vacuum, and the present book is not meant to imply that African policy-makers are free to create whatever developmental futures they care to imagine for themselves and their countries. Like Wiener's book in relation to the United Kingdom, however, mine does aspire to contribute in a small way to a process of consciousness-raising, whereby decision-makers in African countries may come to see more clearly how their habitual ways of imagining the future have held them back from choosing those courses of action which would have led to the greatest good for the greatest number of their compatriots.

The Tracking Development project was in many respects a bumpy ride, but for me it was also an inspiring intellectual adventure, and I hope others will remember it that way too. I remain deeply grateful to the colleagues with whom I shared it. Above all my thanks go to Deborah Bryceson, together with whom I conceived and launched the project, and to Jan Kees van Donge, my counterpart 'regional coordinator' on the African side during the final phase of the endeavour. Although he may not agree with me, Jan Kees is actually one of the few Africanists with whom I usually agree, and this book owes a lot more to him than he probably thinks it does. Special thanks also to my co-researchers in the Indonesian part of the project, Ahmad Helmy Fuady and Riwanto Tirtosudarmo, and to 'project officer' Ursula Oberst, who frankly had an awful lot to put up with, and did so with great strength of character. Ursula also had a direct input into this book, as some of the South-East Asia regional aggregate statistics in Chapter 1 were calculated with her help. Among the other 'TD-ers' I would like to mention Akinyinka Akinyoade, Han ten Brummel-huis, Joseph Fernando, Hamidin Abdul Hamid, Blandina Kilama, Bethuel Kinuthia, André Leliveld, Un Kheang and Un Leang. The departure of Tran Quang Anh from the team due to chronic illness was an unforgotten loss to the project and indeed to the academic world, as well as a personal tragedy.

Many others less directly connected with Tracking Development have played important roles in the writing of this book, whether as key inform-ants or as sources of intellectual guidance and inspiration. They include Ari Kuncoro, David Booth, Jan-Paul Dirkse, Do Duc Dinh, Stephen Ellis, Richard Gozney, Arie Kuijvenhoven, Peter Lewis, Othieno Nyanjom, Seth Kaplan, Tim Kelsall, Emil Salim, Howard Stein, Thee Kian Wie and Ali Wardhana.

Tracking Development was supported institutionally by the Royal Netherlands Institute of Southeast Asian and Caribbean Studies (KITLV) in Leiden, and by the African Studies Centre (ASC), University of Leiden. In addition it enjoyed strong and consistent personal support from KITLV director Gert Oostindie, from KITLV Head of Research Henk Schulte Nordholt, and from ASC director Ton Dietz, who also had his own direct research input into the project. In concluding the writing of this book subsequent to the formal termination of the project at the end of 2011, I have benefited from the support of my current employer, the Leiden Institute of Area Studies, Faculty of Humanities, University of Leiden.

Outside the Netherlands a large number of international partner institutions was involved at one stage or other in Tracking Development. Among them I would especially like to thank the Asia–Europe Institute of the University of Malaya, Kuala Lumpur, and the independent research institution REPOA (Policy Research for Development) in Tanzania, which were responsible for the organization of conferences held under the auspices of the project in Putrajaya and Dar es Salaam respectively.

Funding for Tracking Development came entirely from the taxpayers of the Netherlands, via the Dutch Ministry of Foreign Affairs. I sincerely hope it can be said that with this and other 'deliverables', they have got their money's worth in terms of results that are of direct relevance to development cooperation in Africa. The ministry and its embassies and ambassadors in several countries also provided efficient practical support for TD-related events, while several ministry officials in The Hague, notably Martin Koper and Maarten Brouwer, were intellectual contributors to the project in their own right. So too was the chairman of the TD Steering Committee, former Netherlands ambassador to Tanzania Bernard Berendsen. To them and to their colleagues at the Ministry of Foreign Affairs, where I and my academic colleagues were always treated both generously and seriously, I am extremely grateful.

The most important figure on the ministry side, without whom this book would certainly never have been written, is diplomat, writer and public intellectual Roel van der Veen. It was a conversation with Roel in 1996 in Jakarta, where he was then stationed, which sowed in my own mind the seeds of the ideas which led to this work. Later, back in the Netherlands, he provided strong initial support for the idea of Tracking Development in ministry circles, and went on to stand by the project through good times and bad. Along the way, Roel's thinking on development issues has on many points so closely paralleled my own that sometimes I am not sure any more whether it was me or him who came up with a particular phrase or idea.

South-East Asia's development miracle has been one of the greatest world events of my lifetime, not just in terms of a spectacular economic and social transformation, but in terms of something much more important: the relief, on a massive scale, of human suffering and deprivation. When I first went to Indonesia in the 1980s, it was in the process of achieving what was at that time the biggest, fastest poverty reduction in all of human history. In the twenty years between 1970 and 1990, some fifty million Indonesians escaped for the first time from the most abject poverty. At the same time the national average life expectancy rose by almost two decades as countless people survived who would previously have died at birth, or in infancy, or later of disease and malnutrition. In Malaysia and Thailand, advances of similarly epic proportions had been achieved at slightly earlier dates; in Vietnam and Cambodia, they are still being achieved today.

It has been a privilege for me to witness something of this miracle with my own eyes, and a privilege too, as part of the research on which this book is based, to speak in person with a few of the people, now old men, who were directly responsible for bringing it about. For the miracle did not happen spontaneously, or by some historical accident. At the level of individuals and households, of course, it owed much to the hard work, resilience and ambition – so often underestimated – of ordinary South-East Asian people. But it also depended on opportunities being available for people to seize, and this would not have been the case if their governments, the privileged few who had power over them, had made the wrong rather than the right decisions. I would like to dedicate the book to the memory of a man whose decisions were both righter and more politically influential than those of any other, and who consequently did more good for more people than almost any other individual in history: Widjojo Nitisastro (1927–2012), the quiet technocrat who steered Indonesia's national development effort throughout its most successful and benevolent years, and who sadly passed away in 2012 in Jakarta. It would have been a great honour for me to meet him.

My greatest thanks, finally, go to those close to me who have been affected by my many absences, physical and mental, as a result of this research: Antoinette and Niamh, who have had to put up with a lot already, and Daniel and Ann, who first taught me that in the end, all the academic stuff doesn't really matter that much.

# 1 | DIVERGING PATHS

Fifty years ago when the colonial empires ended, most of the globe, including the Asian as well as the African tropics, was inhabited by peasantries facing very low living standards. Since then, the tropical world, the South, has diversified into a wide spectrum of development outcomes. On the one hand, there are successful countries with export-oriented manufacturing industries and productive, commercialized agricultural sectors. At the other end of the spectrum are countries where, despite increasing urbanization, subsistence farming still forms the backbone of the economy, and where the only significant export industry is oil or mineral extraction. While the successful developers have experienced vast improvements in living standards, many of the countries left behind are still almost as poor as they were fifty years ago.

The reasons for this great divergence are of obvious importance to everyone concerned with development and development cooperation today. This book sets out to investigate them in the context of the two regions of the world which most clearly exemplify the diverging paths to prosperity and poverty: South-East Asia and sub-Saharan Africa (Figure 1.1). The present chapter introduces some basic data and briefly summarizes my main arguments and conclusions. For more detail on any point, readers are referred to the more complete information and argumentation presented in subsequent chapters.

In South-East Asia the 1960s, 1970s and 1980s all saw sustained and accelerating economic growth. By the 1990s only Burma, among the major countries of the region, was still missing out on what was acclaimed as an Asian development miracle (World Bank 1993). Although the financial crisis of 1997–98 revealed vulnerabilities in South-East Asia's economies, it only very briefly halted their expansion. In Africa, by contrast, such dynamism remained absent. By the early 1990s even those few African countries where security and policy conditions had long been considered promising, such as Kenya and

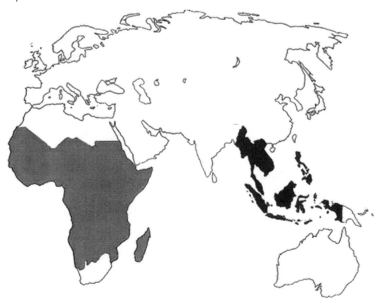

**1.1** Sub-Saharan Africa and South-East Asia

Côte d'Ivoire, were falling into the continental pattern of instability and stagnation. Scholars identified a negative 'African dummy' as a statistical predictor of comparative economic performance (Barro 1991), and counterposed an African 'growth tragedy' to the Asian miracle (Easterly and Levine 1995).

Since the late 1990s there has been sustained growth in national incomes in Africa due to improved macroeconomic policies and liberalization of markets, together with increased world demand for minerals, coffee, cotton and other primary products. But by most accounts, there is little sign yet of this rapid aggregate growth translating into comparably rapid poverty reduction. If poverty is still present among marginal and dispossessed groups in South-East Asia, in Africa it is still the norm. And whereas the bulk of South-East Asian exports now consists of manufactured goods, Africa still manufactures almost nothing which the rest of the world wants to buy. South-East Asia, to complete the irony, has outstripped Africa even in the export of traditional African agricultural products such as palm oil, coffee and cocoa.

Historically, both regions formed part of the world's economic periphery, exporting forest products (spices, ivory) and later commercial tree crops, and importing manufactures. At the local level their economies were subsistence-oriented and their societies organized on a peasant or tribal basis, often without educational or business institutions of indigenous origin. Commerce, in both regions, was associated with trade-specialized ethnic minorities – historically often Islamic, later also Asian (Indian/Chinese) and European. Over large parts of South-East Asia as well as most of Africa, indigenous state formation was limited prior to colonial intervention. In the middle of the twentieth century, both regions were still substantially under European rule. Climate and soil conditions in both regions are generally problematic for arable farming, and people and livestock are subject to similar health problems.

These historical and geographical similarities make the comparison of South-East Asia with sub-Saharan Africa a sharp tool for the analysis of development issues. Insofar as the research on which this book is based has precedents, they have most often involved the comparison of Africa with economically successful Asian countries in general, including Taiwan, South Korea and even Japan (Lawrence and Thirtle 2001; Lindauer and Roemer 1994; Nissanke and Aryeetey 2003a; Stein 1995a). But North-East Asia, by almost any measure, was already much more different from Africa fifty years ago than was South-East Asia: better governed, more educated, more industrialized (Booth 1999, 2007). In analytical terms, selecting South-East Asia as the unit of comparison helps to reduce the number of potential explanations for the observed developmental divergence. By the same token South-East Asia's policy experience, as the World Bank's *East Asian Miracle* study rightly noted (1993: 7), is more relevant than that of North-East Asia to other developing countries, including those of Africa.

Another good reason for comparing Africa with South-East Asia is that since the 1960s both regions have been characterized by corruption and a notorious lack of 'good governance'. Certain features of African politics which are often said to explain economic stagnation in Africa (Chabal 2009; Chabal and Daloz 1999; Van der Veen 2004; Van de Walle 2001) are also present in economically successful South-East Asia. In both regions, rent-seeking is common in government positions in connection with what has been called 'neo-patrimonialism': a fusion of public and private spheres in which patron–client relations structure political behaviour. Some of the same cultural phenomena currently blamed for development failure in Africa, including a preference for personalistic power relationships, have been equally pervasive aspects of the South-East Asian political scene (Robison and Hadiz 2004; Scott 1972). In South-East Asia, some have even argued, patron–client ties between politicians and businessmen may serve precisely to facilitate economic development (Braadbaart 1996; Khan and Jomo 2000).

Corruption and clientelism, then, cannot in themselves explain African economic retardation. Correlations between indices of 'good governance' and economic growth rates, as Mushtaq Khan (2007: 8–16) has shown, all but disappear once already rich countries are excluded from the database. Among developing countries, those with rapidly growing economies hardly differ from slow growers in terms of corruption and institutional quality (Wedeman 2002).

Some authors have tried to qualify this observation by distinguishing between 'organized' (Asian) and 'disorganized' (African) forms of corruption, the former being centralized and predictable and the latter competitive, unpredictable and incompatible with growth (Lewis 2007; Kelsall 2013; Macintyre 2001). On close inspection, however, this distinction is not entirely convincing either, since some African countries have seen long periods of political stability during which illicit rents have been centrally managed by dictators or tight-knit ruling oligarchies. A particular aim of this book is to take issue with the influential school of thought which ascribes developmental failure in Africa to the ways in which political power is *organized* on that continent, as opposed to the ways in which it is *used* (Bates 1981, 1983; Lewis 2007; Ndulu et al. 2008; Van de Walle 2001). I argue that the great developmental divergence of the last fifty years between Africa and South-East Asia has been caused first and foremost by differences in the *policy choices* of governing elites, and that in both regions, as Bannerjee and Duflo (2011: 271) also conclude in their book *Poor Economics*, 'it is possible to improve governance and policy without changing the existing social and political structures'.

Accordingly, this will be a book on development in which the voices of the historical actors who have actually made development policy in practice, and of contemporary eyewitnesses to the policy-making process, will take precedence over the voices of academic commentators on development. While theoretical debates are certainly not ignored, politicians and planners whose decisions have influenced the development trajectories of their countries will be quoted as often and extensively as will canonical writers in the field of development studies. In my view it is the first-hand experience of key historical decision-makers which provides the best insights not only into which policies work and do not work, and why, but also into the reasons why particular policies are chosen, or not chosen, in particular times and places.

## Scope of the divergence

In 1960, South-East Asians were on average much poorer than Africans; by 1980 they had caught up, and by 2010 they were two and a half times richer. In South-East Asia the whole of the intervening half-century was a period of almost continuous growth, apart from a brief hiatus at the turn of the century caused by the Asian financial crisis. In Africa, per capita income stagnated in the 1970s, declined in the 1980s, grew weakly in the 1990s, and in 2010 was still barely higher than it had been in 1975 (Figure 1.2).

The recent aggregate growth in Africa has caused the 'Afro-

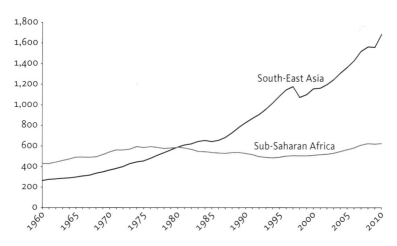

**1.2** South-East Asia and sub-Saharan Africa: GDP per capita (constant 2000 US$), 1960–2010 (*source*: calculated from online World Development Indicators/ World DataBank, World Bank)

pessimism' of the 1990s to be replaced in some circles by a conviction that the Asian tiger economies are now being joined by a fast-developing group of 'African lions' (McKinsey Global Institute 2010; Radelet 2010). But there is a vital difference. Although some researchers believe that recent progress in African poverty reduction has been underestimated (Sala-i-Martin and Pinkovskiy 2010), the consensus is that the aggregate growth in Africa since the 1990s, like that of the 1960s and 1970s, has not translated into commensurate reductions in poverty (OECD 2011: 12, 62–5; UN Economic Commission for Africa 2011: 3).

In South-East Asia, by contrast, spectacular economic growth from the 1960s onward was accompanied by even more spectacular reductions in poverty. In Thailand the proportion of the population living below the national poverty line fell from 57 per cent in 1963 to 24 per cent in 1981 (Rigg 2003: 99); in Malaysia, from 49 per cent in 1970 to 18 per cent in 1984 (Crouch 1996: 189); in Indonesia, from 60 per cent in 1970 to 22 per cent in 1984 (BPS-Statistics Indonesia et al. 2004: 13); and in Vietnam, even more dramatically, from 58 per cent in 1993 to 19 per cent just eleven years later in 2004 (Nguyen et al. 2006: 9). In 2005, according to World Bank and United Nations figures, the proportion of South-East Asia's population living on less than the equivalent of US$1.25 per day was 19 per cent, against 39 per cent in 1990. In sub-Saharan Africa it was 51 per cent, against 58 per cent in 1990 (UN 2011: 6).

The same divergence is evident in other indicators of material well-being. In the 1960s, life expectancy at birth for inhabitants of both regions was still under 50 years (although South-East Asia was aready slightly ahead owing mainly to a somewhat less malign disease environment). In 2010 it was 54 years in Africa, and 70 years in South-East Asia (Figure 1.3).

The absolute decline in African life expectancy between 1987 and 1997 was partly due to Africa's AIDS epidemic, but also reflected generally poor healthcare and nutrition, with levels of infant and child mortality much higher than in South-East Asia. In education, too, Africa, although making more progress than in other fields, still lags well behind South-East Asia, where universal primary education is the norm (UN 2011: 16).

South-East Asia, like Africa, emerged from colonial rule with

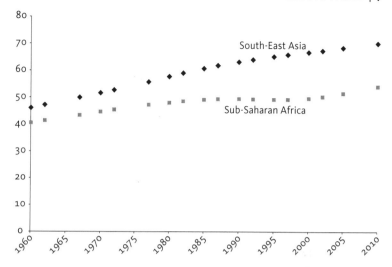

**1.3** South-East Asia and sub-Saharan Africa: life expectancy at birth (years), 1960–2010 (*source*: calculated from online World Development Indicators/World DataBank, World Bank; missing data estimated using WDI 'method of gap filling')

predominantly rural economies, based on peasant farming and the export of primary agricultural products. Subsequently, oil exports also became important in Malaysia, Indonesia and Vietnam. Unlike exporters of oil and primary commodities in Africa, however, South-East Asian countries have succeeded in diversifying their economies and their exports, notably into manufacturing. In 1970 only 5 per cent of Thai exports by value consisted of manufactures; by 1995 they constituted almost three-quarters, including integrated circuits and office machines as well as clothing, footwear and plastics. In 1980 less than 3 per cent of Indonesian exports consisted of manufactured goods; by 1995, they constituted more than 50 per cent. By the end of the twentieth century Malaysia alone, a country of under 25 million people, was exporting more manufactures each year than the whole of sub-Saharan Africa, with its population of more than 600 million (online World Development Indicators/World DataBank, World Bank).

## Origins of the divergence

In the search for the origins of the developmental divergence between Africa and South-East Asia, the methodology of this book is not to compare aggregated statistics for the two regions. Instead the analysis concentrates on three sets of paired nations which, while broadly representative of the general regional contrasts, are also in important respects particularly comparable with each other: Indonesia/Nigeria, Malaysia/Kenya and Vietnam/Tanzania. No claim is made to absolute consistency here: the three pairs do not receive strictly equal attention (Indonesia and Nigeria playing a somewhat privileged role), while evidence from certain countries not included in the pairs, notably Thailand and Rwanda, will also be adduced in passing. Nevertheless, my core method is to compare the divergent development trajectories of the paired countries, looking carefully for clues as to the causes of the divergence.

The comparison of Nigeria and Indonesia is an obvious one that has already attracted considerable scholarly attention (Thorbecke 1998; Bevan et al. 1999; Lewis 2007). Both countries have experienced long periods of military rule, and are similarly ranked in terms of Corruption Perception Index. Both are also large, densely populated and well endowed with natural resources, notably oil. The second pair, Kenya and Malaysia, consists of two countries that have opted rather consistently for a 'capitalist road' to development, relying to a great extent on private ownership of the means of production, and on foreign investment. Tanzania and Vietnam, by contrast, are both countries which for a long time relied on state ownership and direct government intervention, and which have subsequently liberalized their economies.

The pairwise method differs from the dominant approaches to cross-country comparison, which attempt to explain growth differentials either through multiple regression analyses of time series data for many countries (Barro 1991; Easterly and Levine 1995; Johnson et al. 2007; Ndulu et al. 2007), or through explicit model-building and the identification of 'anti-growth syndromes' (Ndulu et al. 2008). While these approaches have produced valuable results, I believe that the one followed here offers sharper insight into the connections between policy choices and economic outcomes. Particularly important is the identification of *successful* policy choices. There is no shortage of critical works on development and development aid, but to compare disappointments with triumphs can be uniquely constructive and inspirational (Bebbington and McCourt 2007). This does not, of course, imply the possibility of infallible prescriptions.

It has been said with some justification that there has been too much planning in development policy, and that attention can more profitably be directed to 'searching' (Easterly 2006). The research reported on in this book has been an exercise in searching. It has also followed Dani Rodrik's (2007) admonition to compare the various policies that have succeeded in particular settings, and to look beyond them in order to extract general principles that can also be applied in other settings.

In my search for these underlying principles, I and my colleagues in the Tracking Development project (outlined in the Acknowledgements at the front of this book) began by putting together comparative narratives of the selected countries and looking for turning points: dates at which two crucial development indicators, per capita GDP and poverty incidence, showed a lasting turn for the better, leading to sustained growth in combination with sustained poverty reduction. Then we attempted in each case to identify the specific circumstances, in particular policy changes, responsible for the turning point. Such positive turning points are found only in South-East Asia, and they function as templates against which to compare and contrast the sub-Saharan cases. In Indonesia, for instance, the year 1967 marked the end of a long period of stagnation in welfare (Van der Eng 2002) and the beginning of a sustained and rapid

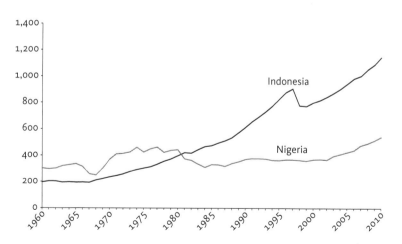

**1.4** Indonesia and Nigeria: GDP per capita (constant 2000 US$), 1960–2010 (*source*: online World Development Indicators/World DataBank, World Bank)

growth in per capita income which, apart from a sharp but brief decline in 1998 and 1999, would continue uninterrupted for the next four decades. Nigeria, by contrast, saw a brief, largely oil-fuelled burst of GDP growth from 1968 to 1974, followed by decline in the 1980s, stagnation in the 1990s and renewed growth only since 2002 (Figure 1.4).

Malaysia's sustained growth, by the same criterion of per capita GDP, began almost a decade earlier than Indonesia's in 1958, gradually accelerating – temporary fluctuations aside – in a gently concave curve for the next fifty years. In Kenya, by comparison, average per capita income has not grown significantly since 1974 (Figure 1.5). In relation to this country pair, however, it should also be noted that in the mid-1950s, before Malaysia began its developmental take-off, its per capita GDP was already more than twice Kenya's.

Our third country pair, by contrast, mirrors the continental pattern (Figure 1.2) of initial African advantage. In the 1980s Tanzania still enjoyed a higher average per capita income than Vietnam, but in 1986 the latter embarked on a steadily accelerating growth trajectory which enabled it to overtake Tanzania in 1994 and exceed it in per capita GDP by more than 50 per cent in 2010. This despite the fact

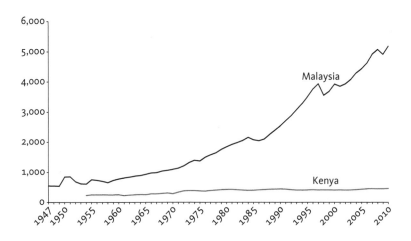

**1.5** Malaysia and Kenya: GDP per capita (constant 2000 US$), 1947–2010 (*sources*: online World Development Indicators/World DataBank, World Bank; Malaysia 1947–59 calculated from Lim 1967: 28; Kenya 1954–59 calculated from Leavy et al. 1963: 339, 341, 359)

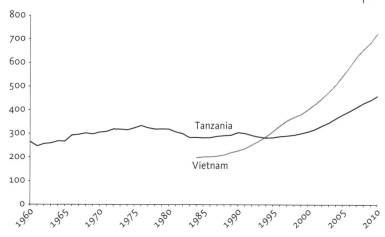

**1.6** Vietnam and Tanzania: GDP per capita, 1960–2010 (*sources*: online World Development Indicators/World DataBank, World Bank; Tanzania 1960–87 calculated from Tanzanian Economic Trends 1991: 73)

that Tanzania itself has also shown growth since 1995, and quite rapid growth since 2000 (Figure 1.6).

Statistics on poverty are available for our paired countries only on a very discontinuous basis, and subject to interpretative difficulties arising from uncertain reliability and definitional changes. However, the poverty data we do have confirm that the recent aggregate growth in Nigeria, Kenya and Tanzania has not yet led to anything like the kind of mass poverty reduction seen in South-East Asian countries during their early years of sustained growth. Poverty levels, of course, do not track per capita GDP precisely because they also reflect the level of inequality in the distribution of national income. Indonesia and Malaysia both saw the proportion of their populations falling under their respective nationally defined poverty lines plummet by tens of percentage points in the 1970s, and Vietnam has seen an even more rapid reduction in the last decade. Poverty incidence in Tanzania, by contrast, is today only a little lower in proportional terms than it was in the early 1990s, while in Kenya it is more or less unchanged, and in Nigeria it actually seems to have increased quite dramatically over the same period (Table 1.1 below).

I will argue that the crucial and persistent contrast between the development performance of the two regions in terms of poverty reduction reflects an equally crucial and persistent contrast in

TABLE 1.1 Poverty in the case study countries, selected dates, 1970–2010 (proportion of population below national poverty line, per cent)

| Indonesia | 1970: 60 | 1984: 22 |
|-----------|----------|----------|
| Malaysia | 1970: 49 | 1984: 18 |
| Vietnam | 1993: 58 | 2008: 14 |
| Nigeria | 1992: 43 | 2010: 69 |
| Kenya | 1992: 45 | 2005: 46 |
| Tanzania | 1992: 39 | 2007: 33 |

*Sources*: online World Development Indicators/World DataBank, World Bank (Kenya, Tanzania); NBS 2012: 11 (Nigeria); for Indonesia, Malaysia and Vietnam, see main text, page 6.

development policy. State-led rural and agricultural development, leading to higher incomes for peasant farmers, has been central to South-East Asia's success, and I infer that its absence has been crucial to sub-Saharan Africa's failure (Henley 2012).

This conclusion is at odds with a very influential opposite view that appears logical at first sight: the view that because South-East Asian economic success is also associated with export-oriented industrialization, it is the emulation of this strategy which should have the highest priority in Africa (Collier 2007; Johnson et al. 2007; Soludo 2003). In the African Economic Research Consortium's treatise on *The Political Economy of Economic Growth in Africa 1960–2000*, 'diversified export growth' is identified *tout court* as 'the Asian model' which the whole of coastal Africa should emulate, while 'rural development' is mentioned only as the *last* of nine second-best growth strategies that may be worth trying in landlocked countries which for geographical reasons 'do not have the option of rapid industrialization' (Ndulu et al. 2008, I: 428, 434). In the last few years, a growing number of writers on Africa have contested this view and argued for a renewed rural focus in development policy (Breisinger and Diao 2008; Cervantes-Godoy and Dewbre 2010; Fan 2008; Losch 2012; World Bank 2007). Nevertheless, authoritative publications encouraging African policy-makers to give priority to industrial transformation continue to appear (African Centre for Economic Transformation 2014; UN Economic Commission for Africa 2014).

Besides state-led agricultural development, sustained growth and poverty reduction in South-East Asia are also associated with two other essential policy preconditions. Sound macroeconomic policy, firstly, is a precondition for economic growth. Economic freedom, at least for peasant farmers and small entrepreneurs, is the other variable associated with positive turning points. Unless farmers are free (subject to certain caveats as discussed below) to choose what to grow and to sell it to the highest bidder, the prospects for reducing rural poverty are poor. But although macroeconomic stability together with economic freedom can generate – at least in the short term – aggregate economic growth, it does not produce rapid poverty reduction unless it is also accompanied by pro-poor policies with respect to agriculture and food. Whether growth *without* commensurate poverty reduction – that is, growth that is accompanied by progressively widening income inequality – can be sustained over the long run is to some extent an open question. In all of our Asian case studies, however, all three policy conditions were realized simultaneously, and there is good reason to think that the speed and duration of the subsequent growth were enhanced by the fact that it consisted of what the *East Asian Miracle* report famously dubbed 'shared growth' (World Bank 1993: 13).

TABLE 1.2 Three preconditions for sustained growth with rapid poverty reduction: dates at which achieved in the case study countries

| | 1. Macroeconomic stability (low inflation, little currency over-valuation) | 2. Economic freedom for peasant farmers and small entre-preneurs | 3. Pro-poor public spending (on peasant agriculture and rural infra-structure) | Date at which all three policy conditions simultane-ously met |
|---|---|---|---|---|
| **South-East Asia** | | | | |
| Indonesia | 1967 | 1967 | 1967 | 1967 |
| Malaysia | always present | no history of over-regulation | 1958 | 1958 |
| Vietnam | 1986 | 1989 | 1976 | 1989 |
| **Africa** | | | | |
| Kenya | only briefly absent (1992) | 1995 | – | – |
| Nigeria | 1997 | 1986 | – | – |
| Tanzania | 1995 | 1985 | 1967–82 | – |

Further discussion of the content of each policy precondition follows in subsequent sections. Meanwhile the table above (Table 1.2), in a schematic and simplified way, summarizes the model and its application to the countries included in the study. Sustained growth with rapid poverty reduction has taken place when, and only when, all three policy preconditions have simultaneously been met: in Malaysia since 1958, in Indonesia since 1967, and in Vietnam since 1989.

In all cases the dates given in the table are those at which the relevant policy decisions were taken. The effects of those decisions, particularly in the case of pro-poor, pro-rural public spending, were often somewhat delayed (see Chapter 5). In Malaysia, for instance, sustained aggregate growth began in 1958, mass poverty reduction perhaps not until a decade later (Snodgrass 1980: 80–1). Most of the Malaysians disimpoverished in the 1970s, however, were rice or rubber farmers reaping the benefits of earlier public investments in agriculture (Othman 1984: 211, 276).

There is little reason to think that current policies in Nigeria, Kenya or Tanzania will shortly generate such a delayed dividend for the poor. In none of the African countries studied have the three policy conditions yet been fulfilled simultaneously, either now or in the past. Tanzania devoted large public investments to rural and agricultural development in the 1970s during the Nyerere era, but since these coincided with an attempt to collectivize the agricultural sector, economic freedom was emphatically absent. Kenya too made respectable budgetary allocations to agriculture during the decade following independence, but since most of this spending targeted large-scale, 'progressive' farmers, it was not pro-poor (Henley 2012: 37–8). Despite Kenya's reputation for economic liberalism, there was also considerable over-regulation; as late as 1984, government agencies were involved in marketing three-quarters of all the country's agricultural produce (Leonard 1991: 210).

Since the 1990s, most African countries have removed the most serious restrictions on the economic freedom of small farmers; the date given in Table 1.2 for the fulfilment of this condition in Kenya (1995) is that at which the last official restrictions on private trade in maize were removed (see Chapter 3). By the beginning of the twenty-first century, macroeconomic stability too had become the norm rather than the exception in Africa. However, the third precondition for sustained growth with mass poverty reduction, pro-poor, pro-rural public spending, remains elusive. In 2003 in Maputo the governments of the African Union did declare a collective intention to raise public spending on 'agricultural and rural development' (a very elastic category) to 10 per cent of national budgetary resources, but so far only a handful of countries have actually done so (NEPAD 2010: 4; ReSAKSS 2011: 29). As a result there has been no breakthrough in the productivity of smallholder agriculture, and the impact of current African economic growth on poverty is weak. The future continuity of that growth, moreover, remains uncertain amid rising inequality, limited domestic market growth and continued food insecurity.

## South-East Asia's road to development: (1) sound macroeconomic management

There is no positive turning point in our case studies without a background of macroeconomic stability. In the first place, this means the presence of policies embodying a clear commitment to combating inflation. The rigour of the target to be achieved here should not be exaggerated: in Indonesia during the 1970s and early 1980s, inflation rates of between 10 and 20 per cent proved fully compatible with growth and poverty alleviation (Figure 1.7). Yet the importance of avoiding *excessive* inflation – meaning, roughly speaking, preventing inflation from exceeding 20 per cent for any length of time – is nowhere clearer than in Indonesia, where the hyperinflation of the late Sukarno years provided a strong negative benchmark for the Suharto regime which seized power in 1965. To help ensure that hyperinflation would never happen again, in 1967 the new government instigated a law whereby parliament could not approve any budget that was not balanced, in the sense of state revenues (including foreign aid and loans) equalling or exceeding expenditures (including debt servicing) (Hill 1996a: 59).

Macroeconomic stabilization also played a central, and seldom fully appreciated, role in Vietnam's Doi Moi or 'Renovation' process of the 1980s and 1990s. In retrospect Doi Moi is mainly associated with liberalization, but at its inception the primary goal was actually the control of inflation, which by 1986 had reached over 400 per cent (Nguyen 2006: 84, 173). In Malaysia, thanks to consistently prudent

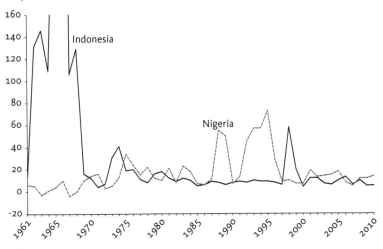

*Note*: Indonesia peak off scale at 1,136 per cent in 1966

**1.7** Inflation, consumer prices (annual per cent), Indonesia and Nigeria, 1961–2010 (*source*: online World Development Indicators/World DataBank, World Bank)

financial policies, macroeconomic stability has never been seriously threatened since independence in 1957.

In our African case studies, macroeconomic stabilization is clearly associated with the return of aggregate growth in the 1990s. In Tanzania an agreement with the international financial institutions to bring down inflation was concluded in 1985, but did not have the desired effect until 1995, when donor conditionality brought discipline to the banking system and to government finances. In Kenya, as in Malaysia, macroeconomic stability has only rarely been a major problem. By contrast the lack of stability in Nigeria during the late 1980s and early 1990s, despite attempts to discipline the economy in the face of falling oil revenues, was strongly associated with negative economic performance (Figure 1.7).

It bears repeating that macroeconomic stabilization is a necessary, not a sufficient, precondition for developmental take-off. Except during the initial stage of liberalization when markets re-establish themselves, it is not strongly associated with poverty alleviation. In many cases it is also more fragile than it at first sight appears, being dependent on large inflows of foreign aid or oil revenue. In New Order Indonesia the development budget was at first financed almost entirely by aid, and in Vietnam the turning point was accompanied by the coming on stream of oil production. Neither aid nor oil, as the African story shows, is in itself a guarantee of macroeconomic stability, still less of sustained growth. Nevertheless, such inflows of foreign money are very useful when it comes to balancing state finances and overcoming foreign exchange constraints.

A second vital aspect of sound macroeconomic management is the maintenance of a competitive exchange rate between the national currency and those of potential export markets. Cross-country statistical studies show that the size of the black market premium on currency deals – that is, the difference between an administratively overvalued official exchange rate and a real (black market) rate for a national currency against the US dollar – is a reliable predictor of poor economic performance (Easterly 2002: 221–3, 238). The successful South-East Asian countries have never overvalued their currencies enough to allow any such black market premium to emerge. Indonesia, in fact, repeatedly devalued its currency by tens of percentage points at a time in the 1970s and 1980s in order to reverse oil-fuelled appreciation of the rupiah and keep its non-oil exports competitive. In Nigeria, by contrast, the value of the naira appreciated throughout the oil boom of the 1970s and early 1980s, and was then maintained for several years at four times the black market level after oil prices fell (Lewis 2007: 193).

### South-East Asia's road to development: (2) economic freedom

Wherever there has been a development strategy based on accumulation by the state, and a more or less successful attempt by the state at comprehensive control of the economy, there has sooner or later been a deep economic crisis. Freedom for economic actors, especially the smaller actors, was essential for a return of growth. This is nowhere clearer than in Vietnam, where the dissolution of the communal farm was a vital part of the transformation of the late 1980s. Economic liberalization in Tanzania from 1985 onward did not immediately bring a return of growth; this did not follow until macroeconomic stability was established in 1995. When growth came it still had only a limited effect on poverty, since the third precondition for development success, a pro-poor agricultural policy, was still lacking.

It would be wrong to equate the need for economic freedom

with a demand to reduce the role of the state to a minimum and expose farmers to 'market forces'. Certain forms of state intervention are important, but they need to be supplementary to, or mediated through, markets. In all of the South-East Asian cases there has been considerable state involvement in the agricultural economy: fertilizer and credit subsidies, provisions for subsidized purchase of crops when market prices fall below guaranteed minimum levels, and restrictions on the import and export of food. However, the South-East Asian governments have as a rule avoided granting monopoly or monopsony positions to state institutions. Indonesia's 'logistics bureau' (Bulog) successfully stabilized rice prices by buying grain at a fixed floor price when the market price was low and selling it at a ceiling price when the market price was high; but the margins provided between the floor and ceiling prices allowed private traders to handle most of the rice marketed. In normal years, Bulog bought and distributed less than 10 per cent of the rice produced and consumed in Indonesia (Timmer 1997: 137).

In South-East Asia, state agencies operated alongside independent agents, frequently providing subsidies to private sector distributors rather than taking over the provision of subsidized goods themselves. Although export and import controls, where present, did affect the economic freedom of small farmers indirectly, in their own environs farmers were as a rule free to sell their produce to any chosen party, and to buy inputs such as fertilizer on the open market. They were usually also free to choose which crops to plant, and at what price to sell them (or not). Price controls were seldom resorted to, except by the indirect means of public subsidy. Although there were exceptions in particular contexts, such as the early days of the Green Revolution in Java and the Federal Land Development Authority (FELDA) land settlement scheme in Malaysia, on the whole the state placed very few coercive restrictions on the economic activity of small farmers and petty entrepreneurs.

The continuation of some types of state intervention under liberalized conditions is nevertheless a common feature of the South-East Asian systems, and an important difference between them and their African counterparts. In Africa there has in recent decades been a sustained withdrawal of the state from its former heavy-handed regulatory role in the economy, but this has not been balanced by the creation of institutional structures through which positive interventions can continue in a relatively hands-off fashion in order to support a growth coalition between state officials and the mass of the farming population. The diffusion of the Green Revolution in South-East Asia has accurately been characterized as state-led, market-mediated and smallholder-based (Djurfeldt and Jirström 2005). This last characteristic is essential to understanding the role of economic freedom in developmental turning points. Whether in sub-Saharan Africa or in South-East Asia, smallholder production stagnates or declines if there is no freedom to choose which crop to plant and who to sell it to.

### South-East Asia's road to development: (3) pro-poor, pro-rural public spending

In the last two decades, macroeconomic stabilization and market liberalization have been important policy goals in Africa as well as South-East Asia. In Tanzania they were associated with a return of quite strong aggregate economic growth in the 1990s. In crucial contrast with South-East Asia, however, they have not been linked with pro-poor policies directed at agriculture and rural development. South-East Asian planners saw that the obvious way to address the problem of mass poverty, given that most of the population lived in the countryside and depended on agriculture, was by raising farm incomes.

One way to do this was to increase the productivity of export crops, such as rubber and palm oil in Malaysia or coffee and cashew nuts in Vietnam. The most concentrated effort, however, went into food production, and was inspired by a desire for national self-sufficiency in food. South-East Asian countries gave the highest priority to promoting the Green Revolution in rice agriculture by means of irrigation, extension services, credit and the subsidization of inputs such as fertilizer and seeds of improved rice varieties. In Africa after independence, food crop agriculture was largely neglected, while export agriculture was openly used as a source of surplus for industrial and urban development, extracted by means of state marketing monopsonies. Although the marketing boards were mostly abolished or reformed during the period of structural adjustment in the 1980s and 1990s, liberalization was not accompanied by public investment in agriculture on a scale remotely comparable to what happened in South-East Asia.

Agricultural output in the African countries is in general erratic. This is partly explained by agronomic factors, but it is also a consequence of policy. The organization of agricultural marketing in the African countries has typically been either dominated by the state, or left to the private sector without any consideration for minimum price guarantees. While the use of fertilizer has grown exponentially in the South-East Asian countries, in Africa it has not. Food crop production, accordingly, has also remained almost stagnant on a per capita basis. The African countries have frequently been dependent on food imports.

For these reasons economic growth in Africa has not usually led to much poverty alleviation in rural areas. In Africa, poverty tends to decrease in urban areas. This is partly explained by disproportionate benefits from the aid flows into the country. It also reflects a pattern of enclave development. Economic liberalization usually leads to an inflow of foreign direct investment, but in Africa this tends to be concentrated in mining and other extractive industries, or in tourism. These sectors have few linkages with the domestic economy, so that the multiplier effects of the investment are limited.

The single most important distinction between South-East Asian and African development strategies is that in South-East Asia, macro-economic stabilization has been paired with a concern for 'shared growth' through agricultural and rural development. South-East Asian government spending tends to show a pronounced 'rural bias'. In the 1970s, when Malaysia was already on the way to becoming an industrial power, the Malaysian government was still spending one quarter of its national development budget – almost ten times its expenditure on industrial development – on agriculture (Second Malaysia Plan 1971: 68; Third Malaysia Plan 1976: 240). In Indonesia too, foreign aid and oil revenues were invested on a huge scale in enhancing the productivity of peasant agriculture by means of irrigation works, the development and dissemination of new high-yielding rice varieties, fertilizer and pesticide subsidies, and subsidized farm credit. In the New Order's first five-year development plan (1969–74), fully 30 per cent of the development budget was allocated to agriculture – not including the large sums also spent on rural roads, electrification, health services and education (First Five-Year Development Plan 1969: 41). Vietnam, after its reunification in 1975, consistently devoted some 20 per cent to agriculture (Tran 1998: 8), investing heavily in technical irrigation projects (Young et al. 2002: 11–12), which later made possible a rapid expansion of rice production.

In Nigeria at the same period, by dramatic contrast, the proportion of development funds spent on agriculture fell to just 6 per cent as Nigerian planners chose to invest the oil windfall of the 1970s in ill-conceived schemes for heavy industrial development (Third National Development Plan 1975: 349). This choice was not a matter of corruption or clientelism: the industrialization effort was 'driven by a (technocratic) economic vision, rather than by the self-interest of the regime' (Collier and Gunning 2008: 211). Even in Kenya, often thought of as one African country that did invest in agriculture rather than 'squeezing' it for the benefit of urban and industrial interests, an initially strong spending focus on agricultural development was largely lost amid the false security of the prosperous 1970s.

Sectoral budgetary allocations are at best a rough first indication of the level of rural/agricultural or urban/industrial bias in a country's development strategy. The allocation of money to rural development may be a different matter from its actual disbursement. Even when it is disbursed, its effectiveness may vary dramatically. Fertilizer subsidies, for example, do not constitute pro-poor public spending if they disproportionately benefit large-scale farmers – a persistent problem in Kenya (Oluoch-Kosura and Karugia 2005: 189). Rural development spending may also be counterbalanced by rural taxation: in Tanzania in the 1970s, impressive budgetary allocations to agricultural development went hand in hand with very heavy indirect taxation of peasant farmers (Ellis 1983).

On the daring assumption of other things being equal, it may be said that an allocation of at least 10 per cent of total public spending, and/or 20 per cent of the total development budget (public capital investment), to the agricultural sector (including research, extension, input, credit and replanting subsidies, irrigation, drainage and land settlement) is indicative of pro-poor, pro-rural public spending. A comparably high proportional allocation to the transport sector may also be a good sign: road building benefits the rural population and is, alongside agriculture, the area in which public spending in Africa has in the past fallen most strikingly below Asian levels (Fan et al. 2008: 25). Ultimately, however, any assessment of whether and how this crucial precondition for development is met must be based on a specific historical narrative which takes account of conditions in the country under study.

### Findings and method in comparative perspective

The conclusions of this book are close to those of the World Bank's *East Asian Miracle* study (1993) in stressing the importance of policies designed to promote 'shared growth', and similar also to those of Campos and Root's *The Key to the Asian Miracle* (1996) in pointing to the 'growth coalition' that underpins such policies and makes them politically feasible. But whereas these studies stress the general need for growth with equity, I argue more strongly that in the case of South-East Asia, development success is specifically associated with a policy focus on agriculture and on food production. It is striking that in *The East Asian Miracle* only five pages are devoted to the importance of a dynamic agricultural sector, compared to twenty-five on the need to create an 'export push' (World Bank 1993: 32–7, 123–48). Even works dealing comparatively with countries within South-East Asia seldom emphasize the pattern of rural and agricultural policy bias which the successful developmental states of the region have in common, or have had in common at crucial stages. Perhaps the closest existing study to this one in spirit and conclusions, ironically, is that of Diane E. Davis (2004) on North-East Asia and Latin America, arguing that the roots of the South Korean and Taiwanese economic miracles lie ultimately in the pro-rural development strategies of the 1960s rather than in the later triumphs of export-oriented industrialization.

In our South-East Asian case studies, certainly, the industrial export boom was a secondary development, preceded and facilitated by mass rural poverty reduction. When export-oriented industrialization did come in South-East Asia, it was largely a private sector response to macroeconomic stability, economic freedom, adequate infrastructure and – perhaps above all – an already healthy rural economy. These conditions ensured political stability, private saving and investment, enlarged domestic markets, and a cheap, reliable food supply for workers. It is important to note that when South-East Asian governments have attempted to nurture specific manufacturing sectors to the point of competitiveness along Japanese or Korean lines, as in the case of the Indonesian and Malaysian car industries, they have most often failed (Aswicahyono et al. 2000; Jayasankaran 1993). The fact that this failure usually had to do with corruption and clientelism should make policy-makers in Africa, which as noted is much more comparable to South-East than to North-East Asia in terms of institutional quality, doubly wary of interventionist industrial strategies.

That said, in general there are strong reasons to be sceptical of explanations for African developmental retardation which emphasize the nature of institutions, or indeed any other 'structural' constraints rooted in culture, history or geography, as opposed to policy choices (Chabal and Daloz 1999; Chabal 2009; Gallup et al. 1998; Easterly and Levine 1997; Lewis 2007; Rodrik et al. 2004; Van der Veen 2004). Although this book presents and analyses narratives of historical development, it does *not* take a *long-term* historical view. The South-East Asian countries were never predestined for developmental success, and even on the eve of that success very few experts predicted it. In the 1970s Vietnam was embroiled in war, Thailand in domestic conflict, and Cambodia in one of the most destructive revolutions in history. In Indonesia the economy had been stagnant for decades: in 1968 the foremost international expert on the subject described Indonesia as 'the number one economic failure among the major underdeveloped countries' (Higgins 1968: 679). The new Suharto dictatorship, established in a bloodbath and riddled with corruption, was not expected to last long. Malaysia too was seen as a fragile polity that could easily be torn apart by racial troubles.

Above all, South-East Asia was considerably poorer than Africa. Any long-term historical theory of the later developmental divergence would need to explain the earlier stagnation and decline of both regions, as well as South-East Asia's eventual success. It follows that the historical determinism implicit in the term 'path dependency' is not productive in this context. Within South-East Asia there are countries that have taken a different path: Burma is a stagnating state-dominated economy, and the Philippines have not developed as strong an agricultural and industrial base as the countries included in our study. Their failure reveals the limitations of the 'neighbourhood' (Easterly and Levine 1998) and 'flying geese' (Akamatsu 1962) effects: policy-making elites may choose to pick up ideas from the development success of neighbouring countries – or they may not. But if development success is a matter of policy choice rather than geography, history, culture or institutions, it still remains to explain why some policy-makers make the right choices, and others do not.

### Factors influencing policy choices

With regard to the adoption of sound macroeconomic policies and the establishment of economic freedom for farmers and small entrepreneurs, the evidence from South-East Asia is that the best learning experience for policy-makers is the experience of a deep national economic crisis (Henley et al. 2012: 64–6). In Indonesia there is an succinct expression for this, 'Sadli's law' (after the economist and technocrat Mohamad Sadli), which states that bad times produce good policies, and good times bad policies. Both in Indonesia in the 1960s and in Vietnam in the 1980s it was severe crises involving hyperinflation and food shortages, transparently the results of macro-economic mismanagement and over-regulation, which triggered the crucial policy reversals in these areas (although Malaysia, where there was continuity of liberal economic policies from colonial into post-colonial times, is a more complex story). Our African countries, by contrast, never experienced crises of quite such severity, or of quite such transparent aetiology. In Nigeria, for instance, the growth collapse of the 1980s did not involve hyperinflation or hunger, and among Nigerians it was widely attributed to 'Dutch disease', the volatility of oil prices and corruption.

With respect to the adoption in South-East Asia of strongly pro-rural, pro-poor development policies, however, a longer historical process seems to be involved. In all cases those policies reflected a strong concern to include the peasantry in the development process, and to do so urgently and on a massive scale. The fate of the poor genuinely mattered to the governments in question. One common explanation for this is that political realities forced Asian elites to take the interests of peasant farmers seriously (Slater 2010; Van der Veen 2010). The successful developmental states of South-East Asia were either counter-revolutionary states facing, or recently having faced, a serious communist threat (Thailand, Malaysia, Indonesia), or liberalizing post-revolutionary states concerned to avoid alienating their mass support base (Vietnam).

On close inspection, however, communism and anti-communism are not the whole story here. Communism in Malaysia was almost entirely an affair of the country's ethnic Chinese minority, whereas the beneficiaries of the rural development effort were Malays who showed few signs of being attracted to communism anyway. By the time Indonesia adopted its pro-poor, pro-rural development policies under President Suharto, the Communist Party of Indonesia had already been bloodily and comprehensively destroyed during Suharto's rise to power in 1965. In interviews conducted by Tracking Development researchers, senior Indonesian technocrats of that time have strenuously denied that political considerations affected their policy choices, which they insist were based purely on economic logic, and indeed on common sense.

What does emerge from these interviews and from other personal testimonies, on the other hand, is a rather consistent difference between Asian and African policy-makers in terms of their personal evaluation of rural ways of life. In South-East Asia, elite attitudes to village life, although condescending, are often also marked by nostalgia and a degree of admiration. Although Africa has had no lack of rulers with rural origins, their attitudes to rural life have mostly been much less positive. Consequently they have tended to see development not as a matter of improving the living conditions of the peasant masses *in situ*, but rather as a question of accelerating the transition from rural backwardness to urban modernity, of which their own lives have been a microcosm. This has led them to favour elitist development strategies aimed at acquiring symbols of developed-country status (universities, steelworks, information technology, human rights) rather than meeting the urgent practical challenge of making poor people richer by whatever means lie immediately to hand. The relevant differences in world-view between African and South-East Asian policy elites, I suggest, may be rooted partly in divergent historical experiences. Colonialism caused a more radical rupture with the past in Africa than it did in South-East Asia, and one legacy of Africa's deeper colonial transformation has been a persistent and counterproductive assumption of dualism, a conviction that economic progress can be achieved only by means of a quantum leap from backwardness into modernity.

## Structure of the book

This introductory chapter has set out the questions to be asked, and provided a preview of the answers. In Chapter 2, 'Studying the divergence', I review some existing comparative research on economic development and development policy in Asia and Africa, summarizing its conclusions and identifying its strengths and weaknesses in relation to the present work. In Chapter 3, 'Setting the stage for development', I examine the significance of two of the three proposed policy-based preconditions for developmental success, macroeconomic stability and economic freedom. The roles of foreign aid and natural resources in financing South-East Asian development without jeopardizing macroeconomic stability are also discussed. Chapter 4, 'Agrarian roots of development success', focuses on the key role of pro-poor public spending in the South-East Asian development story, with particular reference to Indonesia and Nigeria, and to the links between the reduction of rural poverty and the subsequent growth of export industry. Chapter 5, 'Varieties of rural bias', extends the same argument to other countries, notably Malaysia, often wrongly thought of as a case of successful urban-industrial policy bias in South-East Asia, and Kenya, often misleadingly portrayed as an exception to the rule that African governments have neglected the potential of the peasant farmer as a driver of development.

Chapter 6, 'Elements of the developmental mindset', attempts to identify some general principles informing the policy choices of planners and politicians in the successful South-East Asian developmental states. I suggest that these underlying principles are threefold: *outreach* (mass impact is more important than technical sophistication); *urgency* (short-term priorities are more important than long-term aspirations); and *expediency* (results are more important than rules). Consideration of the last principle leads into a discussion of the limits to the significance of institutions to developmental outcomes. Attention is paid to the continuing lack of urgency, outreach and expediency in the policies of our African case study countries today.

In Chapter 7, finally, I return to the Indonesia–Nigeria comparison for a review of the factors influencing successful and unsuccessful policy choices on the part of technocratic planners in these two countries during the period 1965–90. The results tentatively confirm the significance of culturally and historically rooted world-views alongside socio-political factors and lessons of personal experience. The chapter, and the book, concludes by suggesting how African policy-makers can nevertheless be encouraged to give higher priority to pro-poor agricultural and rural development, the neglect of which, judging by the South-East Asian evidence, has been their most crucial error up to now.

# 2 | STUDYING THE DIVERGENCE

The World Bank's 1993 report on *The East Asian Miracle* prompted a wave of comparative research aimed at extracting practical lessons for African countries from the development achievements of Asia in the late twentieth century. This chapter briefly surveys the existing comparative literature on African and South-East Asian development experiences, discusses the merits of that literature in relation to the cross-country statistical regression analyses which dominate the comparative study of development performance, and explains the approach followed in the present book.

## Chalk and cheese? Africa and the lessons of Asian development

As recently as the 1970s, income levels in Africa and South-East Asia were still similar. Both regions had overwhelmingly rural and agricultural economies, and both were regarded as belonging to a 'tropical' or 'third' world in which economic progress was held back by a similar set of environmental, social and political constraints. Examples of classic comparative studies stressing such common constraints (although identifying them differently) are Gourou's *Les Pays tropicaux* (1947), Boeke's *Economics and Economic Policy of Dual Societies* (1953), Rostow's *The Stages of Economic Growth* (1960) and Frank's *Dependent Accumulation and Underdevelopment* (1978).

These and other early attempts to formulate general theories of development and underdevelopment were to founder on the divergent experiences of Asia, Africa and Latin America in the late twentieth century. By around 1990 it was evident even to sceptical observers that the old Third World, in the sense of an equatorial belt of stagnant, poverty-ridden countries stretching from Latin America through Africa to South and South-East Asia, was no more. In South-East Asia, Malaysia, Thailand and Indonesia, following the lead of Singapore at the heart of their own region and of Hong Kong, Taiwan and South Korea farther north, had all been developing rapidly, according to almost every conceivable (non-political) measure of development, for more than two decades. A whole new vocabulary was invented to characterize them: 'Newly Industrializing Countries', 'Asian Tigers', the 'East Asian Miracle'. The economic rise of neighbouring Vietnam, and of course China, was confidently foreseen.

At the same time it was also becoming clear that this miracle had its antithesis in the 'growth tragedy' (Easterly and Levine 1995) of sub-Saharan Africa, where during the 'lost decade' of the 1980s per capita income had actually fallen at a rate of more than 1 per cent per annum (Stein 1995b: 1). A negative 'African dummy' had been identified as a statistical predictor of comparative national economic performance (Barro 1991), and sub-Saharan Africa was already being identified as the site of 'underdevelopment's last stand' (Chege 1995).

The World Bank's 1993 report *The East Asian Miracle; economic growth and public policy* summarized the achievements of East and South-East Asia, offered a canonical explanation for them, and prompted a wave of further comparative research aimed at extracting practical lessons from the Asian development experience in the late twentieth century. According to this report, the eight 'High Performing Asian Economies' (HPAEs) – Japan, South Korea, Hong Kong, Taiwan, Thailand, Malaysia, Singapore and Indonesia – had succeeded by a number of common means: by ensuring low inflation and competitive exchange rates; by creating an effective banking system; by investing in human capital through education; by supporting rather than neglecting agriculture; by insulating civil servants from political pressures; by forging institutionalized alliances between government and business; and – most characteristically – by emphasizing the growth of exports as at once a goal, strategy and touchstone of development (World Bank 1993: 347–68).

Although the decisive export successes had been achieved in manufacturing, in the eyes of the World Bank the most successful state economic interventions' (other than the supply of education and infrastructure) had involved the promotion of food production and the control of food prices. The effectiveness of certain 'market-distorting' industrial policies, such as the temporary protection of promising infant industries with export potential, was acknowledged in the cases of Japan, South Korea and Taiwan, but denied as far as South-East Asia was concerned. This was important in terms of the implications of the study for Africa, since it was South-East rather than North-East Asia which the World Bank held out in the first instance as a model for the rest of the developing world (ibid.: 7).

A year later, the first specific policy-oriented comparison between the development histories of Asia and Africa appeared in the form of a collective volume published for the Africa Bureau of USAID by the Harvard Institute for International Development (Lindauer and Roemer 1994). Here too the emphasis was on the newly industrializing countries of South-East Asia (excluding Singapore) as the most appropriate comparators, and development models, for sub-Saharan Africa. Like Africa but unlike East Asia, South-East Asia is rich in natural resources – minerals, forests and farmland – but poor (at least until recently) in human capital; commercially dominated by ethnic minorities of foreign origin; and weak in terms of the administrative capacity of its states, which are prone to inefficiency and corruption (ibid.: 6).

The USAID/HIID study echoed that of the World Bank in noting that the successful South-East Asian economies had followed 'outward-looking, market-friendly policies' on international trade and foreign investment (ibid.: 4); accommodated rather than alienated their entrepreneurial minorities (ibid.: 7); invested heavily in domestic agriculture and infrastructure (ibid.: 9); and 'seldom strayed from balanced macroeconomies' (ibid.: 12). Government budget deficits had been kept low, inflation under control, exchange rates realistic, currencies convertible, and capital flows unrestricted. Weaknesses in the sphere of governance had been circumvented by relying for the purposes of industrial development on the effects of macroeconomic management and market forces, rather than attempting direct state interventions which were bound to be thwarted by 'clientelism and rent-seeking' (ibid.: 8). In all these respects, Lindauer and Roemer argued, South-East Asia offered realistic policy blueprints for Africa.

> We reject the pessimism that surrounds so much discussion of African prospects [...]. The continuing successes in Asia provide both help and guidance. It is important to remember that Asia's achievements were neither automatic nor inevitable. Each country had to overcome major barriers to growth, including war, revolution, political instability, ethnic competition, corrupt regimes, and grinding poverty. The policy agenda, although ambitious,

has been proven under conditions in Southeast Asia that have important similarities to those in Africa. Most of what can be accomplished in Southeast Asia beginning thirty years ago can be accomplished by several African countries today. (Ibid.: 22)

Early policy-oriented comparative studies of specific African and South-East Asian countries shared this optimism. Chhibber and Leechor (1995), in an article on lessons from Thailand and Malaysia as applied to Ghana, recommended that Ghana should expand spending on basic education (if necessary at the expense of higher education) and maintain macroeconomic stability to encourage private investment. Harrold, Jayawickrama and Bhattasali (1996), in a World Bank discussion paper on 'Practical lessons for Africa from East Asia in industrial and trade policies', briefly compared Nigeria with Indonesia, Côte d'Ivoire with Malaysia, and Tanzania, Ghana and Thailand with each other. They too confirmed the *East Asian Miracle* conclusion that macroeconomic stability, with low inflation to encourage saving and investment, was an indispensable foundation for economic success that many African states had not yet laid, and that currency exchange rates should be kept low to encourage exports rather than overvalued as African governments had tended to prefer. They also recommended that formal consultation mechanisms should cautiously be developed in Africa to foster a more cooperative relationship between business and state. On the other hand African countries were 'not yet ready for industrial targeting and directed credit' along North-East Asian lines, because they lacked the 'necessary institutional conditions' to implement such policies (ibid.: 110).

Bevan, Collier and Gunning (1999), in a book-length study on Nigeria and Indonesia likewise sponsored by the World Bank, reached similar conclusions in the sphere of industrial and trade policies while also highlighting major divergences with respect to agriculture, the priority attached to which had 'differed radically and consistently' between the two states (ibid.: 417). In Indonesia much more had been done for farmers, and for the poor in general, than in Nigeria. Agricultural exports, in Nigeria, were heavily taxed through monopolistic marketing boards, and food crops largely ignored. In Indonesia, by contrast, there were active state agricultural extension efforts to promote new Green Revolution technologies in rice farming, and 'deliberate manipulation of the rice/fertilizer price' to support rice production and control food prices for the benefit of the poor (ibid.: 405).

Nicholas and Scott Thompson (2000), in an anecdotal Africa–Asia comparative study entitled *The Baobab and the Mango Tree* and looking mainly (but not exclusively) at Ghana and Thailand, focused on the personal characters and qualities of political leaders: impractical, bombastic and bellicose in most African cases, prudent, pragmatic and unpretentious in the case of their Thai counterparts. Bad policies were sometimes pushed upon governments by circumstance, or as inheritances from the past: examples include export crop marketing boards, which, 'like smallpox, were introduced into Africa by the colonialists' (ibid.: 114). But whereas Asian leaders had the courage to reject them even in the face of vested interests, Africans did not.

Brian van Arkadie and Do Duc Dinh's (2004) comparative commentary on economic reform in Tanzania and Vietnam since 1986 supported the conclusions of the World Bank with respect to the effectiveness of market-oriented economic reforms, the crucial importance of exports, and the need for public investment in agriculture, education (human capital) and rural infrastructure. But it also noted that Vietnam's explicit policy emphasis on industrialization, combined with its retention of state ownership in some sectors, has produced better results than has the wholesale privatization undertaken in Tanzania. 'When the private sector is weak', Van Arkadie and Do concluded, 'it is wrong to advise a country to virtually abandon its State sector – such advice destroys the leaking house at the very moment it needs maintenance and renovation.'

In recent years, Asia–Africa comparative development studies that conclude with clear policy recommendations like these have become less common. This is partly because of the improving performance of many African economies, which has reduced the poignancy of the Asian comparison and revived hopes that Africa will chart its own path to economic success, perhaps along lines closer to Western than to Asian experience. Steven Radelet's optimistic *Emerging Africa*, for instance, notes in passing the 'phenomenal progress' of 'countries like China and Indonesia', but both its analysis of Africa's emerging strengths, and its prescriptions for future consolidation, make a resolutely Eurocentric impression – stressing for instance the benefits of democracy, political accountability and the control of corruption, none of which have played central roles in South-East Asian development success (Radelet 2010: 21, 47–69). Lately, Asia has figured in African development literature less as a source of comparative inspiration than as a source of direct opportunities and challenges in the form of Asian, particularly Chinese, engagement and investment in Africa (Alden 2007; Bräutigam 2009; Van Dijk 2009).

Insofar as comparison between Asian and African development trajectories has continued in the academic literature, however, the tendency has been to reflect increasingly on the constraints to which African policy-makers have been subject – consciously or not – when choosing between particular courses of action, and also on the impediments to effective implementation of Asian policies under African conditions. Concern for promoting particular policies in the present, in other words, has partly given way to a concern for understanding why in Africa those policies were either not adopted, or not successfully implemented, in the past.

### From choice to constraint

In 1996 the African Economic Research Consortium (AERC) instituted a research programme on comparative development experiences in Asia and Africa. In the resulting publications (Aryeetey et al. 2003; Nissanke and Aryeetey 2003b) the emphasis is on constraints rather than choices, and on the fact that those constraints are tighter in Africa than in South-East Asia. For ecological reasons, note Nissanke and Aryeetey (2003a: 51), Africa's agriculture did not benefit as much as Asia's did from the Green Revolution of the 1960s in farming technology, which mainly affected irrigated rice cultivation. In the 1970s and 1980s, African countries accumulated too much debt, rescheduling of which was made conditional on programmes of 'structural adjustment' that starved them of public investment, destroying their institutions and infrastructure (ibid.: 52). Africa inherited from the colonial state 'a distorted set of economic structures that blocked indigenous opportunities for autonomous growth'. Africa suffers from a 'cumulative institutional impoverishment' which makes even good policies impossible to implement effectively (ibid.: 53). African economies are 'continuously exposed to large aggregate external and policy generated shocks as well as to high political instability, civil strife and natural calamity' (ibid.: 57). Africa, add Elbadawi, Ndulu and Ndung'u (2003: 88-91) in a similar vein, has a less highly skilled and educated labour force than Asia's, has been more prone to violent changes of government, and also lacks regional 'growth poles' to stimulate development (and good policy choices) via the kinds of 'spillover' effect that have served to disseminate growth across national boundaries in East and Southeast Asia.

Turning from geographical to historical constraint, Deborah Bräutigam (2003: 107) argues that 'Southeast Asia's lead over Sub-Saharan Africa is not simply a response to good policies undertaken in the past two decades, but also reflects the different ways in which each area first engaged with the capitalist world'. The similarities between the two regions in terms of economic structure and stand-ards of living in the mid-twentieth century mask a number of deeper historical contrasts. South-East Asia was 'well integrated into Asian and European maritime trading networks several centuries before maritime trade reached most of Sub-Saharan Africa'. This gave South-East Asian traders a long lead in developing 'business skills', and also drew to the region many immigrants, especially from China, who already possessed such skills. At every subsequent stage, this qualitative – if not quantitative – lead in economic development was maintained. Import-substituting industrialization began, albeit on a small scale, in the late nineteenth century, 'three or more decades before any significant industrial development occurred in Africa'. Proximity to Japan, the first industrial country outside Europe, 'served as a powerful catalyst for entrepreneurial development in Southeast Asia' through the medium of direct investments and joint ventures. To this, Soludo (2003) adds in his contribution to the same volume that 'many African countries are too small and balkanized to provide substantial economies of the scale to support profitable investment' (ibid.: 256), and that for geographical as well as institutional reasons, 'Africa faces the highest transport and telecommunications costs in the world' (ibid.: 261).

A key implication of this emphasis on constraint rather than choice is that African political actors who behave differently from their counterparts in Asia are not necessarily either misguided or reprehensible. Rather, they are rational individuals responding to different sets of problems and incentives. Essentially there are two versions of this 'rational choice' approach to development failure in Africa. In the first, the development strategies of Asia are simply not realistically available to Africa – for instance, 'because few, if any, SSA countries could identify a manufacturing sector in which they have or are likely to acquire a comparative advantage' (Morrissey 2001: 46). In the second version, such strategies are potentially feasible but are not chosen because the individual or collective interests of those in power are systematically at odds with the broader public or national interest. An early application of this second model was proposed by the doyen of rational choice theory among Africanists, Robert Bates (1981, 1983). Because of the limited development of indigenous export agriculture in most African countries in the late colonial period, Bates argued, after independence African states were typically 'captured' by bureaucratic, intellectual and urban groups more immediately interested in redistributing wealth away from the export sector than in enlarging it. And since power, in Africa as elsewhere, has a natural tendency to flow to where the money is, governments made up of consumers and redistributors often felt that even in the long term they had little reason to allow producers and exporters to become rich.

## Explaining divergence: Nigeria and Indonesia

The way in which explanations for the Asia–Africa development divergence have evolved is well illustrated by a succession of studies comparing Nigeria and Indonesia. As big, oil-rich states of great ethnic diversity and with tendencies to both authoritarian military rule and regional separatism, these two countries form a natural pair and have been the object of many comparative studies; those considered below do not amount to an exhaustive list.

An early contribution by Brian Pinto (1987), published well before the *East Asian Miracle* study, was a pure policy comparison looking at responses to the 'Dutch disease' problems caused by booming oil exports. It concluded that Nigeria should pay attention to how Indonesia's prudent macroeconomic management had prevented oil earnings from causing a decline in the agricultural sector, and leading to budget deficits and indebtedness, following the end of the boom. In the same period two further studies underlined the same conclusion, again without investigating the reasons why the policy responses of the two countries had differed (Ajoku 1992; Scherr 1989).

The 1996 World Bank discussion paper on industrial and trade policy in Africa and Asia by Harrold, Jayawickrama and Bhattasali also dealt partly with Nigeria and Indonesia. It too concluded that simply getting interest and exchange rates right would in itself help put Nigeria on the right developmental track. However, it added in passing that two of the deeper principles informing Asian growth policies would be difficult to implant in Nigeria: the assumption that what is good for business is in principle also good for the nation and the state, and the conviction that (non-oil) exports are both a measure and a source of development success (Harrold et al. 1996: 108–9). Two years later Dibie (1998), in a brief survey of 'cross-national economic development in Indonesia and Nigeria', concluded that the Nigerian state should 'gear its spending towards promoting competitiveness in the private sector' (ibid.: 81). Besides 'pragmatic government policies', however, Indonesia's achievements had also been based on 'political stability and a disciplined, hard-working population that responds to the right incentives' (ibid.: 65).

Also in 1998, economist Eric Thorbecke looked again at macroeconomic management in Nigeria and Indonesia in a contribution to a volume on *The Institutional Foundations of East Asian Economic Development*. Thorbecke noted the policy decisons which enabled Indonesia to maintain macroeconomic stability, surmount the 'Dutch disease' problems associated with disproportionate reliance on oil exports, and promote exports and investment. These included the adoption in 1967 of a balanced-budget rule prohibiting domestic financing of the budget either by debt or by money creation; and repeated currency devaluations to maintain export competitiveness. Thorbecke's focus, however, was not on the decisions themselves but on the 'initial conditions' which had made them possible.

Drawing on the work of Douglass North (1990) – and prefigured to some extent in a doctoral dissertation by De Silva (1996), which was also inspired by North – Thorbecke argued that Indonesia's centralized institutions of government, revolutionary origins and domination by a single ethnic group (the Javanese) had all inclined those in power to adopt policies reflecting an encompassing, national interest. By contrast Nigeria's federal constitution, lack of nationalist solidarity and greater ethnic fragmentation had encouraged conflict and the pursuit of narrow group interests. Currency overvaluation, for instance, benefited elite urban consumers of imported goods at the expense of almost all other sections of society. Large import-substituting industrial projects, protected behind tariff walls, gave more scope for kickbacks which could be used to reward personal followers and ethnic constituencies than did (for instance) agricultural extension services or free trade zones. In Nigeria 'the *raison d'être* of most of these projects was blatant corruption' (Thorbecke 1998: 133).

Bevan, Collier and Gunning's lengthy World Bank comparative study on Indonesia and Nigeria leaned generally towards an optimistic voluntarism, concluding that 'policies are not deeply embedded in unchanging structures' (Bevan et al. 1999: 425). Nevertheless, it too conceded that a number of differences in initial conditions had predisposed Indonesia to 'good' and Nigeria to 'bad' policy choices (ibid.: 418–20). Indonesia's preoccupation with food production, for example, reflected the fact that it was a major importer of its staple food, rice, and so faced the danger that in years of poor harvests it would drive up international prices against itself. Nigeria, by contrast, did not have a single staple crop and imported on a smaller scale, mainly grains for which the world market was much larger. The greater priority attached to poverty alleviation in Indonesia had to do partly with the revolutionary origins of the Indonesian army and its leaders, while Indonesia's greater export orientation is explained partly by the fact that at independence foreign trade was already more important there than in Nigeria. The clear demographic predominance of the Javanese in Indonesia meant that ethnicity was less of a destabilizing factor in politics than in Nigeria. The dominant entrepreneurial group in Indonesia, consisting of ethnic Chinese, was too small to be a threat to the indigenous political elite, which formed an alliance with it. In Nigeria, where a greater proportion of commerce was in indigenous hands, northerners feared the greater business expertise of southerners and consequently 'used the state to restrict the operation of market capitalism' (ibid.: 420).

The trend towards assessing policies as consequences of institutional contexts reaches a possible apogee in Peter Lewis's book

*Growing Apart; oil, politics, and economic change in Indonesia and Nigeria* (2007). Written in the same tradition as Thorbecke's earlier essay, this is pitched almost entirely at the level of institutions – or rather, the lack of them in Nigeria.

> Nigeria's elites, divided along communal and factional lines, have not consolidated stable political regimes or fostered capable state organizations. Insecure leaders employ patronage and ethnic cooptation as a basis of rule [...]. Ruling groups have been unable to cement a producer coalition or resolve central pressures for distribution. Military and civilian governments construct bases of support through clientelism, rent seeking, and the disbursement of largesse. In a setting of weak formal institutions and myriad conflicts over distribution, the Nigerian state has succumbed to a social dilemma: individuals and groups focus on particular gains at the expense of collective goods and general welfare. (Ibid.: 77–8)

Under these conditions of disunity, distrust and uncertainty, precariously incumbent governments have 'little incentive to establish a developmental regime' (ibid.: 280). Lewis concludes by giving tentative support (somewhat surprisingly given his central thesis) to further administrative decentralization in both countries, and by expressing the (perhaps unconvincing) hope that in the future, if 'different ethnically defined producer groups can develop interethnic economic linkages and complementarities', then even in Nigeria 'the promise of "gains from trade" can encourage new plural coalitions in a developmental project' (ibid.: 295).

### The paradox of African economic nationalism: in search of capable states

In conversation, Africanists – and indeed Africans – are seldom enthusiastic about the idea that the solutions to Africa's problems lie in emulating Asia. This is especially so when the interpretation of Asian success proffered to them is that of the World Bank with its emphasis on free trade and privatization, at least in the industrial sector. What does tend to interest Africanists is the 'heterodox' interpretation of the East Asian miracle, which stresses the importance of state intervention to protect and support promising 'infant industries' up to the point where they can compete in export markets (Amsden 1989; Chang 2003; Wade 1990). This is not only closer to traditional African economic ideologies, but also resonates with realistic fears that if protected African industries are suddenly exposed to the full force of international competition, they will simply be destroyed, leaving no foundation on which to build in pursuit of export-oriented industrialization.

> It is important when liberalising trade not to 'throw the baby out with the bath water'. Infant industry protection has a rationale in both theory and practice, and many economists have argued that countries should *first* promote exports and only later open up to imports. (Bräutigam 2003: 123)

Some Africanists, accordingly, have looked to industrial Asia for evidence of viable alternatives to the systematic abandonment of interventionist economic policies that was required of African governments by donor agencies in the 1980s and 1990s under the banner of 'structural adjustment'. A major problem arises here, however. Even those who believe that neoclassical economists have underestimated the role of state intervention in East Asia tend to agree with them that such intervention was more successful in North-East than in South-East Asia, and that one reason for this is that the deliberate nurturing of industries from protected infancy to competitive adulthood makes heavy demands on the quality of governance and the capability of state institutions. Where these are low, interventionist policies will tend to be subverted by rent-seeking private interests. As Roemer put it in relation to Thailand, Malaysia, Indonesia and the Philippines (the 'ASEAN four'):

> Interventions that, in Korea or Singapore, would lead quickly to new export industries more often have other outcomes in the ASEAN four. Treecrop exports are cartelized, ostensibly to stabilize domestic prices, but actually to protect processors by reducing prices to farmers. Log exports are banned or heavily taxed to promote cartelized plywood industries that use political influence to retain their protection. Steel mills and cement plants are constructed by clients of the regime, or by the regime itself, behind high protective barriers that remain in place long after the industry is mature, stifling export growth from downstream

industries. Technological advances, such as the auto industry in Malaysia and the airplane industry in Indonesia, are disciplined neither by competition nor by ambitious export targets. Many public enterprises are notably inefficient, with little prospect of selling overseas. (Roemer 1994: 251)

As far as South-East Asia is concerned, even heterodox economists have concentrated on highlighting successful state interventions in agriculture, and on questioning the depth and sustainability of the industrial transformation, rather than trying to argue that successful export industries grew out of an earlier stage of strategic protectionism.

Whereas much export-oriented manufacturing in Northeast Asia developed from import-substituting industries, such firms in Southeast Asia have been much less linked to the rest of the host economies, creating the impression of new manufacturing export enclaves, not unlike the primary producing export enclaves from the colonial era. (Jomo and Rock 2003: 165)

But if South-East Asia's states were not competent to manage an industrial revolution, then what hope for Africa, where states were equally notorious for incompetence and corruption? In the 1980s and 1990s, scholars vied with one another to coin new epithets expressing the dysfunctionality of African government: 'lame Leviathan' (Callaghy 1987), 'politics of the belly' (Bayart 1989), 'predatory rule' (Fatton 1992), 'shadow state' (Reno 1995), 'neopatrimonialism' (Chabal and Daloz 1999). By the turn of the century there was broad agreement on the one hand that African countries would not develop until they had competent governments committed to development, and on the other hand that in their present state of development, such governments were beyond their reach. 'One remarkable feature of the discourse on the state and development in Africa', observed Mkandawire (2001: 289), 'is the disjuncture between an analytical tradition that insists on the impossibility of developmental states in Africa and a prescriptive literature that presupposes the possibility of their existence'.

This irony is much in evidence in a volume edited by Howard Stein entitled *Asian Industrialization and Africa; studies in policy alternatives to structural adjustment* (Stein 1995a). Stein opens the introduction to the book by arguing that the principles of liberalization, deregulation, privatization and austerity demanded by the World Bank and the IMF in Africa are at odds with the reality of strategic planning and economic nationalism underpinning East Asian success, and that managed economic growth and integration along Asian lines offers an alternative development model for Africa (Stein 1995b). Other authors in the volume, however, are not so sure. Bräutigam (1995: 178) finds that the political and institutional context in Taiwan, featuring a state with 'considerable capacity and a high degree of autonomy', is so different from that of any African country that she cannot recommend that Africans attempt to emulate Taiwanese policies. Edwards (1995: 255), likewise, doubts whether 'industrial targeting' is likely to succeed in the African context of 'pervasive but not efficient' state intervention. At the end of his introduction, Stein is obliged to acknowledge the scepticism of his contributors.

> Finally, most of the studies in this volume have contrasted the nature of the state in Asia relative to Africa. States in Africa have generally been weaker, less professional and much more subject to patronage and clientage. This greatly delimits their capacity to implement and sustain an industrial strategy. (Stein 1995b: 19–20)

Other publications discussing the transferability of East Asian development lessons to Africa invariably make the same point (Evans 1999; Morrissey 2001; Hanatani 2008).

'Weak' states, of course, are disadvantageous for many other purposes besides industrial intervention. Stein (1995b: 20), in his defence, argues that 'the enforcement of a distortion-free (and rent-free) set of markets itself requires a "strong" state', since liberalization alone 'does not ipso facto remove rent seeking in Africa'. A point stressed in much of the comparative literature is that governments like those of Thailand and Indonesia in the 1970s and 1980s, however limited their ability to control patronage and corruption in the implementation of certain types of development policy, were at least capable of insulating the process of economic policy-making from politics to a degree rare in Africa. This meant that the high-risk policies were to some extent avoided on the advice of 'technocratic' experts, rather than deliberately seized upon under the influence of those who stood to gain (Lindauer and Roemer 1994: 7). Soludo (2003: 269) sums up the consensus of opinion as follows: 'an enduring lesson of the Asian countries, Northeast or Southeast, is that there is no detour around a capable state'.

## According to the statistics: Africa against the geographical odds

Increasingly comprehensive statistical investigations into the determinants of economic growth have shown that when it comes to geographical impediments, Africa does seem to have the odds stacked against it (Bloom and Sachs 1998; Bosker and Garretsen 2008). After a long period of neglect, the rise of the New Economic Geography, pioneered by Paul Krugman (1991), attracted scholarly attention once more to the geographical factors affecting economic development. One result was renewed appreciation for the specific obstacles to development in the tropics, including generally poor soil quality and a malignant disease environment (Sachs 2000). National per capita income levels, it turns out, are as significantly correlated with distance from the equator as they are with openness to trade (Rodrik 2003).

This particular correlation, of course, cannot help explain the contrast with the equally tropical region of South-East Asia; but other geographical factors can. Gallup, Sachs and Mellinger (1998) ran regressions of per capita income and its growth (from 1965 to 1990) against several geographical variables and showed that income growth, holding other variables constant, is over one percentage point per year slower in landlocked than in coastal countries. In sub-Saharan Africa there are fifteen landlocked countries, in South-East Asia only one (Laos).

A positive correlation also exists between population density and both income and income growth, at least in coastal areas (ibid.: 4, 39, 42). This has to do with the effects of transport costs and economies of agglomeration both on commerce, and on the supply of public goods such as education and medical services (Platteau 2000: 42–53). Low population densities may also discourage local investment in 'landesque capital' such as terracing, tree crops and irrigation, either because the requisite labour force cannot be assembled or because collective landownership, which is typical of sparsely populated areas, forms a disincentive to land improvement.

The average population densities in the two regions are respectively about 30 and 140 persons per square kilometre (online World Development Indicators/World DataBank, World Bank). Africa between the tropics is five times larger than South-East Asia in terms of land area, yet until recently its total population was smaller.

The importance of two other aspects of Africa's geography was demonstrated statistically by World Bank economists William Easterly and Ross Levine (1995, 1997, 1998). The first of these factors has to do with a propinquity or contagion effect, also referred to as 'neighbour spillover', in cross-national economic performance. In any region of the world, countries with economically successful neighbours are much more likely to experience growth themselves than are countries bordering on less dynamic states. This effect has served to spread and amplify the development 'miracle' in East and South-East Asia, while its almost complete absence in Africa has held the whole continent back. In addition to the direct spillover effect, neighbouring countries also tended to imitate each other's policies, which amplifies the overall importance of contagion.

The second factor, more intractable and presumably more important in terms of ultimate causation, is the level of ethnic diversity within the nation-state. In Africa this is generally high, due to the small scale of African socio-political organization in pre-colonial times and the well-known arbitrariness ('lines on a map in Berlin') of the national boundaries inherited from the nineteenth-century colonial scramble for the continent. The main index of ethnic diversity used by Easterly and Levine in their calculations measures the probability that two randomly selected individuals in each country will belong to the same ethnic group. Of the fifteen lowest-rating countries according to this index, only one (India) is not in Africa (Easterly and Levine 1997: 1220). Africa's greater-than-average ethnic diversity, they calculate (1995: 13), accounts for about 35 per cent of its growth differential with the rest of the world between 1960 and 1990. In 'some extreme country cases', these authors go so far as to claim, ethnic diversity alone may *fully* explain the growth differential between African and East Asian nations (Easterly and Levine 1997: 1237).

The diversity theory certainly makes intuitive sense in terms of the contrast with South-East Asia. Most South-East Asian states are themselves highly heterogeneous: over 500 languages, for instance, are spoken in Indonesia, and in Malaysia the descendants of immigrants from China and India make up a third of the population – no African country, not even South Africa, contains allocthonous groups on that scale. But if South-East Asian countries are very diverse in ethnic composition, almost all are still permanently dominated by a single large ethnic group: Burmese, Thai, Lao, Khmer, Kinh, Malay, Javanese, Tagalog. There are only two states, the Philippines and East Timor, in which the largest ethnic group makes up less than 40 per cent of the population, and only one, Malaysia, in which it is (just) less than twice the size of its nearest rival. In sub-Saharan Africa, by contrast, it is common for the largest ethnicity to include less than a third of the national population, and for another group, or even two others, to be almost as large. Although there are exceptions, notably Botswana, in general African nations, unlike their South-East Asian counterparts, lack a clear ethnocultural 'core'.

TABLE 2.1 Major ethnic divisions in selected African and South-East Asian countries

|  | 1 | 2 | 3 |
| --- | --- | --- | --- |
| Cambodia | Khmer 90% | Vietnamese 5% | Chinese 1% |
| Vietnam | Kinh (Viet) 87% | Tay 2% | Thai 2% |
| Thailand | Thai/Lao 75% | Chinese 14% | Malay 4% |
| Malaysia | Malay 49% | Chinese 26% | indigenous non-Malay 10% |
| Indonesia | Javanese 42% | Sundanese 15% | Madurese 3% |
| Ethiopia | Oromo 32% | Amhara 30% | Tigrawai 6% |
| Nigeria | Hausa/Fulani 29% | Yoruba 21% | Ibo 18% |
| Kenya | Kikuyu 22% | Luhya 14% | Luo 13% |
| Uganda | Baganda 19% | Bahima 10% | Bakiga 9% |
| Tanzania | Sukuma 13% | Nyamwezi 4% | Chaga 4% |

*Sources*: UN Statistics Division Demographic Yearbook, CIA World Factbook.

In Nigeria, for instance, the political scene is dominated by three major ethnic groups, the Hausa, Yoruba and Ibo, which make up respectively 29, 21 and 18 per cent of the population. Later refinements of the Easterly and Levine model indicate that this kind of coarse fragmentation into a few large ethnic blocs may be even more strongly associated with slow growth than is ethnic diversity as such, and is certainly more closely associated with civil conflict (Montalvo and Reynal-Querol 2005; Posner 2004). In Nigeria it led to civil war from 1967 to 1970, and its continuing ramifications since the end of that war have already been alluded to. One is 'competitive rent-seeking' – that is, engaging in competition for limited existing wealth at the expense of rival groups, rather than in a common endeavour to produce more wealth in the future. In the worst cases, this has led to a 'tragedy of the commons' in which productive activities are taxed out of existence by groups which fear that if they do not do this themselves, their rivals will (Easterly and Levine 1997: 1215). More generally, the policies of governments which reflect ethnic interests in environments of intense interethnic competition tend to be short-sighted owing to the fear of losing power in the future.

As noted, two existing comparative studies of Indonesia and Nigeria, by Thorbecke (1998) and Bevan, Collier and Gunning (1999), both attribute Indonesia's greater success partly to the secure political position of its largest ethnic group, the Javanese.

> [T]he fact that the Nigerian government never focused on poverty as such surely reflected the priorities of Nigerian society: ethnic rivalry and the politics of perceived disadvantage precluded cross-ethnic interventions. By contrast in Indonesia the Javanese secured undisputed control from the late 1950s, but it was still politic to balance the interests of Java against those of the outer islands, and continued legitimacy required that the government spread wealth regionally. (Bevan et al. 1999: 419)

The circumstance that the Javanese have no rival as Indonesia's predominant ethnicity arguably helped the country to avoid the kind of self-destructive contest for state resources seen in Nigeria, where the Hausa of the north enjoy only a 'precarious plurality' (ibid.: 420).

### According to the statistics: the irrelevance of governance?

With respect to the commonly heard argument that Africa has failed because of the 'weakness' of its political institutions, on the other hand, the evidence from cross-country statistical analyses is much more mixed. Some influential authors have certainly claimed to demonstrate that cross-country variations in economic performance are best accounted for by differences in institutional quality, as measured by indices of such variables as the strength of property rights and the rule of law (Acemoglu et al. 2001; Rodrik et al. 2004). However, as noted in Chapter 1, Khan (2007) has shown that correlations between institutional quality measures of this kind and economic growth rates all but disappear once already rich countries are removed from the database. Among developing countries, those with rapidly growing economies hardly differ from those with slowly growing economies on scales of what Khan calls 'market-enhancing governance'.

This is consistent with the casual observation that in terms of corruption, South-East Asian countries do not seem to differ significantly from their African counterparts. In the 1980s Indonesia was judged among the international business community to be a considerably more corrupt country than Nigeria, and even today its corruption rating is only slightly better.

TABLE 2.2 Corruption perception indices, selected countries, 1980–85 and 2010

|  | 1980–85 | 2010 |
|---|---|---|
| Netherlands | 8.4 | 8.8 |
| United Kingdom | 8.0 | 7.6 |
| Malaysia | 6.3 | 4.4 |
| Kenya | 3.3 | 2.1 |
| Thailand | 2.4 | 3.5 |
| Nigeria | 1.0 | 2.4 |
| Uganda | 0.7 | 2.5 |
| Indonesia | 0.2 | 2.8 |
| Ethiopia | – | 2.7 |
| Vietnam | – | 2.7 |
| Tanzania | – | 2.7 |
| Cambodia | – | 2.1 |

*Sources*: 2010 – Transparency International Corruption Perceptions Index (CPI) 2010; 1980–85 – Internet Center for Corruption Research (University of Passau), based on surveys by Business International (1980) and the Political Risk Service, East Syracuse, NY (1982, 1984, 1985), adjusted for comparability with the Transparency International CPI.

Such corruption indices, it is true, are crude and do not distinguish between unpredictable, chaotic forms of corruption and the more predictable, centralized, organized form, resembling informal taxation, which is often said to have been a redeeming feature of the Suharto regime in Indonesia (Macintyre 2001; McLeod 2000). The deeper political economy of corruption and development has so far been little studied by cross-country statistical means. There is some interesting evidence, at least from within Africa, that a history of pre-colonial political centralization is positively correlated with effective provision of public goods in the present (Gennaioli and Rainer 2007). In South-East Asia the big states of the mainland (Vietnam, Thailand, Cambodia and Burma) are all directly descended from major pre-colonial kingdoms with few parallels in Africa. In Java, too, state formation in the pre-colonial period had proceeded farther than in most parts of Africa.

If this difference is crucial to the broad contrast in development performance between the two regions, on the other hand, then why should Ethiopia, Africa's most important and successful indigenous state, have come to epitomize the African tragedy in the late twentieth century? And why should Malaysia – an ad hoc federation of thirteen territories including nine petty sultanates each about the size of an English county, and arguably a country as artificially colonial in origin as any in Africa – have performed so much better?

## Comparative method and common sense

Similar simple, comparative thought experiments can be used to cast grave doubt on some of the most common popular 'systemic' explanations for the Asia–Africa economic divergence. For this purpose it is not always necessary to resort to large databases and complex statistical methods. A combination of common sense and some basic historical facts about our two regions is often sufficient. For instance: the things that are now sometimes said about the lack of a work ethic in Africa were said about South-East Asia too in the nineteenth and early twentieth centuries, when the 'myth of the lazy native' was as unquestioned among Europeans in Indonesia, Malaya and the Philippines as it was in Africa (Alatas 1977). Later, however, it became clear that the laziness of the population had either been gravely exaggerated or was rapidly disappearing as economic development created improved economic incentives to work. 'Post-war Malayan padi farmers, and in fact the Malayan community in general [...] are psychologically different from their pre-war counterparts,' wrote one observer in 1967. 'Their attitude towards work, towards progress and many other matters, is in process of rapid transformation' (Lim 1967: 156). By the end of the 1980s, the 'present point of view on Javanese society' among scholars of Indonesia was described as one in which 'Javanese villages nowadays, and, to some lesser degree, even in the past, are peopled by ruthless individualists and (proto-) capitalists' (Schweizer 1989: 276).

Some writers imply that what really made the difference in South-East Asia was the culturally conditioned industriousness and business skill not of the indigenous population, but of the thirty million or so people of Chinese descent who live in the region (Hofstede and Bond 1988; Redding 1993). But it is important to note that what is now glibly called the 'Chinese spirit of capitalism' did not do China itself much good until the Chinese government began to make the right policy choices in the late 1980s. Moreover, it is less than a hundred years since the great sociologist Max Weber wrote a learned treatise arguing that Chinese culture was inherently *incompatible* with capitalism (Weber 1951 [1915]: 241–9). Other observers try to explain South-East Asia's success in terms of its strategic importance during the Cold War, which enabled its non-communist countries, particularly Thailand and Indonesia, to benefit from large amounts of Western aid (Stubbs 2005). But if aid was so important, then how can it be that Africa, as every newspaper reader knows, has swallowed billions of dollars of Western aid over the years, with very little to show for it (Easterly 2006)? And if aspects of South-East Asia's geography – its relative agricultural fertility, for instance, or its proximity to international trade routes – predestined it for success in comparison with Africa, then how to explain the case of Burma, which shares these advantages yet has not been able to translate them into anything like the same rates of growth or poverty reduction as other countries of the region?

In this book I will show that even in the most successful South-East Asian countries, development got under way only once certain crucial *policy* decisions were taken by those in power. In other words, I reaffirm the value (although not necessary all of the results) of the early policy-oriented approaches to comparative Africa–Asia development study (World Bank 1993; Lindauer and Roemer 1994; Bevan et al. 1999). Geographical, cultural and institutional factors may have facilitated the implementation of the vital decisions in South-East Asia, or even made it easier to take them. The question of whether all the policies chosen in Asia could potentially be implemented in Africa is a difficult one, to which attention will be given at several points in the coming chapters. However, at this point in history it is also a rather abstract one given that in reality African leaders, at least in my case studies, have so far never *tried* to implement all of them, and given that there is not much evidence that the reasons for not doing so included doubts regarding their technical feasibility.

What is in any case clear is that if African conditions did not necessarily preclude the correct policy choices, nor did South-East Asian conditions make them automatic. If this had been so, then the policies in question would have been adopted in Asia from the start, and there would have been no marked developmental 'turning points'. As it was, the fulfilment of the policy preconditions for sustained development often brought about a dramatic transition from prolonged stagnation to growth more rapid than anybody, including the policy-makers themselves, had predicted.

## History is not destiny

The ethnic fragmentation of most African states arguably presents them with a somewhat greater structural obstacle to economic development than most of South-East Asia has had to face, and the same can be said of aspects of Africa's physical geography. Nevertheless, this does not mean that the obstacles cannot be overcome. Forty years ago in South-East Asia the impediments to growth also appeared, and indeed were, severe enough. The wisdom that identifies structural preconditions for South-East Asia's success in the situation and condition of the region prior to that success is very much the wisdom of hindsight.

Pessimism regarding African development prospects has usually been based on a tendency to explain African political and economic behaviour in cultural terms (Chabal and Daloz 1999; Hyden 1983), and on a fascination among Africans and Africanists with the burden of history. It is no accident that three of the most prominent dependency or 'world-systems' theorists, Immanuel Wallerstein, Samir Amin and Giovanni Arrighi, were originally Africa specialists. Their work on the systematic nature of African underdevelopment, continuing deep into the 1980s (Amin 1989; Wallerstein 1986), influenced Africanists even after the undeniable fact of Asia's economic rise at last began to give them and other *dependentistas* second thoughts (Arrighi 1996; Frank 1998). And well into the 1990s, Africanists were still devoting major monographs to post-mortem attacks on colonialism as the root cause of Africa's contemporary problems (Davidson 1992; Mamdani 1996). Since then expectations have improved sharply as a result of renewed growth in Africa, but an undertone of historically based pessimism has persisted (Meredith 2005; Van der Veen 2004).

South-East Asianists are no longer much interested in this sort of argument, nor in the pessimism with which it is associated. But that was not always so. Most of what has been said in the last three decades to explain, and predict, persistent African underdevelopment was once said about South-East Asia too. In 1968 Benjamin Higgins, a prominent development economist and at that time the leading specialist on the Indonesian economy, published the second edition of his textbook *Economic Development; problems, principles, and policies*. The chapter on Indonesia was entitled 'Indonesia: the chronic dropout', and it began with the following passage.

> Indonesia must surely be accounted the number one economic failure among the major underdeveloped countries. No other large and populous country presents the same stark picture of prolonged economic stagnation [...] throughout centuries of colonial rule and continuing throughout a decade and a half of independence. Stagnation – in the form of virtually constant levels of per capita income or an unchanging structure of employment and production or both – is certainly not unknown among underdeveloped countries; but the Indonesian experience, in which a whole series of concepts of economic organization, first in a colony and then in an independent nation, failed to bring significant or lasting improvements in levels of living at any time, seems to be unique. (Higgins 1968: 679)

In 1966, when this was written, per capita income in Indonesia was lower than it had been in 1930, budget deficits had reached 50 per cent of government expenditures, inflation over the past year had exceeded 800 per cent, hunger was widespread, and the country was the world's biggest importer of rice.

Thirty years later in 1996, Higgins's successor as leading foreign expert on the Indonesian economy, Hal Hill, published a book on *The Indonesian Economy since 1966*. This book is subtitled 'Southeast Asia's emerging giant', and in his introduction Hill outlines why:

> Real per capita GDP has more than trebled in just a little over one generation, and [...] economic decline [...] has given way to strong positive growth for almost the entire period since 1966. Virtually all sectors of the economy have performed impressively. Rice yields have risen quickly, virtually doubling in the case of Java. [...] Rising output has resulted in a sharp increase – almost 50 percent – in average daily calorie consumption. [...] The transport infrastructure has experienced a virtual revolution [...]. Underpin-ning these changes has been macroeconomic stability, as reflected in reduced inflation. [...] External debt has [...] been sustainable [...]. Investment has [...] risen sharply [...]. The share of industry [in GDP] has more than trebled, and manufacturing overtook agri-culture in terms of value added in 1991. [...] Poverty incidence has fallen sharply, in virtually all regions of the country. (Hill 1996a: 4)

Not all commentators were quite this sanguine, and the timing of Hill's book, published a year before the Asian financial crisis shook the country, was unfortunate. Nevertheless, although the crisis highlighted vulnerabilities in the Indonesian economy, as we have seen it only very briefly halted the country's growth.

It is important to observe that Indonesia's economic problems in the 1960s were not thought at the time to result merely from revers-ible policy errors or temporary political difficulties. They were also thought to reflect structural impediments to growth, impediments with deep historical roots. Indonesia was the country which, through the work of J. H. Boeke (1953), had given the world the pessimistic idea of 'economic dualism'. According to Boeke, non-Western societies, both for cultural reasons and because of the particular ways in which the West and its capitalism had affected them in the past, were more or less impervious to economic development. Worse, such societies were said to respond to any aggregate economic growth which did occur by increasing in numbers rather than in standards of living, so that development efforts only served to fuel a population 'explosion'. Java's dense and growing population, far from being an economic asset, as more recent writers have argued, was thought at this period to be symptomatic of a 'low-level equilibrium trap' (Nelson 1956) – or, worse, of a process of 'agricultural involution' (Geertz 1963) involving diminishing returns to farm labour and progressive impoverishment.

Indonesia's long interaction with the world economy as the 'cradle of colonialism' (Masselman 1963), far from giving it a head start in the accumulation of commercial skills, had stifled the development of any indigenous capitalist class and instead produced a 'plural society' (Furnivall 1939) in which almost all commerce was controlled by foreigners. 'In essence', as Higgins himself put it (1968: 683), 'the Indonesian tragedy is a story of a repeated nipping off of a budding entrepreneurial upsurge by a political elite essentially hostile to it'. Nor did there appear to be much prospect of the country acquiring strong, efficient political institutions, whether for 'nipping' or for more constructive purposes. The concept of the 'soft state' – one in which corruption is rife and 'policies decided on are often not enforced, if they are enacted at all' (Myrdal 1968: 66) – is today mostly applied to Africa, but it was introduced in the 1960s to describe a range of Asian countries, including Indonesia. The eventual success of Indonesia in overcoming its institutional and other barriers to development confirms that history is not destiny, and that the human decisions which change history are worth searching for and learning from.

### The present methodology: rigorously comparative study of development histories

The approach followed in this book is based on the rigorously comparative study of the development histories of a number of selected countries. The Tracking Development research project on which the book is based adopted pairwise comparison of development trajectories as its methodical starting point. It then proceeded to construct pairwise narratives of development, and to search heuristically for the factors that had the greatest value in explaining divergences in development trajectories. Broadly speaking I maintain this methodology here, although much less equal attention is given to each country pair than first envisaged.

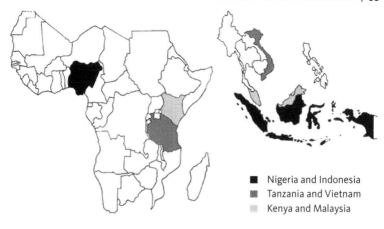

**2.1** The country pairs

The pairings (Figure 2.1) are useful in that they bring together countries which are particularly alike in important aspects of history, society and geography. This means that as is the case with the pairing of South-East Asia (as opposed to East Asia) with sub-Saharan Africa at the level of the regional comparison, the similarities between the paired countries sharpen the comparative analysis by helping to cut down the number of potential explanations for observed divergences in their development trajectories. In particular, the selected pairings will help test some common assumptions regarding the roles played in the African predicament by resource endowments, ethnicity and ideologies.

The reasons for re-examining the classic comparison of *Indonesia and Nigeria* have already been outlined. Indonesia and Nigeria are both huge, populous, multiethnic nations created by colonialism. They also have in common a rich endowment of mineral resources, particularly oil. In the 1960s Indonesia and Nigeria had similar standards of living, similarly stagnant economies, and faced similar problems of political conflict and instability. By the end of that decade, however, Indonesia had come under a competent developmentalist regime and Nigeria had not. The oil export boom of the 1970s provided windfall revenues which in Nigeria were largely siphoned out of the country or wasted on prestige projects, but which in Indonesia helped to fund investments in agriculture, infrastructure and education that provided the foundations for export-oriented industrial development in the 1980s. By the 1990s average living standards in Indonesia were more than twice as high as in Nigeria, and Indonesia was also much the more equal society in terms of wealth distribution. This despite comparable levels of corruption – throughout this period, both countries ranked among the most corrupt in the world – and despite the so-called 'resource curse', which the Indonesian experience shows can be escaped by means of appropriate policy choices.

*Malaysia and Kenya* are both artefacts of British colonialism which became independent at a relatively late date amid episodes of unrest (the Malayan Emergency and the Mau Mau revolt) in which much of the political elite effectively made common cause with the British. Both countries became Western allies during the Cold War, pursued market-friendly economic policies, and remained politically stable despite tensions arising from the presence of market-dominant ethnic groups: Chinese in Malaysia, Asian, European and Kikuyu in Kenya. Both countries have been among the most economically successful in their respective regions. Kenya's growth performance, however, began to falter in the 1980s and has since fallen ever farther behind that of Malaysia, which Prime Minister Mahathir was able to portray in the 1990s as a new model for the developing world.

Opened up to European capitalism under colonial rule, after independence *Vietnam and Tanzania* both experienced more than thirty years of socialist government under Ho Chi Minh and Julius Nyerere respectively. Trading and business communities were marginalized, agriculture partly collectivized or bureaucratized. Communist Vietnam's command economy, the establishment of which led among other things to mass emigration of entrepreneurs of all kinds, was in many ways more radical and destructive than that of Nyerere's Tanzania, and Vietnam also suffered from decades of war at a time when Tanzania remained impressively tranquil. Yet when both countries eventually returned to more orthodox capitalist paths in the 1980s, it was still Vietnam which benefited more quickly and dramatically from re-engagement with the global economy.

Comparison, in this study, is a choice of method, not a choice of subject. The subject is development, and the idea of studying it by means of the comparative method emerged out of the realization that analyses of African politics in terms of neo-patrimonial regimes could be made with equal validity in South-East Asia, where development outcomes were nevertheless very different. It should be stressed that the model of neo-patrimonial politics played no further role in the research. Indeed, there was no elaborate construction of hypotheses of any kind. There were merely similarities between regions and countries, and contrasting development outcomes. These similarities and contrasts provided the starting points for an inductive, iterative process of confronting ideas with emerging data. When exactly did major divergences in key development indices, such as income and poverty levels, become evident? How did these divergences relate to changes and contrasts in other economic variables? Above all, how closely did they correspond to major policy changes and other political events?

## Agency and policy relevance

My methodology here is based on a belief in the importance of *agency* in the sense defined by Anthony Giddens (1976: 75): a series of 'causal interventions', by actors who 'could have acted otherwise', in a world which 'does not hold out a predetermined future'. I agree with Nicholas and Scott Thompson (although without fully underwriting their moralistic intent) that history must hold Asian and African leaders personally responsible for their choices, and that good choices have made, and still can make, a difference.

> Thailand, whose prospects seemed so quaint and modest in the 1950s, had joined the big leagues by the millennium, overtaking many European economies. [...] Ghana, whose prospects were so trumpeted at that earlier time, was still struggling merely to get back on its feet [...]. Little of this happened by chance. The decisions that made it so were made at identifiable times by real people with names which need to be remembered, for better and for worse. (Thompson and Thompson 2000: 184)

This does not mean that I am not interested in the reasons why some interventions were undertaken, and not others. Having established what policy decisions were associated with developmental turning points, an important part of my task then consists of explaining why those decisions were made. If it is evident that factors such as geography, resource endowments or ethnic fragmentation played a role in the decision-making process, then that role will be duly acknowledged. The point, however, is that the influence of such factors can never be assumed, only empirically established. Nor will it be assumed, unless the historical facts strongly indicate otherwise, that the decision-makers in question had no choice but to do what they did.

The assumption of freedom – albeit not unlimited freedom – on the part of policy-makers is essential not only to the research method employed here, but also to the aspiration of this study to generate policy-relevant conclusions. Ultimately, the aim of the book is to indicate what kinds of choices, on the part of governments, aid donors or any other agents, might help to make African development paths converge with those of the successful South-East Asian countries. Without becoming overoptimistic, and without underestimating the large and real problems to be surmounted, the intention is in this way to help make development debates and development policies, particularly in Africa, less problem-oriented and more opportunity-oriented.

# 3 | SETTING THE STAGE FOR DEVELOPMENT

This chapter deals with two of our three proposed preconditions for sustained growth with rapid poverty reduction: macroeconomic stability, and economic freedom. It shows how the transition to growth in Malaysia, Indonesia and Vietnam was underpinned by low inflation and realistic exchange rates, and describes the part played by foreign aid and resource revenues in making rapid growth possible in a context of moderate, but at the same time resolute, fiscal conservatism. African governments, by contrast, were for a long time reluctant to accept the need for conservative macroeconomic policies. Partly as a consequence of this reluctance, they had more difficulty in accessing the capital they needed to make adequate development spending compatible with low inflation. Kenya, Nigeria and Tanzania were also slower than their respective South-East Asian counterparts to accept the need for deregulation of domestic markets, another key precondition for growth.

## Indonesia: macroeconomic stability and productive use of foreign aid

The Suharto regime which seized power in Indonesia in 1965 did so amid a severe hyperinflationary crisis, and immediately made the control of inflation its first and absolute policy priority (Widjojo 2011: 56). Guided by a team of economically trained 'technocrats' led by Widjojo Nitisastro (1927–2012), it did so partly by means of budgetary austerity, partly by using foreign aid to cover the remaining budget deficits, and partly by negotiating the rescheduling of existing foreign debt. The measures taken were extremely successful and established a crucial foundation of public confidence in the regime, subsequently known as Indonesia's New Order. Consumer price inflation fell from over 1,000 per cent in 1966 to just 16 per cent in 1969, and has since exceeded 20 per cent only three times – of which the last, in 1998, led to the fall of Suharto after thirty-two years in power (Chapter 1, Figure 1.7).

To ensure that hyperinflation could not happen again, in 1967 the new government instigated a law whereby parliament could not approve any budget that was not balanced, in the sense of state revenues (including foreign aid and loans) equalling or exceeding expenditures (including debt servicing). 'No slogan', noted Hal Hill (1996a: 59), 'has been more central in the New Order's economic philosophy than that of the balanced budget (BB)'. Strictly speaking the balanced-budget rule was a fiction, since aid and external borrowings were counted as revenue. In conventional terms, Indonesia in the 1970s and 1980s averaged budget deficits of between 2 and 5 per cent of GDP (Husain 1991: 10). Nevertheless, domestic financing of the deficit by the central bank was ruled out. This provided an important safeguard against overspending and inflation, boosting public and investor confidence in the economy.

Another important macroeconomic reform followed in 1970 when the technocrats made the controversial move of removing all restrictions on the flow of capital into and out of Indonesia, and making the rupiah freely convertible into other currencies.

> It might be argued that the opening of the capital account was premature, in the sense that it occurred too quickly after the control of inflation, when the newly won stabilization was still fragile. However, policy-makers knew [...] that an open capital account would impose a discipline on government and, in particular, a check on populist demands for a more adventurous monetary and fiscal policy. (Hill 1996a: 41–2)

An immediate benefit of this measure was the repatriation of a large amount of private capital (equivalent to about 20 per cent of the foreign aid received during the initial stabilization period) which had fled the country during the previous regime (Siber 2007: 110). Despite these self-imposed safeguards against deficit spending, government expenditure rose rapidly from less than 10 per cent of GDP in 1966, to 15 per cent in 1971 and over 20 per cent from 1975 to 1997 (Hill 1996a: 45). It was heavy public investments in agriculture and rural infrastructure which powered the spectacular poverty reduction of the 1970s and 1980s, and set the stage for Indonesia's subsequent industrialization (Chapter 4). These expenditures were made possible by the largest and most successful aid programme in history.

In the first few years of Indonesia's growth all development expenditures, and more than a quarter of the total state budget, were paid for by foreign aid (Siber 2007: 109). During the late 1970s, aid was eclipsed as a source of development finance by revenues from oil and gas production, which rose to form more than half of all government revenue (Hill 1996a: 46). When world oil prices fell sharply in the mid-1980s, however, Indonesia's aid donors once again stepped into the breach to prevent a reduction in public spending, which would have endangered growth, and to give the government time to implement reforms designed to boost domestic tax revenues (Sugema and Chowdhury 2007: 116). Similar support was to be forthcoming following the Asian financial crisis of 1998. During both of these crises, aid was actually even more important to Indonesia, at least in quantitative terms, than it had been in the early years of the New Order. In 1971, aid formed a quarter of government revenue and almost 70 per cent of the development budget; in 1988, by comparison, almost 40 per cent of revenue and 80 per cent of development spending; and in 1999 more than a quarter of revenue and 90 per cent of development spending (Chowdhury and Sugema 2005: 191-2).

'Perhaps the central lesson of the experience', concludes Peter McCawley (2007: 94), 'is that provided the conditions are right, international aid can be very helpful in promoting the development process.' Other classically trained economists who have studied the Indonesian story tend to come to the same conclusion.

> In the longer term, the objective of the Government should not be just filling the fiscal gap, but actually to create fiscal discipline. [...] However, the dilemma is that the arithmetic of closing the fiscal gap, that is, increasing tax and lowering expenditures, is not very simple. Public investment may be very crucial for sustaining growth, and increasing taxes may not be an easy task. [...] Therefore, over the short run, the Government may still have to rely on aid inflows to finance public investment [...]. (Sugema and Chowdhury 2007: 120)

As a result of its reliance on aid, Indonesia accumulated substantial foreign debt. In the 1980s its public external debt averaged around 35 per cent of GDP, and total debt around 50 per cent (Chowdhury and Sugema 2005: 205). The cost of debt servicing rose from less than 10 per cent of government expenditures in 1980 to over 25 per cent in 1990 (Hill 1996a: 53). However, thanks to excellent national economic performance and a highly cooperative relationship with its creditors, the costs of this indebtedness never became unsustainable. 'Today, Indonesia is certainly one of the highly indebted developing countries in the world,' wrote Widjojo (2011: 253) in 1994, 'but fortunately Indonesia has been successful in preventing any foreign debt crisis during the past twenty-four years.'

Especially in the early years, foreign aid to Indonesia was provided on generous terms. In the late 1960s more than 60 per cent of it took the form of outright grants; in the 1980s and early 1990s, the grant component was still above 30 per cent. In 1970 the average annual interest rate on non-grant aid was 2.4 per cent, with a grace period of nine years and a maturity period of thirty-five years (Chowdhury and Sugema 2005: 194). Following a number of interim agreements, in 1970 Indonesia was also able to negotiate a once-and-for-all settlement of its old, pre-New Order debts with the Paris Club group of major creditor countries. The principal sums owed were to be repaid over thirty years in equal annual instalments. Repayment of contractual interest would take place over a period of fifteen years beginning in 1985, and no further interest would be charged on the amounts deferred (Widjojo 2011: 256–7).

The favourable terms on which Indonesia was able to repay its existing debts, and access further foreign finance, had much to do with the international political context. Suharto had destroyed communism in Indonesia, and his rise was hailed by *Time* magazine (15 July 1966) as 'The West's best news for years in Asia'.

> There is no doubt that the diplomatic implications of a good cooperation between Western Powers and Indonesia, in the then prevalent context of the cold war, had a great weight in negotiations. The United States was clearly advocating a very generous settlement and its position, during the long process of discussions, was of course influential on most of its partners. (Deguen 2007: 143)

Cold War politics, however, are not the whole story here. Another very important – and more permanent – factor in the uniquely cooperative relationship between Indonesia and its creditors was that the top Indonesian economic policy-makers, the technocrats, were consistently in agreement with the international financial institutions on matters of macroeconomic policy.

No policy change was ever imposed upon Indonesia by IGGI (the Inter-Governmental Group on Indonesia, set up in 1967 to coordinate Western aid to the country), or by the World Bank or the IMF, as a condition for financial support. On the contrary, all liberalizing initiatives, including the thoroughgoing trade and financial deregulation of the mid-1980s (Basri and Hill 2004; Resosudarmo and Kuncoro 2006), proceeded from Widjojo and his colleagues themselves. In political terms, the international agencies were allies for the technocrats in their endeavour to get their policies adopted against sometimes strong opposition from other parts of the Indonesian establishment (see Chapter 7). In terms of policy-making, agencies such as the World Bank simply acted as on-demand advisers to their Indonesian counterparts.

> I like to think that the Bank's role in Indonesia has been an important one, but it was certainly not one of leadership. What success the Bank has had in helping Indonesia to develop has stemmed from a support rather than a starring role. [...] The Indonesians run their country. They take all the decisions. But they have done so with an unusual willingness to listen to advice and to learn from the experience of other countries. (Kaji 2007: 248)

Another senior World Bank official, posted to Jakarta in 1990 as head of the Bank's Resident Staff in Indonesia (RSI), was surprised to find that Widjojo (by then formally retired, but still very influential in national policy-making) 'saw the RSI as a secretariat', and was in the habit of ringing its director on Saturday morning to summon him to an immediate advisory meeting (Hope 2007: 227). As a former US ambassador likewise recalls: 'it was clear from the outset that Indonesia was in charge and that foreigners should curb their tendency to control' (Masters 2007: 68).

In McCawley's view, it is from this issue of policy 'ownership' that the most important practical lessons regarding the role of aid in development are to be drawn.

What, then, are the right conditions which may help improve the effectiveness of international assistance? Indonesian experience casts some light on this matter. One important characteristic of the aid relationship between donor agencies and Indonesia since the late 1960s has been *the strong involvement of Indonesian policy-makers themselves in the aid process.* Widjojo's own close work with IGGI is, perhaps, the clearest example of this. In the current jargon, it is very clear – and very significant – that senior Indonesian policy-makers themselves had strong ownership of the aid process in Indonesia. In other words, aspects of Indonesian nationalism have [...] always been clearly evident in the relationship between donor agencies and Indonesian recipients. (McCawley 2007: 94)

The role of nationalist sentiments in inspiring successful development policy in South-East Asia will be a recurrent theme in the following chapters. Economic nationalism in Africa, however, has taken subtly different forms, the effects of which in relation to macroeconomic policy and development finance have usually been negative rather than positive. This is illustrated by the case of Nigeria.

### Nigeria: economic nationalism and macroeconomic mismanagement

Nigeria, like Indonesia, benefited (at least in terms of GDP per capita) from the oil boom of the 1970s, but whereas in Indonesia living standards continued to rise during the oil price slump of 1980–86, in Nigeria they fell sharply (Chapter 1, Figure 1.4). Comparative accounts of the development trajectories of the two countries identify the oil slump as a decisive point of divergence (Bevan et al. 1999: 378; Lewis 2007: 87, 157–9). The usual explanation is that whereas Indonesia responded by further deregulating its economy and opening up to foreign investment, paving the way for a boom in export-oriented manufacturing industry and an expansion of its non-oil domestic tax base, Nigeria failed to liberalize and was therefore left with no alternative source of income, either for its government or for its people, to compensate for shrinking oil revenues.

While there is certainly truth in this account, it also bears repeating that Indonesia was able to weather the crisis of the 1980s, without severely cutting public spending, thanks only to a renewed influx of foreign aid even larger than that of the late 1960s and early

1970s (Chowdhury and Sugema 2005: 190). This not only bought the country crucial time in which to implement trade and tax reforms, but also ensured the continuity of its ongoing public investments in smallholder agriculture and rural infrastructure (Chapter 4).

In Nigeria, by contrast, the government of Ibrahim Babangida refused in 1985 to accept an IMF structural adjustment loan offered conditional on liberal reforms, despite the fact that Babangida himself was in principle sympathetic to deregulation. While the personal interests of other members of the political elite were to some extent involved here, the decision to reject the IMF loan was essentially a popular one, made for nationalistic reasons and because of popular disenchantment over how public money had been spent in the past.

> How do we account for the very widespread opposition to the loan? Beyond a nationalist response to the infringement of national sovereignty that the dictates of the IMF elicit in all countries and a more specific anti-imperialist opposition to the leading organ of international finance capital from the Left, there was a widespread feeling that additional foreign loans were not the answer to Nigeria's economic problems. It was felt that Nigeria's rulers should not again be given the opportunity to mismanage and waste resources on a grand scale. [...] After three months of debate, negotiations for a loan with the IMF were suspended [...]. The outcome was widely seen as a democratic victory for popular forces. (Forrest 1993: 211)

The result of this 'victory' was an immediate halving of development spending (Bevan et al. 1999: 80) and a scramble for alternative but more expensive sources of foreign credit, which increased the burden of debt and debt servicing. Budgetary discipline was abandoned (Lewis 2007: 165, 171) and inflation quickly soared to over 50 per cent, remaining at damagingly high levels for most of the following decade (Chapter 1, Figure 1.7).

This is not to argue that if only Nigeria had taken advantage of IMF credit in 1985, its future would have resembled Indonesia's. Its public spending priorities during the oil boom, as we shall see in the following chapter and as the previously quoted passage already suggests, were so misguided that in the long run enabling it to indulge them for longer would probably not have helped much.

Nevertheless, Nigeria clearly paid a price for its failure to manage development finance effectively, whereas Indonesia benefited greatly from its consistently prudent macroeconomic management and its cooperative relations with international donors.

Another persistent macroeconomic policy contrast between Nigeria and Indonesia can be seen in the area of exchange rate management. Cross-country statistical studies show that the size of the black market premium on currency deals – that is, the difference between an official and a black market exchange rate for a national currency against the US dollar or other international currencies – is a reliable predictor of poor national economic performance (Easterly 2002: 221–3, 238). Currency overvaluation was deliberately favoured by many countries during the 1950s and 1960s in connection with import-substituting industrial strategies calling for the purchase of expensive foreign production equipment. But it had serious disadvantages, the most important being that it made exports uncompetitive. Among the first acts of the New Order in 1966 was to devalue the rupiah, which had become massively overvalued as a result of over-regulation combined with hyperinflation, by 90 per cent against the dollar (Wing 1988: 340).

Although Indonesia maintained a pegged rather than floating dollar exchange rate, once every few years over the next two decades further stepped devaluations took place – by 10 per cent in 1971, 34 per cent in 1978, 28 per cent in 1983, and 31 per cent in 1986 (Simatupang 1996: 60–1) – to promote exports and to compensate for domestic inflation, which was fuelled by oil, aid and public spending. Consequently, no significant black or 'parallel' currency exchange market emerged. In Nigeria, by contrast, no devaluation was undertaken, with the result that at its peak in 1986, the official dollar value of the naira stood at over ten times its black market value (Figure 3.1). Rather than change the official rate, the Commissioner of Finance (equivalent to finance minister) of the time, Onaolopo Soleye, preferred to tighten administrative controls on foreign exchange in an attempt forcibly to eliminate the parallel market (Rimmer 1985: 439).

This situation was disastrous for non-oil exporters, whose products were priced out of international markets, and for agriculture in general, which suffered heavily under competition from imports.

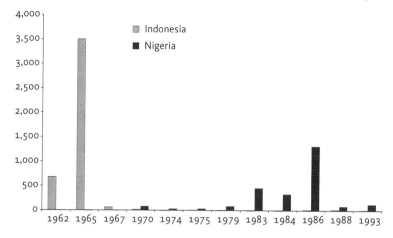

**3.1** Black market premium (per cent) of US$ banknotes against national currency, Indonesia and Nigeria, 1962–93 (*source*: Pick's Currency Yearbook/World Currency Yearbook)

During the early 1980s, Nigeria imported between two and five times more food per head of its population than did Indonesia (Pinto 1987: 434). When devaluation finally did become inevitable – to the tune of fully 69 per cent – in 1986, structural dependence on imported goods meant that unlike the Indonesian devaluations, it contributed to a burst of rapid inflation (Orubu 1995: 115).

One reason why devaluation was so much delayed in Nigeria was that, in the early 1980s, members of the political elite enjoyed illicit rents obtained from access to scarce foreign exchange at the official rate. A more constant underlying factor, however, was that policy-makers in Nigeria suffered from a nationalistic 'exchange-rate fetishism' which dictated that 'the naira should remain at least as valuable as the dollar' (Bevan et al. 1999: 81). More will be said about the nature and effects of this variety of economic nationalism in Chapter 7.

### Vietnam and Tanzania: macroeconomic crisis, reform, growth

Like Indonesia twenty years earlier, Vietnam and Tanzania in the mid-1980s faced severe macroeconomic crises involving excessive inflation (in Vietnam, hyperinflation), associated with budgetary imbalances (Figure 3.2), and shortages of foreign exchange and import goods, associated with overvaluation of the domestic currency (Figure

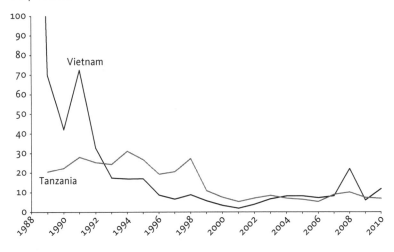

*Note:* Vietnam 1988 off scale at 411 per cent

**3.2** Inflation, GDP deflator (annual per cent), Vietnam and Tanzania, 1988–2010 (*source:* online World Development Indicators/World DataBank, World Bank)

3.3). It was when they began to tackle these problems effectively that their per capita incomes began to grow: respectively in 1987 in Vietnam and 1995 in Tanzania (Chapter 1, Figure 1.6).

In retrospect Doi Moi tends to be mainly associated with liberalization, but at its inception the primary goal was actually the control of inflation, which by 1986 had reached over 400 per cent (Nguyen 2006: 84, 173). This was tackled by drastically reducing public expenditure – over three-quarters of a million workers in state enterprises, for instance, were laid off within three years (Irvin 1995: 730); by renouncing domestic deficit financing by the central bank; and by beginning to draw on foreign loans for public finance. State revenues from oil and gas, which Vietnam began to export at the same period, also played an important role. Foreign exchange restrictions were removed, and US dollar bank accounts legalized (Goujon 2006). Although it took until 1993 before inflation fell below 20 per cent, the credibility of these drastic measures was such that aggregate growth began immediately. A rapid agricultural response, to be discussed below and in Chapter 5, also led to mass poverty reduction (Chapter 1, Table 1.1).

Tanzania's inflation problem, by comparison, took longer to solve. This was due partly to a lack of domestic enthusiasm for what was

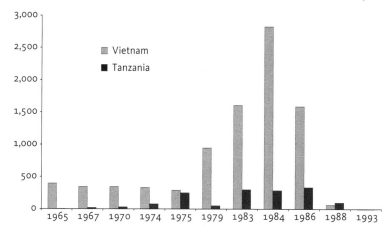

*Notes*: Vietnam up to 1975 = North Vietnam; Vietnam 1979 interpolated; in Tanzania in 1965, and in both Tanzania and Vietnam in 1993, the black market premium was below 5 per cent

**3.3** Black market premium (per cent) of US$ banknotes against national currency, Vietnam and Tanzania, 1965–93 (*source*: Pick's Currency Yearbook/World Currency Yearbook)

seen as a donor-driven policy agenda, and partly to the continuing power of credit-hungry state enterprises over the central bank (Eriksson Skoog 2000). Overvaluation of the currency, although initially much less severe than in Vietnam, likewise took somewhat longer to correct (Figure 3.3).

By 1995 both problems had, however, been addressed, with the result that sustained aggregate growth began and good access to concessional sources of international development finance was secured. Nevertheless, for reasons connected with public spending priorities (Chapter 5), this growth still did not lead to rapid poverty reduction.

### Malaysia and Kenya: stability a necessary but not sufficient condition for growth

The other country pair under consideration, Malaysia and Kenya, presents a different picture in that both countries have a history of relatively successful inflation control, without this having led in the Kenyan case to rapid aggregate growth. Although the Kenyan record is not as good as Malaysia's (Figure 3.4), with inflation exceeding 20 per cent in only three years since 1960, it is on the face of it comparable

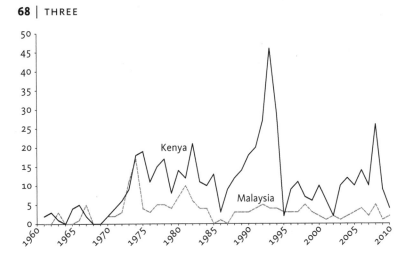

**3.4** Inflation, consumer prices (annual per cent), Malaysia and Kenya, 1960–2010 (*source*: online World Development Indicators/World DataBank, World Bank)

to Indonesia's (Chapter 1, Figure 1.7). It might be argued, however, that political commitment to keeping inflation down was less solid in Kenya (Swamy 1994), and that this affected investor confidence. Currency overvaluation was much more evident in Kenya than in Malaysia, where no significant parallel currency market emerged (Figure 3.5). On the other hand this problem, although persistent,

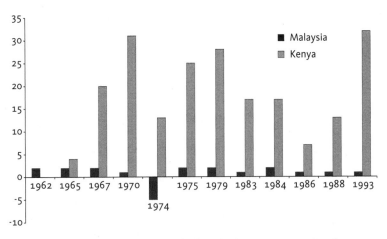

**3.5** Black market premium (per cent) of US$ banknotes against national currency, Malaysia and Kenya, 1962–93 (*source*: Pick's Currency Yearbook/World Currency Yearbook)

was still mild compared to the levels of hundreds of per cent reached in Nigeria and Tanzania.

Malaysia began its growth period with a healthy export economy, providing an adequate basis for savings and taxation. Aid has never been important in Malaysian development, and initially even non-concessional foreign loans played only a limited role, supplying 28 and 31 per cent of development expenditure respectively under the first (1956–60) and second (1961–65) national development plans (Drabble 2000: 163). Later Malaysia had the additional benefit of income from oil and gas, the contribution of which to total government revenue rose from 12 per cent in 1975 to a peak of 36 per cent in 1985, before declining thereafter (Von der Mehden with Troner 2007: 29). At this period there was also more foreign borrowing, by the state as well as by the private sector. External finance helped the country weather the oil and trade crisis of the mid-1980s, in the same way as foreign aid helped Indonesia in that period. In 1986 Malaysia's total foreign debt reached 76 per cent of national income, a figure which Drabble (2000: 261) notes was 'far above the average' for a developing country. Thereafter, however, renewed growth quickly enabled debt to be brought down again.

> Overall, the Malaysian government succeeded in maintaining monetary and fiscal stability, together with low inflation throughout this period by a combination of pragmatic and moderate policies. These counteracted the periodic fluctuations arising out of the country's exceptional openness to the international economy, and accelerated the recovery in export values after the slump of the mid-1980s. (Ibid.: 262)

In Kenya, by contrast, a combination of more thoroughly stalled growth and a growing lack of trust on the part of donors and creditors gave rise to a vicious circle of rising indebtedness from 1980 onward. When deregulatory trade reforms (of which more below) prescribed as conditions for concessional loans were only partly and reluctantly implemented (Swamy 1994), Kenya found its access to international credit constrained.

> Kenya progressively lost the confidence of the IMF and donors because of its lax adherence to the terms of previous programmes

and mounting concern about corruption and malpractice [...].
For a while, Kenya was able to borrow commercially, short-term,
to overcome its foreign-exchange liquidity difficulties, but by the
early 1990s mounting debt-service obligations blocked further recourse to commercial borrowing. (Roberts and Fagernäs 2004: 37)

This is not to claim, however, that Kenya's debt problem was
itself the root cause of the economic stagnation after 1975 (Chapter
1, Figure 1.5). In Chapter 5 it will be argued that, like Nigeria, Kenya
was already failing in the 1970s to invest in the kind of broad-based
rural development which was ultimately the most important cause
of the resilience of Indonesian and Malaysian growth in the 1980s
and 1990s. Over-regulation of the domestic economy, although the
donors may have exaggerated its severity, was a real problem too
(see below). When assessing the impact of the debt crisis, finally, it
is important to note that total public spending in Kenya remained
at the high level of about 30 per cent of GDP throughout the 1980s
and early 1990s, and that while development expenditure was cut to
compensate for the rising debt-service burden, the amount spent
on the wages and salaries of the country's oversized civil service
actually grew (ibid.: 43).

## Vietnam and Tanzania: the importance of economic freedom

Besides a stable macroeconomic environment, sustained growth
also depends on the provision of a reasonable degree of economic
freedom for farmers and entrepreneurs, particularly small farmers
and small entrepreneurs. Where farmers are not free to make their
own production decisions and sell their produce on competitive
markets, their incomes are not likely to grow. This is most clearly
demonstrated by the cases of Vietnam and Tanzania.

The rationalization of macroeconomic management in Vietnam
from 1986 onward formed one part of a more general move away from
state ownership and regulation of the economy, and towards reliance on private ownership and market forces. Since independence
in 1954, communist Vietnam had pursued a radical collectivization
of agricultural production. By the early 1980s more than 90 per cent
of farmers in North Vietnam – although still far fewer in the South,
which had remained a separate, non-communist state until 1975 –

were members of cooperative farms. On these farms all work was carried out by production teams using communally owned equipment, and payment was based on 'the quantity and quality of work performed' rather than on the quantity or value of the crops produced (Pingali and Xuan 1992: 699).

Well before 1986, deep popular dissatisfaction with the results of this system had induced the Vietnamese government to dilute it with liberal elements (Kerkvliet 2005). A household contract system, whereby farmers could sell a regulated proportion of their surplus on the open market, was introduced as early as 1981. In 1988 a resolution was passed enabling farmers to buy, own and sell all agricultural inputs, and to lease land for up to fifteen years. In 1989, all compulsory state purchase of farm products was eliminated. The two state food marketing corporations became actors in a fully competitive domestic market, retaining monopoly and licensing powers only with respect to rice imports and exports, which they regulated with a view to stabilizing domestic prices in the face of international price fluctuations.

Rice production in Vietnam doubled between 1981 and 1992, and in 1989 the country began to export rice for the first time in decades (Dang and Tran 2008: 207). Although other factors were also involved (Chapter 5), this growth was due in major part to the improved production incentives created by the decollectivization of production and the liberalization of agricultural product markets. Statistical analysis of disaggregated data from the 1980s confirms that productivity was significantly higher on farms operating under the contract system than on fully collectivized farms (Pingali and Xuan 1992: 712–13). Likewise, although state-owned industrial enterprises have remained important in Vietnam since Doi Moi, the strong growth of export-oriented manufacturing industry since the 1990s, not to mention the explosion of coffee, cashew nut and other non-rice agricultural exports, would have been inconceivable without the abandonment of state socialism and the progressive liberalization of trade and investment regulations (Hill 2000a; Nguyen and Grote 2004).

In Tanzania, the 1970s saw a brief but intense attempt at full state control of agriculture in the name of *ujamaa*, a variety of 'African socialism' embraced by President Julius Nyerere in 1967. Scattered peasant households were to be regrouped into big new villages where, by working collectively and sharing equipment such as tractors, it was hoped that they could reap economies of scale without becoming wage labourers in the service of capital owners.

> One of the most important objectives of Ujamaa is to modernize agriculture, creating a framework in which the advantages of large-scale production can be reaped without the negative social consequences of capitalist agriculture. [...] Emphasis on development through the individual farmer, which has been the basis of previous extension practice, will be ended. (Second Five-Year Plan 1969: 29)

Envisaged at first as a consensual process, in 1973 collectivization was made compulsory, and by 1976 at least five million people had been relocated into new villages (Scott 1998: 223). At the same time state agencies attempted to take full control of all rural trade, including retail trade (Hyden 1980: 132). Although collective production in the new settlements was only partly realized, the damage caused to the economy – in particular to agricultural exports – by the social upheaval, the destruction of private trade and the mismanagement of the macroeconomy under state socialism was so serious that the resulting crisis lasted a decade. It culminated in the end of the socialist experiment and the 'capitulation' (Cooksey 2003: 69) of Tanzania in 1986 to the terms of an IMF structural adjustment programme which required it, among other things, to reopen all markets in agricultural products and inputs to private traders.

## Indonesia and Nigeria: market-oriented pragmatism versus regulatory nationalism

Like Vietnam, Indonesia began its successful development trajectory by correcting policy errors which had previously plunged it into an economic crisis. In the early 1960s the Indonesian government had not only caused hyperinflation by mismanaging public finances, but also damaged agricultural and other production by restricting almost all kinds of commercial activity in the pursuit of a state-dominated 'guided economy' to match President Sukarno's 'guided democracy' (Hill 1996a: 1–3). This systematic over-regulation, sometimes described at the time as '*étatisme*' (statism), was the background against which Widjojo Nitisastro and his fellow technocrats formulated their corrective strategies from 1966 onward.

The evil of 'free fight liberalism' has often been described and heard. On the other hand, the term 'etatism' is rarely heard, although actually this system, also known as statism, has become a reality in Indonesia lately. In the system of 'etatism' the state and the state's economic apparatuses are fully dominant and push back, as well as kill, the potential and creativity of the economic units beyond the state sector. (Widjojo 2011: 85)

The need to free the 'potential and creativity' of private enterprise from excessive state regulation, first under the banner of 'debureau-cratization' and later in the name of 'deregulation', was to be a constant theme in the thinking of the leading Indonesian economic policy-makers over the next thirty years.

Despite their special concern with rural interests and poverty reduction (Chapter 4), the Indonesian technocrats were in most respects orthodox neoclassical economists. Their attitude to foreign capital, for example, was strikingly liberal. In 1967 the New Order passed new investment laws and established a Technical Team for Foreign Investment, the role of which was essentially to extend an open welcome to investors. As its first chairman, Mohamad Sadli, later recalled (1993: 43), with incentives including '100 percent foreign equity ownership, absence of exchange controls, tax holidays, and the opportunity of exploiting Indonesia's abundant natural resources', there was no shortage of interested parties.

In the 1970s, with the economy stabilized and oil income coming on stream, there was a temporary move back towards the economic nationalism of the Sukarno years, as 'technicians' (technology enthusiasts with a belief in infant industrial protection) and 'patri-monialists' (soldiers, bureaucrats and managers with a personal interest in protected industries) once again acquired a measure of policy influence (Resosudarmo and Kuncoro 2006: 343–4). The technocrats, however, were able at crucial junctures to reassert their authority – notably when a dangerous debt crisis hit the patrimonially managed state oil company Pertamina in 1974, and again when falling oil revenues in the years from 1982 to 1988 enabled them to convince President Suharto to authorize a second wave of deregulation aimed among other things at promoting investment, both foreign and domestic, in export-oriented manufacturing industry.

By deregulating trade and investment, Indonesia integrated itself into the international economy more tightly and extensively than ever before. Indonesia made the world its market-place and reciprocated by inviting the world to take a stake in the nation's development. Investors from around the world have responded most obligingly. [...] Many businesses have suffered, and many have chastised the government for abandoning protectionist policies. However, Indonesia as a nation has profited. Most of Indonesia's businesses have risen to the challenge of international competition. The competition has made them stronger and all Indonesians have benefited from lower costs, as well as better quality and a broader range of goods and services. (Prawiro 1998: 277–8)

Widjojo and his colleagues were no Chicago School ideologues; their professed guideline was 'pragmatism, that is, the principle that what is good is what works' (Sadli 1997: 243), and they 'saw the need of planning to influence the market through intervention in supply or demand' (Salim 2011: xv). But their 'default position' was one whereby market forces were allowed to dominate the economy, and whereby the economic freedom of entrepreneurs, including small entrepreneurs and peasant farmers, was respected. Only in 'extremely exceptional circumstances' (Prawiro 1998: 146) did they favour price controls. One such exception occurred immediately following the currency devaluation of 1978, when the regime resorted to the temporary use of force to prevent retailers from instituting 'irrational' price rises, quickly lifting price controls once the inflationary momentum had been broken (Baneth 1997: 286).

The form of state economic intervention consistently preferred by the technocrats was not *regulation*, but *subsidy*. Their founding father, Dutch-trained economics professor Sumitro Djojohadikusumo (1917–2001), once said: 'I believe in the active role of the state but [...] I don't believe in regulations' (Sumitro 1986: 37). State subsidies on fertilizer, credit and fuel, as well as education and other public goods, were used to allocate resources and influence behaviour in non-market ways without compromising the freedom of consumers. It is worth noting that even fundamental subsidies like the one on fertilizer, of which more in the next chapter, were intended as temporary, not permanent, measures.

The fertilizer subsidy constituted what I would call a 'structural adjustment subsidy'. The intent of the subsidy was [...] to encourage a particular behaviour that the government hoped would become habit forming, that is, the use of modern farming technologies, such as advanced seed strains and fertilizers. [...] The government believed that when Indonesia's farmers had become 'married' to modern farming techniques, they would never get divorced. The government could then remove the subsidy. This proved to be correct. (Prawiro 1998: 146)

One area in which the New Order was particularly aware of the danger of market failure and instability was the production and distribution of Indonesia's staple food and most politically sensitive commodity, rice. At one point during a rice production crisis in 1972, Widjojo (2011: 166) went so far as to declare that 'the government has never had any intention of letting the market decide the rice prices'. In practice, however, the chosen policy reflected a careful compromise between market and non-market mechanisms. A 'logistics agency', Bulog, was set up to stabilize both farm-gate and retail prices by buying rice at a fixed floor price when the market price was low, and selling rice from the resulting buffer stock, or out of imported supplies, at a fixed ceiling price when the market price was high.

Bulog had no monopsony or monopoly rights (except over imported food) and did not seek to displace the private sector from the domestic rice trade. The margins provided between the floor and ceiling prices allowed private traders to handle most of the rice marketed. In normal years, Bulog bought and distributed less than 10 per cent of the rice produced and consumed in Indonesia (Timmer 1997: 137). As the government was at pains to stress, the fact that state-sponsored cooperatives linked to Bulog were allocated a role in rice marketing did not mean that the system was designed to involve any compulsion.

In order to make the policy succeed [...] the government will purchase food from the farmers through the Village Unit Cooperatives. This does not mean that the cooperatives are given a monopsony position. The farmers are free to sell to anyone they want. But whenever the market price drops below the floor price

the Village Unit Cooperatives will purchase from farmers at the
floor price. (Third Five-Year Development Plan 1979: 33)

If the rice market interventions did not limit the freedom of rice
producers, neither did they significantly restrict the operations of
private sector rice traders, except by discouraging speculation and
hoarding. The continued dominance of an essentially unregulated
private sector in the rice marketing system provided an inbuilt safeguard against abuse of power by the bureaucrats responsible for
the operation of the state-owned component of that system. Even
this limited state participation in crop marketing, moreover, was
restricted to rice; other food crops, and all export crops, were bought
and sold exclusively through private sector channels.

In Nigeria at the same period, it was a different story. State-owned
marketing boards enjoyed exclusive control over the marketing of all
the major export crops: cocoa, palm oil, palm kernel, groundnuts and
cotton. As in other African countries, these boards were originally
introduced by colonial administrators, and in the 1950s they were
already being abused as 'a fiscal base for the politicians to whom
control of the new regional governments was now devolved' (Williams 1985: 6). After independence in 1960, nevertheless, they were
retained by the Nigerian planners. Partial reforms in the 1970s left
their export monopolies intact; in the case of cotton, the board also
retained its domestic buying monopsony. It was not until 1986 that
they were abolished, partly under pressure from foreign aid donors
(Forrest 1993: 194–5). It has been calculated that over the whole period
1942–85, the cotton board, without in practice providing any net price
stabilization benefit, imposed an effective tax on Nigerian cotton
farmers equivalent to 72 per cent of the value of all the cotton they
produced; for none of the other major export crops was the figure
lower than 30 per cent (Ilorah 2006: 37). Together with the simultaneous currency devaluation, which raised prices for agricultural exports
and reduced competition from imported food, the abolition of the
marketing boards and the lifting of price controls in 1986 created
new incentives for Nigerian farmers (Olomola 1995: 100). Per capita
agricultural production rose rapidly to higher levels than before the
oil boom, although growth slowed once more after 1993 (Figure 3.6).

When it came to manufacturing industry, an area much closer to

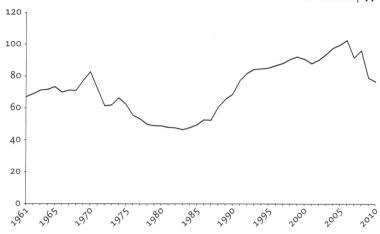

**3.6** Nigeria: gross per capita crop production index (2005 = 100), 1961–2010
(*source*: FAOSTAT online)

their hearts, the interventionist impulse of the Nigerian policy-makers was stronger still. They were proponents of a classic import-substitution industrialization strategy, with its usual policy implications: tariffs and quantitative restrictions (quotas) on the import of foreign manufactured goods, and an overvalued domestic currency in order to cheapen imported capital goods for use in the industrialization process. In addition, there was a pervasive concern with foreign ownership in the industrial sector. The underlying assumption here seems to have been that 'indigenization' was not just an instrument of development policy, but a form of development in its own right. Whereas in New Order Indonesia the technocrats stood in radical opposition to the 'technicians' and the 'patrimonialists' on this point, in Nigeria it was the technocrats themselves who championed intervention and regulation in the name of economic nationalism.

> National Planning should be aimed at the transformation of the whole society, and must be directed at the power centres of economic and political decisions. In the circumstances of Nigeria, a major segment of those centres from the point of view of development possibilities is still dominated by foreign interests. These interests cannot always be expected to coincide with those of the nation. (Second National Development Plan 1970: 31)

The 1970s, accordingly, saw the enactment of much legislation excluding non-Nigerians altogether from particular areas of business, and restricting foreign ownership in others (Forrest 1993: 153–7).

This is not to argue that Nigerian economic interventionism was either particularly effective in interfering with market forces, or particularly pronounced by the developing-country standards of its day. Nigeria under Yakubu Gowon (head of the Federal Military Government, 1966–75) was hardly comparable with socialist Tanzania under Nyerere, and Lewis (2007: 273) notes the paradox that in Indonesia, public attitudes to private enterprise have always tended to be more critical, not less critical, than in Nigeria. The regulatory urge of Nigerian policy-makers was inspired more by bureaucratic self-interest and bourgeois nationalism than by any deep hostility to private enterprise as such. Nevertheless, it is fair to say that the Nigerian technocrats, especially in the 1970s when they were at the height of their power and autonomy (Chapter 7), had a greater propensity to interfere with the operation of markets than did their counterparts in Indonesia, where regulatory and protectionist policy impulses, where present, usually originated from other quarters and were opposed by the technocrats.

## Kenya and Malaysia: market economies with and without parastatal monopsonies

Kenya, even more than Nigeria, is an African country with a reputation for following a liberal development path which acknowledges the importance of private capital and entrepreneurship. Yet government and government-controlled ('parastatal') institutions have played a very major role in the Kenyan economy, especially in the important area of agricultural marketing. In 1984, according to a World Bank study, the state played at least some part in marketing 78 per cent of Kenya's agricultural production, and 34 per cent of all crops and animal products were owned at some point by government agencies. The price of maize, the staple crop, was administratively set, at least in principle, by the cabinet, as were the prices of milk, beef, wheat, sugar and cotton (Leonard 1991: 210).

Since the colonial period, the government had purchased and marketed most major agricultural products more or less monopolistically via official marketing boards. Private sector participation was either banned, or severely restricted.

The boards maintained tight controls over the marketing of the main food items [...] in spite of the fact that Kenya was regarded as one of the leading countries in Africa in terms of strong orientation to a liberal market-based economy. The rationale for the regulations on food marketing was the widespread public belief in the 1960s and 1970s that they were the most appropriate forms of protecting the interests of both producers and consumers. (Ikiara 1998: 99)

The Maize Marketing Board was not only responsible for the maintenance of a floor price using a buffer stock, but also had legal monopsony power over all maize produced in the country as soon as it was harvested, unless the grain was consumed by the farmer or his family or 'bartered by him to an individual in the same district' (Report of the Maize Commission 1966: 6). This power was retained by the National Cereals and Produce Board (NCPB), established as the successor to the Maize Marketing Board in 1979. To complement its monopsony, the NCPB was given control of all movement of maize within the country, an NCPB licence being required for any transport of more than a single bag (90 kilograms) across a district boundary. The weight threshold was progressively raised after 1988, but domestic maize transport was not completely decontrolled until 1993, and maize prices not until 1995 (Wangia et al. 2004: 12).

Unlike many of its counterparts elsewhere in Africa, the NCPB was not a predatory institution taxing farmers for the benefit of bureaucratic, urban and industrial elites. Indeed, the main reason why the World Bank was hostile to it in the 1980s was not because it was paying farmers too little, but because its efforts to 'support high producer prices in good times and in bad' were costing the state too much (Swamy 1994: 10). Nevertheless, the way it operated had serious shortcomings. The restrictions on grain movements imposed costs on producers and consumers by generating rents for those who granted and obtained licences. Moreover, in practice the whole official system served only a limited proportion of Kenya's rural maize farmers and consumers. The rest relied on a huge 'informal' marketing system, handling perhaps half of all maize traded (Wangia et al. 2004: 11), but technically illegal and subject to police harassment and extortion (Ikiara 1998: 104). Even for those farmers who were able to obtain the official price, bureaucratic inefficiency often meant that payment was disastrously delayed.

> NCPB made every effort to ensure prompt payment to large-scale farmers in order to maintain their political support. But small farmers might have to wait months for payment, or might have to pay a bribe or sell at a distress price to larger farmers. This was often a critical problem for poor farmers who needed immediate cash to purchase inputs, pay debts, purchase other foodstuffs, and pay school fees. (O'Brien and Ryan 2001: 504)

After the last restrictions on private trade in maize were finally abolished in 1995 as a result of sustained pressure from international donors, a nationwide survey of 1,540 households found that both the availability of maize (in rural as well as urban areas), and the convenience of selling it, had improved dramatically since the heyday of the Board's monopoly.

> In spite of the fact that grain wholesale prices have declined during the post-liberalization period, the overwhelming major-ity of households in all regions (88%) stated that it was more convenient to sell grain since liberalization [...]. There are two reasons for this: First, most traders buying maize now pay cash immediately at the time of the transaction, in contrast to sales to NCPB, which often took months for reimbursement. Second, most farmers are now able to sell their grain at or very near the farm premises. (Argwings-Kodhek et al. 1998: 33)

Since its reduction after 1995 to the status of a 'buyer of last resort', approximately comparable to Bulog in Indonesia, the NCPB has re-portedly been successful in stabilizing national grain prices without creating disincentives to production and trade (Jayne et al. 2008: 324).

In Malaysia, which, as we shall see (Chapter 5), achieved much greater progress than Kenya in the production of both food and ex-port crops between 1960 and 1990, the role of the state in agricultural marketing was much more limited. For the export crops, with the minor exception of pepper, there were never any marketing boards or equivalent institutions. Price stabilization in the face of global fluctuations was considered important, but this was achieved by the indirect means of an adjustable export tax (in the case of rubber, which was produced mainly by smallholders) or production tax (in the case of palm oil, which was produced mainly on large plantations). The tax was raised when the world price of the commodity was high, and lowered when it was not (Jenkins and Lai 1989: 69–70).

In the politically sensitive case of rice, there was more intervention. A minimum price, at which the state guaranteed to buy any rice offered to it, was introduced in 1949. Rice purchased (almost entirely from traders rather than direct from farmers) at the minimum price formed a national buffer stock which could be released to reduce prices in times of shortage (Brown 1973: 166–7). The import of rice, meanwhile, was controlled by quotas and tariffs. Until 1974, the price support policy was not financed directly by the government budget. Instead, licensed importers were required to purchase, at a high fixed price, a certain proportion of rice from the government buffer stock for every unit of rice imported. As in Indonesia the main aim, at least up to 1980, was not to subsidize the rice price on a permanent basis, but to stabilize it, encouraging production by reducing the risks involved in rice cultivation (Jenkins and Lai 1989: 90, 93). Over the long run, the level of protection afforded to domestic rice producers was low: between 1960 and 1981, the domestic rice price in Malaysia was as often below as it was above the world price (Timmer 1993: 167).

In 1966, a Padi and Rice Marketing Board was created with the aim of reducing the monopsony power of rice traders and millers in the domestic market. In 1971 this was replaced by a National Padi and Rice Authority (Lembaga Padi dan Beras Negara, LPN). In 1974, partly in reaction to an international rice shortage and partly in connection with domestic political changes, the LPN acquired two new powers which its predecessor had not enjoyed: monopoly control of rice imports, and the power to impose direct price controls on the private sector, rather than simply operating in (subsidized) competition with it as an alternative rice buyer and seller.

Two important caveats, however, are immediately in order in relation to the apparently high level of regulation which existed from 1974 onward. First, by that stage Malaysia's great leap forward in rice production had already been achieved: the year 1974, in fact, saw the all-time peak of national rice self-sufficiency, the level of which subsequently declined (Chapter 5). Secondly, even in the regulatory era after 1974, the LPN did not aspire to monopolize rice marketing. In 1975 it purchased 8 per cent of West Malaysian rice production; in 1985, 29 per cent (Pletcher 1989: 375). Today (2014) the LPN's privatized successor, Bernas (Padiberas Nasional Berhad), purchases just under a quarter of national rice production, and continues to act as a buyer of last resort in support of the guaranteed minimum price (www.bernas.com.my).

The willingness of successive Malaysian governments to leave the bulk of the rice market in private hands is consistent with their essentially liberal stance in other spheres. Although Malaysia's unexpected use of controls on international capital movement during the financial crisis of 1998 has given the country a reputation in some circles for macroeconomic heterodoxy, the extreme briefness of that episode (Beeson 2000) reflects a keen awareness in Malaysia that the nation's long-term success is based on 'exceptional openness to the international economy' (Drabble 2000: 262). And although Malaysia under Mahathir Mohamad (prime minister 1981–2003) saw some spectacular (and mostly rather unsuccessful) state-led, technology-rich, capital-intensive national industrial projects, as a whole the industrial sector continued to be characterized by a very large component of foreign investment, and by labour-intensive production (Akyüz et al. 1999: 20–1). Until as recently as 2012 it also featured a complete – and globally almost unique – absence of minimum wage legislation.

### Conclusion: economic stability, resources, freedom as preconditions for development

From the above discussion, the following conclusions can be drawn. First, despite the scepticism of some heterodox economic thinkers (Stiglitz 2005; Stiglitz et al. 2006; Stein 2008), the prevention of excessive inflation and the avoidance of currency overvaluation are necessary conditions for growth. Arguments to the contrary are usually based on consideration of short-term fluctuations rather than long-term policy commitment. Second, even under very fortunate initial conditions like Malaysia's, access to substantial external finance, and/or domestic resource revenues, is likely to be essential at some point in order to make the maintenance of macroeconomic stability consistent with the maintenance of adequate development spending. The fact that Indonesia, Malaysia and Vietnam all made productive use of oil income for development purposes supports the emerging view that the so-called 'resource curse', whereby resource endowments handicap rather than benefit developing nations, is a politically contingent phenomenon (Robinson et al. 2006; Rosser 2007), or even a statistical illusion (Brunnschweiler and Bulte 2008), rather than a law of economic motion.

A third conclusion is that given appropriate public spending priorities and cooperative relations between donors and recipients, foreign aid can make a vital contribution to successful development finance. The Indonesian story here is radically at odds with the popular (Easterly 2006; Moyo 2009) and even technical (Collier 2006; Djankov et al. 2008) literature which suggests that aid, like oil, is a curse rather than a blessing for developing countries. Although the cases of Malaysia and Vietnam are different in this respect, the Indonesian experience is paralleled to some extent by that of Thailand (of which more in Chapter 5), where one quarter of the cost of the crucial Chao Phraya basin irrigation project of the 1950s was met by a World Bank loan, and where US government grants made possible heavy investment in rural roads during the 1950s and 1960s (Ellsworth et al. 1959: 38, 285; Warr 1993: 45).

To this it can be added that although geostrategic considerations were often also involved, and although international institutions were not necessarily correct in all their policy prescriptions, generally speaking access to concessional development finance, like access to non-concessional overseas loans, was itself a function of the adoption of prudent, growth-friendly macroeconomic policies and the removal of excessive restrictions on economic freedom. Political leaders and policy-makers in Malaysia, Indonesia (after 1966) and Vietnam (after 1986) were fully and genuinely committed to restraining inflation, maintaining realistic exchange rates, and avoiding or ending over-regulation, and this commitment greatly facilitated their coopera-tion with international financial institutions. The same was true in Thailand, where many of the policy reforms prescribed by the World Bank and the IMF as preconditions for Structural Adjustment Loans during the 1980s had already been anticipated and implemented by the Thai government by the time the World Bank announced them (Sahasakul et al. 1991: 81, 99).

Although the South-East Asian experience shows that the state has a legitimate and important role in the stabilization of agricultural product markets, in conjunction with African data it also indicates that there is no case for government or parastatal monopsony or monopoly control of any agricultural product or input. Although there were occasional exceptions to this rule in South-East Asia, such as the obligation of participants in Malaysia's FELDA farmer resettlement scheme (which was, however, voluntary) to use official marketing channels (Pletcher 1991: 628–9), and the fertilizer monopoly which the Indonesian Village Unit Cooperatives enjoyed for a short period in the 1970s (Booth 1988: 149), these were minor anomalies in a history characterized by the use of subsidy rather than regulation as the major instrument of rural development policy.

Finally, the continuing weakness of poverty reduction in our African case studies following successful liberalization and stabilization reminds us that neither of these policy changes, nor indeed the availability of development finance as such, is a sufficient condition for pro-poor growth. That depends on the application of the available finance through policies designed specifically to raise the incomes of the mass of the population. The nature of such policies is the subject of the next two chapters.

# 4 | AGRARIAN ROOTS OF DEVELOPMENT SUCCESS

One common answer to the question of what Africa can learn from South-East Asian development, perhaps the most common answer in recent years, can be summed up in three words: 'export-oriented industrialization'. Africa's poverty, in this view, can be transformed directly into riches if only cheap African labour can be used, as cheap Asian labour has repeatedly been used in the past, to produce manufactured goods for export at internationally competitive prices. In his influential book *The Bottom Billion*, Paul Collier argues that foreign aid to Africa (and other very poor parts of the world) can best be concentrated on helping carefully selected countries to follow the Asian example by breaking into world markets for cheap, labour-intensive industrial products.

> For a start, the aid can be spent on helping the export sector – for example, improving infrastructure at the ports. [...] What is required is a once-and-for-all push, country by country. Such aid would be targeted at lowering the costs that potential exporters would face. [...] The bottom billion would look a lot more hopeful if a few of their coastal economies really started to take off in global markets. (Collier 2007: 121–2)

In combination, ironically, with protection against competition from (for the time being) even cheaper Asian manufactures on European markets, this kind of focused financial aid could help to create in Africa pioneering successes in export-oriented industrialization – successes which would then inspire neighbouring countries to imitate them, just as they did in Asia four decades ago when Malaysia, Thailand and then Indonesia followed Singapore, Taiwan and Hong Kong into the ranks of the newly industrializing countries. But concentrating the necessary international resources on the promotion of African industrial exports, Collier warns, will not be easy given the strength of other, competing lobbies within aid agencies – notably those favouring rural and agricultural development.

> Every aid agency is divided into fiefdoms – rural development, education, health, and so forth. Trying to get an aid agency to focus its resources on an export growth strategy runs afoul of all these interests, for if there is more money to be spent on the country, you can be absolutely sure that the rural development group will lobby for its share of the spending, whether that is important for export growth or not [...]. (Ibid.: 122)

This kind of insistence on the priority of industrial exports, although ostensibly based on Asian experience, reflects a mistaken interpretation of that experience. In fact, if the South-East Asian evidence is anything to go by, then aid agencies interested in reducing poverty and promoting growth – even *industrial* growth – in Africa might be well advised to forget about industry for the time being, and instead concentrate precisely on the rural and agricultural development which Collier dismisses as a distraction from the main concern. In what follows, this is argued with particular reference to the comparison between Indonesia and Nigeria.

### Indonesia: a two-stage development miracle

Is it really true that an industrial export push was the key to growth in South-East Asia? The biggest and most important country in South-East Asia is Indonesia, with fully 40 per cent of the region's population. Although still a poor country compared to some of its neighbours, Indonesia is very much part of the Asian economic miracle, having increased its per capita national income from US$200 (at constant 2000 prices) in 1965 to more than US$1,000 today. In terms of per capita GDP growth over the years 1965–85, Indonesia ranked higher than any other South-East Asian country except Singapore. The contrast with Nigeria, where growth stagnated in the 1970s and collapsed in the 1980s, is dramatic (Chapter 1, Figure 1.4).

Since 1993, consistent with the export-oriented industrialization model, more than half of Indonesia's exports have consisted of manufactured goods. Here again there is a sharp contrast with Nigeria, where oil has remained overwhelmingly the most important source of foreign exchange, industrial exports are negligible, and the overall

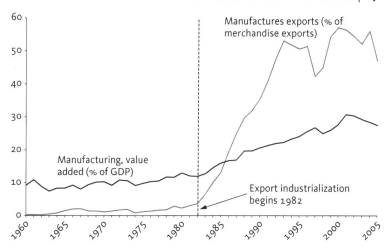

**4.1** Indonesia: industrialization, 1960–2005 (*source*: online World Development Indicators/World DataBank, World Bank)

contribution of manufacturing to GDP has never risen above 10 per cent. If, however, we compare the timing of the boom in Indonesian industrial exports with that of the rise in Indonesian GDP, a striking discrepancy emerges. Rapid income growth began abruptly in 1967 and was sustained until 1982, when there was a slight and temporary dip. Yet up to and including 1982, less than 5 per cent of Indonesia's exports consisted of manufactured goods. The great expansion of manufactured exports began in 1983 and was complete a decade later in 1993 (Figure 4.1). Indonesia's economic take-off, in other words, preceded its emergence as an industrial exporter by a full fifteen years. It follows that in the Indonesian case, the take-off cannot possibly have been caused by the industrial exports.

If we look specifically at the record of poverty reduction, in the last analysis surely the primary goal and measure of development, then the importance of the period prior to export-oriented industrialization becomes even clearer (Figure 4.2). Statistics based on a nationally defined poverty line were collected in Indonesia from 1976 onward, and show a decline in the proportion of the population living in poverty from 40 per cent in 1976 to just over 20 per cent in 1984. The equivalent figure for 1970 is conventionally estimated at 60 per cent. Indonesia's spectacular (albeit not complete) victory over poverty was essentially won in the first fifteen years of economic growth.

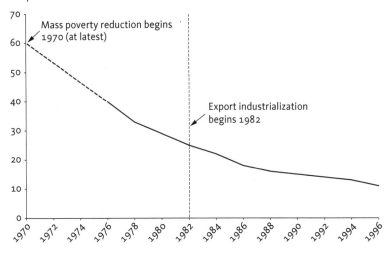

**4.2** Indonesia: proportion of population living in poverty (according to national poverty line, per cent), 1970–96 (*source*: BPS-Statistics Indonesia, Bappenas and UNDP (2004: 13); 1970: estimate; 1976–96: survey data)

Although the number of Indonesians living in poverty continued to fall thereafter, it did so more slowly, declining from 20 per cent in 1985 to 11 per cent in 1996.

Retrospective studies of Indonesia's development success have often concentrated on the economic 'deregulation' of the 1980s, involving financial liberalization and the removal of obstacles to foreign trade and investment, which was the immediate trigger for the industrial export boom (Basri and Hill 2004; Resosudarmo and Kuncoro 2006). But the most important policy lessons for Africa must surely come from the 1970s, when some fifty million Indonesians were lifted out of poverty without the aid of the kind of 'export push' which some now regard as the *sine qua non* of the Asian Miracle. 'Despite its creditable export performance', observes Hill (1996a: 14), 'Indonesian economic development since 1966 has not really been "export-led" in the way it has in some of the smaller East Asian neighbouring economies.'

What, then, actually happened in Indonesia during the first two decades of the New Order and the first fifteen years of sustained economic growth? The most important changes took place in the agricultural sector, and particularly in food crop agriculture (Figure 4.3). Between 1968 and 1985 areal yields of rice, the staple food, rose

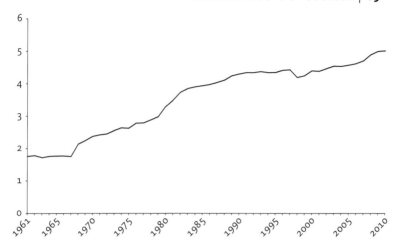

**4.3** Indonesia: average rice yield (tonnes per hectare, unhusked), 1961–2010 (*source*: FAOSTAT online)

by almost 80 per cent (Booth 1988: 140), and total rice production grew almost three times faster than population growth (Dasgupta 1998: 213). In 1974, Indonesia was the largest rice importer in the world; by 1984, it was self-sufficient. The main cause of the surge in food production was a massive application of technological and capital inputs in agriculture. Per hectare use of artificial fertilizer in food crop farming rose by a factor of ten between 1968 and 1985 (Booth 1988: 143). The effects of this Green Revolution on farm incomes, and on the health of the rural economy in general, go a long way towards explaining the impressive record of poverty alleviation in the early New Order years. Cross-country statistical analysis indicates that throughout South-East Asia, poverty reduction depends primarily on growth in agriculture and services, industrial growth having much less consistent impact on poverty levels (Warr 2005).

The Green Revolution in Asia has been described as a 'state-driven, market mediated and small-farmer based strategy to increase the national self-sufficiency in food grains' (Djurfeldt et al. 2005b: 3). In the Indonesian case this is accurate on all three points. Indonesia's Green Revolution was small-farmer based because most of the country's farmers, and almost all of its rice farmers, have always worked very modest areas of land; in Java in the 1970s, only 2 per cent of all agricultural holdings were larger than three hectares (Booth

1988: 52). It was market mediated because the trade in agricultural products, including rice, remained largely in private hands. And it was state driven because the state set the goal of rice self-sufficiency and supplied the technologies, and most of the investments, which made it possible to achieve that goal.

The state made available to farmers the new high-yielding, fertilizer-responsive rice varieties developed at the International Rice Research Institute (IRRI) in the Philippines, or in Indonesia itself by government scientists as derivatives of the IRRI types (Fox 1991: 66). The state subsidized, sometimes to the tune of more than half of the international price, the fertilizers needed to make them yield to their full potential (Van der Eng 1996: 118). It provided subsidized credit for the purchase of this and other inputs (Henley 2010). Crucially, it also rehabilitated and extended Java's irrigation systems, the improved rice varieties being suitable only for cultivation in flooded fields. Between 1968 and 1989 the area under irrigation in Java expanded by almost one third (Bottema 1995: 196), while existing irrigation systems were repaired and improved after years of neglect that had reduced them by 1967 to less than a quarter of their capacity. In many years, expenditures on irrigation accounted for more than half of the total agricultural development budget (Van der Eng 1996: 61–2, 161). Finally the government established a Logistics Agency (Bulog) to stabilize rice prices, both farm-gate and retail, by buying rice at a fixed floor price when prices were low and selling at a fixed ceiling price from the resulting buffer stock when prices were high (Timmer 1997).

During the 1970s and early 1980s, agriculture was typically the largest item on the development budget. As a proportion of total public spending, including routine expenditure as well as public investment, it accounted on average for over 10 per cent (IMF 2005). This reflected a heavy political commitment to agricultural development on the part of the New Order leadership – most importantly Suharto himself, who cultivated an image as personal benefactor of the rural masses. In 1985, addressing the Food and Agriculture Organization of the United Nations in honour of Indonesia's success in becoming self-sufficient in rice, Suharto underlined the sustained, consistent nature of his regime's commitment to agricultural development.

Our goals were gradually to achieve self-sufficiency in food production, improve nutrition, raise the income and standard of living of farmers and boost economic development in general. [...] The political decision to focus attention on the development of agriculture was clearly reflected in the government's development budget for the agricultural and irrigation sectors, which, for many years, [...] absorbed the greatest share of the budget. (Soeharto 1991: 2)

The rural development effort did not end with agriculture. Much of the concurrent spending on roads, electrification, marketplaces, schools and public health also took place in rural areas, where more than 70 per cent of the Indonesian population lived. The total length of roads in Indonesia increased by almost 50 per cent in the ten years 1967–77, while the existing network was repaired and upgraded. Much of the new rural infrastructure was built using labour-intensive techniques, creating mass employment for the poor (Timmer 2005: 4, 44). Indonesian development spending, in short, was targeted substantially at agriculture, the countryside and the poor.

It has been calculated that government expenditure on agricultural development in the 1970s and 1980s was more than thirty times higher, in real terms, than in the late colonial period (Van der Eng 1996: 160). How was this unprecedented rural spending made possible? Not by rural taxation: under Suharto as under his predecessor Sukarno, the tax burden on the poor remained much lighter than in colonial times. The answer is simple: oil – or rather: oil and aid. From 1967 to 1973, foreign aid provided about a quarter of all government revenue and paid for almost the whole of the development budget; from 1974 to 1985 the oil and gas industry provided about half of all revenue, and foreign aid around another 15 per cent (Hill 2000b: 47). To the extent that the economic take-off was export-led, it was led not by manufactures, but by oil. Which is to say, it was export-led only to the extent that it was state-led, since it was mainly through the redistributive activities of the state that oil income, and aid, was transformed into pro-poor growth. The purpose of the later transition to manufactured exports, facilitated by deregulation, was twofold: to substitute for oil as a source of state revenue, and to provide a second, complementary source of mass employment and labour-intensive economic growth alongside peasant agriculture. The Indonesian development miracle, as its key architect, technocrat Widjojo Nitisastro, emphasized in an illuminating retrospective in 1994, came in two distinct stages.

> Of key importance to poverty reduction in the 1970s and early 1980s was the high rate of growth in the agricultural sector, on which most of the population and the poor depended. [...] The sources of rapid growth in rice production have been a combination of the rapid spread of irrigation, the provision of key inputs, and the spread of high-yielding varieties. At the same time, investment in rural infrastructure, as well as price policy, public procurement, and price stabilization, increased the level and stability of the prices received by the farmer. [...] In the second half of the 1980s and the 1990s, a different process became important in generating high growth and reducing poverty – the rapid growth of exports of labor-intensive manufactures, which generated employment growth in manufacturing of about 7 percent a year after 1985. [...] Indonesia was able to reduce poverty rapidly, first, through sustained, broad-based and labor-intensive growth based on rapid growth of agriculture, and then through rapid growth of labor-intensive manufacturing exports. (Widjojo 1995: 177–80)

Export-oriented industrialization, then, helped to make development sustainable in the long term, but it did not start the development process, and it was not the key to poverty reduction.

## Nigeria: the cart before the horse

In Nigeria, neither the initial agricultural nor the subsequent industrial stage of this transformation took place. One factor here was no doubt the well-known lack of a uniform technological 'quick fix', along the lines of Asia's Green Revolution in intensive wet rice agriculture, for the more diverse and less area- and labour-intensive farming systems of Africa. But this point should probably not be exaggerated. Major breakthroughs in maize and cassava breeding, some of them achieved on Nigerian soil at the International Institute of Tropical Agriculture in Ibadan, took place in Africa in the 1970s. But in Nigeria as elsewhere on the continent, weak agricultural extension services, combined with lack of input subsidies and inadequate transport, storage and credit facilities, prevented the potential of the new varieties from being realized (Holmén 2005: 70). The proportion of development spending allocated to the agricultural sector was much lower in Nigeria than in Indonesia, and particularly so during the oil boom when the potential availability of funds was at its peak (Table 4.1).

TABLE 4.1  Proportion of national development budget allocated to agriculture (per cent), Indonesia and Nigeria, 1961–85

| Indonesia | | Nigeria | |
|---|---|---|---|
| National Overall Development Plan, 1961–69 (pre-New Order)[1] | 10.5 | National Development Plan, 1962–68[2] | 13.6 |
| First Five-Year Development Plan, 1969–74[3] | 30.1 | Second National Development Plan, 1970–74[4] | 10.5 |
| Second Five-Year Development Plan, 1974–79[5] | 19.1 | Third National Development Plan, 1975–80[6] | 6.0 |
| Third Five-Year Development Plan, 1979–84[7] | 14.0 | Fourth National Development Plan, 1980–85[8] | 12.6 |

*Notes*: 1. Broad Outlines 1961: 21 (excludes industrial and plantation crops, other than tobacco); 2. National Development Plan 1962: 35; 3. First Five-Year Development Plan 1969: 41; 4. Second National Development Plan 1970: 274 (excludes livestock); 5. Second Five-Year Development Plan 1974: 170; 6. Third National Development Plan 1975: 349 (includes livestock); 7. Third Five-Year Development Plan 1979: 15; 8. Fourth National Development Plan 1981: 49.

The decline in Nigerian federal spending on agriculture in the 1970s took place despite the fact that in this period 'the federal government took over many agricultural responsibilities from the regions – an act probably motivated more by the desire to emasculate the regions than to stimulate agriculture' (Bevan et al. 1999: 171). At state level, meanwhile, the priority accorded to agriculture in government spending was similarly low (Fuady 2012: 106).

The focus of Nigerian development planning was not on agriculture but on industry, especially large-scale, capital- and technology-intensive heavy industrial projects: car and truck assembly, machine tool manufacture, cement, petrochemicals, and a hugely expensive state-owned integrated steel plant. Under the oil-fuelled Third National Development Plan (1975–80), direct state spending on the manufacturing sector rose to 16 per cent of the development budget, while the proportion going to agriculture fell to just 6 per cent. Much of what little was spent on agriculture, moreover, took the form of subsidies for large plantations (including state farms) and mechanized equipment, with the aim of bypassing, rather than modernizing, peasant agriculture (Mwabu and Thorbecke 2004: 136; Okolie 1995: 205).

Besides neglecting public investment in smallholder agriculture and the rural economy, it is worth repeating from Chapter 3 that Nigeria also grossly failed to create the macroeconomic and institutional conditions for agricultural growth.

> Indonesia, from the outset, supported its agricultural sector through its exchange rate management and, more directly, though large-scale investment in irrigation, other physical infrastructure, and a fertilizer subsidy scheme, among others. On the other hand, Nigeria squeezed agriculture unmercifully throughout the whole period – directly, through the regional and, later, national marketing boards, and indirectly, through the negative impact of distorted trade and exchange rate policies on domestic agricultural production. (Thorbecke 1998: 134)

In Indonesia the technocrats' insistence on economic freedom, low inflation and a competitive exchange rate was not divorced from their agricultural and rural development priorities. On the contrary, they saw macroeconomic policy as an essential concomitant of those priorities.

> [P]erhaps [...] Widjojo's greatest contribution to Indonesian food security has been his ever-present role as a formulator of a food-friendly macro policy. Many countries throughout the world, and especially those with oil resources, have learned the hard way that poor macro policy obliterates good agricultural projects and programs. [...] Widjojo [...] believed strongly that exchange-rate and interest rate policies, if done poorly or wrongly, would mean the downfall of the food and agricultural sectors. (Falcon 2007: 29)

In Nigeria, by contrast, macroeconomic policies were intended more to support urban consumers of imported goods, and to some extent also import-substituting manufacturing industries, which were heavily dependent on imported raw materials and therefore lobbied against devaluation of the naira (Fuady 2012: 145).

Capital-intensive industrial projects provide lucrative opportunities for politicians and their associates to pocket public funds, and the Nigerian predilection for them is sometimes dismissed as a matter of 'blatant corruption' (Thorbecke 1998: 133). But the decision to use the oil windfall of the 1970s to launch an all-out industrialization drive was taken by technocrats rather than politicians (see Chapter 7), and has in fact been identified as one of the few cases in post-colonial Africa in which 'public spending was driven by a (technocratic) economic vision, rather than by the self-interest of the regime' (Collier and Gunning 2008: 211). The policy of accelerated industrialization was based on a perceived need for 'diversification' of the Nigerian economy, not only away from its new dependence on the oil sector, but also away from its old dependence on agriculture.

> An economy that is not diversified is especially vulnerable to changing economic situations. This is so whether the economy is dominated by agriculture or by oil production. It is, therefore, intended under the next Plan to achieve greater diversification by a rapid expansion and broadening of industrial activities in the economy. It is expected that, in real terms, value added in industry will more than double during the plan period. (Third National Development Plan 1975, I: 31)

In the future, as the Indonesian planners also acknowledged, agriculture was bound to play a proportionally less and less important role in the economy. For this reason there was, and often still is today, a great temptation to concentrate directly on non-agricultural sectors rather than worrying about one which will soon be relegated to history anyway. But history strongly suggests that the Indonesians were right to resist that temptation, and the Nigerians wrong to succumb to it.

## The role of population policy

As McNicoll (2011) has emphasized, the contrast between Indonesian and Nigerian development performance in per capita income terms would have been considerably smaller if population growth

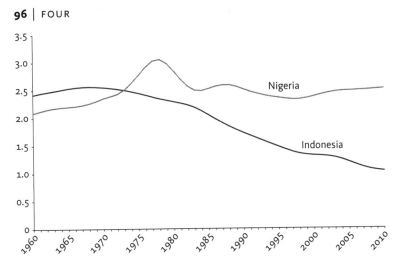

**4.4** Population growth (annual per cent), Indonesia and Nigeria, 1960–2010 (*source*: online World Development Indicators/World DataBank, World Bank)

in Indonesia had not slowed quite dramatically towards the end of the twentieth century owing to a strong decline in the birth rate.

Whereas fertility among Nigerian women hardly changed between 1970 and 1990, in Indonesia the total (completed) fertility rate fell over the same period from almost five and a half children per woman to just over three (Figure 4.4). This transformation owed much to a vigorous state-sponsored family planning programme which was 'one of the first orders of business of the New Order government' after it came to power in 1965, and which became 'a signal success story in population policy annals' (ibid.: 199). Although much less coercive in its methods than contemporary programmes in China and India, the Indonesian birth control effort involved a strong commitment of state resources to the goal of distributing contraceptives, together with information on their use and propaganda for family planning, on a massive scale in both urban and rural areas.

The high priority accorded to birth control in New Order develop-ment strategy reflected a Malthusian, sometimes almost apocalyptic, understanding of the seriousness of the population problem (see Chapter 6), together with the fact that the principal Indonesian technocratic planner, Widjojo Nitisastro, was trained in population studies and 'first thought of himself as a demographer' (Keyfitz 2007: 34). In Nigeria, by contrast, population policy was characterized by 'a lack of urgency about the issue at high levels of government' (McNicoll 2011: 199). Among the reasons for this indifference were a lack of relevant expertise among policy-makers, a general conviction that Nigeria as a resource-rich country had little need of fertility control, and a preoccupation with ethnic rivalry in the electoral – and, by extension, demographic – sphere (no region was keen to see its share of the national electorate reduced).

Despite the clear contrast between Indonesia and Nigeria in the area of population policy and the priority accorded to it, it would be wrong to assume that population policy as such was the only, or even the main, determinant of the divergence in fertility rates between the two countries. Although the forces driving the current global transition from high to lower fertility remain partly obscure, it is clear that many of them result from economic development itself, notably in relation to its effects on female wages and on the availability and cost of education, rather than from changes in the availability of knowledge or means of birth control (Schultz 2001). Hence Paul Collier's well-justified objection to the argument by Bloom and Sachs (1998: 243–51) that Africa's 'delayed demographic transition' is a key reason for its economic retardation.

> I agree that Africa's high population growth rate has been costly for per capita growth, but this may well be largely endogenous to poor economic performance. If parents saw prospects of growth in wage employment, they would have an interest in investing in educational quality, and thus would find large families uneconomic. (Collier 1998: 275)

Declining fertility in late twentieth-century Indonesia was a result, as well as a cause, of Indonesia's economic success, and it is not likely that in the absence of economic policies similar to Indonesia's, a more vigorous population policy alone could have made a decisive difference to Nigeria's development performance. Perhaps the most important thing to note about the Nigerian state's neglect of population control is not that it made, in itself, a crucial contribution to Nigeria's development failure, but rather that it reflected the same general lack of concern with the fate of poor and rural Nigerians which was also responsible for the errors committed in other policy areas (Chapters 6 and 7).

## Linking rural poverty and industrialization: the surplus labour fallacy

There is an influential idea, old (Lewis 1954) but periodically resurgent (Karshenas 1995, 1998, 2001) and frequently endorsed in comparative studies (Edwards 1995: 252; Mwase and Ndulu 2008: 430; Wood and Mayer 2001: 389), that industrialization in developing countries is predicated on a reserve of cheap 'surplus labour' maintained by persistent unemployment and underemployment in the countryside. According to this theory, first conceived (as prediction rather than observation) by Caribbean economist Arthur Lewis on a Bangkok street in 1952 (Lewis 1980: 4), it was the very poverty of rural Asia, caused largely by overpopulation, which predestined the continent for industrial success by ensuring that 'an unlimited supply of labour is available at a subsistence wage' (Lewis 1954: 189).

> In the case of the Asian countries, the existence of an abundant supply of labour in agriculture allowed fast rates of industrial growth to take place at low and competitive wages. This also meant that, after a short period of learning and skill acquisition, the new industries in Asia could become competitive enough to export [...]. (Karshenas 2001: 338)

In the light of what has been said above and in preceding chapters, it should be clear that this model of the Asian industrialization process is *not* applicable to South-East Asia. Quite apart from the fact that since the 1980s most parts of rural Africa have been poorer, not richer, than rural Indonesia, it is important to note that rapid agricultural and rural growth in Indonesia preceded industrialization, and that the labour-intensive technologies of the Green Revolution (more frequent planting and harvesting, fertilizer application, irrigation maintenance) tended to expand employment and raise wages in the agricultural sector, not to displace labour out of it (Booth 1988: 179–89; Manning 1998: 89–91).

Rising farm incomes also spearheaded a general boom in the Indonesian rural economy, including its non-agricultural sectors – trade, transport, construction, handicraft industry and informal sector services – along the lines formulated by Mellor (1995: 235–9). Together with the rise of formal sector manufacturing industry, this soon all but eliminated rural underemployment (Manning 1998: 91).

Even in the most densely populated parts of Java, *shortages* of agricultural labour as a result of *competition* from off-farm employment were already apparent as early as the 1980s (Preston 1989). Teenage Javanese girls who worked in factories increasingly did so not in order to susidize the low income of their parental households, but rather in defiance of their parents, who would rather have kept them at work in the fields or the home (Wolf 1992: 171–8). All of this came as a surprise to even the most optimistic experts on Indonesia. 'It was only 30 years previously', as one of them has observed, 'that everyone, and I mean *everyone*, simply knew unequivocally that Java could not rid itself of surplus rural labor in the 20th century' (Falcon 2007: 31).

Elsewhere in South-East Asia it was a similar story. In the 1990s, labour shortages in agriculture were also widely felt in Malaysia and the Philippines (Rigg 2001: 102–21). The spectacular growth of non-agricultural employment opportunities in Malaysia, indeed, raised the opportunity costs of labour to such an extent that agricultural expansion on the forest frontier was halted and reversed (Vincent and Rozali 2005: 124, 173, 369). Wages in Malaysian manufacturing rose fast and steadily almost from the very beginning of the export-oriented manufacturing boom of the 1970s, doubling between 1973 and 1985 (Mazumdar 1993: 364, 370).

All this confirms that if industrial labour costs for a long time remained more competitive, on average, in South-East Asia than in Africa (Karshenas 1998: 44), the reasons for this had nothing to do with a 'labour squeeze' in agriculture. A more credible factor here was the lack of wage regulation in Asia: Indonesia had only a partial and haphazard system of regionally determined minimum wage levels until 1989 (Agrawal 1995: 16), while Malaysia never legislated an official minimum wage, in manufacturing or any other sector, until as recently as 2012. The power of organized labour to secure wage privileges by means of industrial action is also greater in most parts of Africa than in South-East Asia. Another reason for the persistence of unexpectedly high manufacturing wages in Africa, however, is the often high, and typically volatile, price of food in African cities. This relates once more to the neglect of smallholder agriculture in African development policy, and will be further discussed later in the chapter.

## From import-substituting to export-oriented industry?

Another classic idea of the relationship between agricultural and industrial development is that the former supports the latter by stimulating demand for the products of domestic industry. In Indonesia, this formed part of the official argument for giving agriculture the highest priority under the New Order's first five-year development plan (1969-74).

> The agricultural sector [...] is the central arena in which all efforts are concentrated and results expected. [...] Increased production in the agricultural food sector will have a major influence on the growth of the Indonesian economy. [...] Increased agricultural output enlarges the market for the industrial sector, which produces basic materials needed by the agricultural sector. The demand for fertilizer, cement, insecticide, pesticide and other chemicals will increase [...]. The producers of agricultural products will earn more because of increased production. Usually they spend additional earnings for commodities not produced by agriculture, thus promoting the industrial sector which supplies the needs of consumers in the agriculture sector. (First Five-Year Development Plan 1969: 11–13)

As noted, strong agricultural growth during the 1970s did have an immediate positive effect on the trade, transport, construction, handicraft and informal sector services. However, substantial growth in the contribution of manufacturing industry to national income (Figure 4.1) did not begin until the onset of export-oriented industrialization in the early 1980s, the immediate trigger for which was trade liberalization. Between 1970 and 1982 the share of manufacturing in GDP rose only from 10 to 12 per cent; between 1982 and 1997, from 12 to 26 per cent. In the 1970s, moreover, the fact that most Indonesian industries enjoyed substantial tariff protection against foreign competition (Fuady 2012: 166, 177) meant that Indonesian consumers were paying a heavy price for what limited industrialization did take place. Given that the penalized groups included low-income consumers of everyday products such as textiles, and given the limited scale of industrial employment in this period, it follows that industrialization at this stage was not a pro-poor aspect of Indonesia's development.

Did this early phase of protected import-substituting industrialization, based partly on markets created by agricultural growth, nevertheless contribute to export success by allowing manufacturers to accumulate capital and expertise which would later enable them to compete on international markets? The fact that Indonesia's most important exporting industrial sector of the 1980s and 1990s, garment manufacturing, was dominated by domestic rather than foreign firms (Thee 2012: 251) makes this on the face of it a credible idea. On closer investigation, however, the garment industry turns out to have been subject to net *negative* protection in the 1970s because the effects of the protection afforded to the domestic weaving industry, from which garment manufacturers were obliged to buy their cloth, outweighed the effects of the tariffs on imported clothing (Hill 1996b: 160). Indonesian clothing manufacturers, in other words, would have been even more successful on international markets in the absence of any interventions of this kind. In neighbouring Malaysia, the dependence of export success on liberalization rather than infant industry protection is even clearer. Here the industrial export boom, when it came, was led by the electronics sector, which was the result of new foreign direct investment, had no roots in the earlier import-substitution phase, and purchased only a tiny proportion of its inputs from locally developed industries (Alavi 1996: 39, 55; Rajah Rasiah 1993: 139–41).

There are some exceptions to this pattern. The Indonesian food conglomerate Indofood, a manufacturer of instant noodles now widely consumed in Africa as well as Europe and Asia, has its origins in a state-backed monopoly over the milling of imported flour granted to Suharto 'crony' Liem Sioe Liong in 1970 (Dieleman 2007: 47). On the other hand, the Salim Group (part of Indonesia's ethnic Chinese business community) which owns Indofood also has components which have been internationally successful without such advantageous initial conditions. Some Indonesian automobile component manufacturers have also been able to move successfully from a protected environment into export markets (Doner 2009: 261). However, they have done so only under the auspices of the foreign auto manufacturers which dominate this sector, and for which they serve as subcontractors (Thee 2012: 283). In general, protected industries in Indonesia have remained an expensive burden on consumers and taxpayers. An example is the Indonesian steel industry, the low-quality products of which are avoided where possible even by domestic manufacturers (Doner 2009: 264).

In Thailand there is evidence of continuity between the import-substituting and export-oriented phases of industrialization in the textile and garment sector, where it was a crisis of overproduction in the protected domestic market which provided the stimulus for a reorientation towards international sales. However, in this case it was the manufacturers themselves, through the medium of the Thai Textile Manufacturers' Association, who took the initiative first collectively to subsidize their (initially unprofitable) export endeavours, and then to lobby the government for additional support in the form of credit privileges and lower electricity rates. Moreover, it is clear that the ability of the sector to break into foreign markets by these means was also a product of the intense and largely unregulated domestic inter-firm competition which had led to the initial overcapacity (Doner and Ramsay 2000).

All this highlights the fact that in contrast to the active (albeit market-friendly) and successful role played by South-East Asian governments in agricultural development, their role in directing industrial growth has been limited and to a large extent inauspicious, at least in comparison with North-East Asian precedents. 'There has been no question', declares Dixon (1999: 242) in relation to Thailand, 'of the state following the Asian NIE pattern of "picking winners" and actively promoting them.' Despite some dissenting voices (Jomo 1997; Rock 1995, 1999), there is broad agreement that in South-East Asia the policies most effectively favouring export-oriented industrialization have not been selective interventions to support particular industries, still less indiscriminate protection of domestic markets for the benefit of infant industries, but rather policies designed to keep the prices of exports in general at internationally competitive levels: infrastructure provision, cost-of-living subsidies (including food price interventions), favourable tax and investment regimes, strategic currency devaluations, and provisions allowing exporting companies to import raw materials and capital goods tariff free.

Where South-East Asian states have attempted to direct industrial development along Japanese or Korean lines by selecting, protecting and supporting promising infant industries up to the point where they can compete in export markets (Amsden 1989; Wade 1990), they have generally failed. The Indonesian automotive industry, for example, has been cited as a case study of 'how not to industrialize': a small, inefficient industry, sheltered from foreign competition by tariffs of up to 200 per cent on imported vehicles, concentrated almost entirely in Jakarta, employing few workers, and characterized by 'uneconomic production runs and minuscule exports' (Aswicahyono et al. 2000: 209). In Malaysia, likewise, the national car manufacturer Proton absorbed huge amounts of public funding but conspicuously failed to achieve export growth, remaining dependent on the relatively small, heavily protected domestic market while multinational auto manufacturers made Thailand their base for regional production and exports (Felker and Jomo 2007: 144). If the attempt to create strictly national car industries has served any purpose, it has been to contribute, probably at disproportionate expense, to the development of labour force skills and the interethnic redistribution of wealth. In broad terms, it has been the same story with other protected heavy and high-tech industries: steel, chemicals and aviation. The performance of enterprises which are actually owned by the state has been particularly poor.

### Linking rural development and industrialization: stability, confidence, savings

The fact that export-oriented industrial development in South-East Asia was not obviously predicated on an earlier import-substitution phase, driven by domestic demand from farmers and rural consumers, does not mean that there were no causal links between agricultural and industrial success. One such link was the effect of increased food production on the level, and especially the stability, of industrial labour costs. This was another element of the justification for rural bias which Widjojo included in the text of the First Five-Year Plan in 1969.

> Increased production in the agricultural food sector will have a major influence on the growth of the Indonesian economy. The price of food in the country can be further stabilized with a positive effect on general price stability. Only in a stable economy can rapid growth be anticipated. [...] The stabilization of food prices

through increased food production will also stabilize wages. Thus the industrial sector can operate with a cost-pattern which is not too unstable. (First Five-Year Development Plan 1969: 11–13)

It is worth emphasizing that Widjojo refers here to the stabilization, not the minimization, of food prices. There is statistical evidence that in Indonesia, Malaysia and Thailand the growth of manufacturing industry was specifically correlated with the successful stabilization, rather than the progressive reduction, of rice prices (Rock 2002: 505). Farm profits were not 'squeezed' for the benefit of industrial employers, but supported in order to achieve the goal of national food self-sufficiency. In South-East Asia, it has pithily been said, 'the shift to an export-led strategy of industrialization was preceded by a shift to import-substitution in food grains' (Djurfeldt and Jirström 2005: 60). In the Indonesian case, self-sufficiency in food had the additional benefit of providing national leaders with a policy option not readily available to their counterparts in food-importing countries: the option of repeatedly devaluing the national currency (Chapter 3), in order to promote non-oil exports, without having to fear dramatic increases in domestic food prices.

Besides helping to stabilize labour costs and macroeconomic conditions, the agricultural growth of the early New Order period in Indonesia also reinforced the country's recently restored political stability and generated crucial confidence in the economy among investors, industrial and otherwise. Regardless of labour costs, capital owners everywhere, domestic or foreign, tend to invest their money more readily in a country that is already growing and thriving than in one that is racked by hunger and deprivation, or perceived as being on the brink of political chaos. In surveys of the determinants of foreign direct investment in Africa, perceptions of risk and existing rates of economic growth are both frequently found to play an important role (Jaspersen et al. 2000; Onyeiwu and Shrestha 2004).

A further link between agricultural and industrial growth lies in the fact that in Indonesia and elsewhere in South-East Asia, rural prosperity provided surplus wealth which helped to fund investment in non-farm enterprises, including industrial enterprises. This intersectoral transfer of resources took place not through the medium of taxation, as the theorists of the 1950s and 1960s had thought necessary, but rather through the medium of voluntary savings, the growth of which in Indonesia during the 1980s and 1990s took even the most optimistic observers by surprise (Henley 2010: 181–3). By 1996 the total value of savings deposited at the village branches of the state-owned Bank Rakyat Indonesia (Indonesian People's Bank, BRI), which served a quarter of all Indonesian households, amounted to almost twice the value of outstanding loans, and the bank's rural microfinance operation was subsidizing its lending to corporate clients (Robinson 2001: 47; 2002: 304, 361). In accordance with their general market-mindedness, the New Order planners, while much concerned with national food self-sufficiency, saw no future for subsistence production at the level of the individual household, and were careful to promote the commercialization of smallholder agriculture wherever possible – partly with the developmental utility of rural savings in mind.

> Through BRI [...] and other such institutions and programmes, the government succeeded in its objective of monetizing the rural sector. Not only did this permit Indonesia's farmers to improve their welfare by integrating their work into the modern economy, the monetized rural sector also generated vast sums of development funds that were essential to the nation's development efforts. (Prawiro 1998: 144)

Whatever the precise causal relationship between agricultural development and industrial breakthrough, it is clear that the sectoral sequence seen in Indonesia – first agriculture, then industry – reflects a near-universal historical pattern. In Asia, as in Europe at an earlier period, the transition to sustained economic growth has usually begun with an agricultural revolution.

In Japan and Korea, technological progress led to improvements in agricultural productivity which preceded the industrial revolution by several decades (Francks 1984; Kang and Ramachandran 1999). In South Korea and in Taiwan, as Davis (2004) has shown, the policies that laid the foundation for development success in the 1960s were much more pro-rural and pro-agricultural than most subsequent commentators have realized. The development model favoured in that period by South Korean president Park Chung-hee was not that of a major industrial nation like Japan or the USA, but rather that of Denmark, a 'modern and advanced agriculturally based economy' which 'had achieved its success without sacrificing its reliance on small-farmer classes and their privileged position in the economy and society' (ibid.: 92).

In India, the industrial growth of the 1990s was preceded by two decades of slow but steady poverty reduction based on the same kind of Green Revolution which preceded industrialization in Indonesia, albeit less vigorously led and financed by the state (Datt and Ravallion 2002). The great bulk of China's historic poverty reduction since 1980, the only episode of rapid disimpoverishment comparable with Indonesia's in scale, took place outside the cities and prior to the onset of industrialization in the 1990s (Ravallion and Chen 2007). Returning to South-East Asia, the following chapter (Chapter 5) will show that essentially the same sequence was also followed in Thailand, Malaysia and Vietnam.

All these observations are consistent with a simple but poorly understood law of economic development formulated by John Mellor (1995: 1): 'The faster agriculture grows, the faster its relative size declines'. Or, as Michael Lipton put it in his classic book *Why Poor People Stay Poor; a study of urban bias in world development*: 'If you wish for industrialisation, prepare to develop agriculture' (Lipton 1977: 24).

### Rural bias and shared growth

Viewed in broader perspective, the 'rural bias' of New Order Indonesia can be seen as one manifestation of a general policy principle, keenly discerned in the World Bank's *East Asian Miracle* study (1993) but often overlooked by critical readers of that document, which has been adhered to by all of the successful Asian developmental states: the principle of 'shared growth'. More than their counterparts in other developing countries, the political leaders of the high-performing Asian economies 'realized that economic development was impossible without cooperation' (ibid.: 13).

> To establish their legitimacy and win the support of the society at large, East Asian leaders established the principle of shared growth, promising that as the economy expanded all groups would benefit. [...] Explicit mechanisms were used to demonstrate

the intent that all would have a share of future wealth. [...] Indonesia used rice and fertilizer price policies to raise rural incomes; Malaysia introduced explicit wealth-sharing programs to improve the lot of ethnic Malays relative to the better-off ethnic Chinese; Hong Kong and Singapore undertook massive public housing programs [...]. Whatever the form, these programs demonstrated that the government intended for all to share the benefits of growth. (Ibid.: 13–14)

Africans still tend to assume that growth and equity are antithetical: that growth, at least in its early stages, must involve widening economic inequalities, as classically predicted by Kuznets (1955). But as the 1993 World Bank study already noted, almost all of the miracle countries in Asia displayed levels of income inequality more comparable to Europe than to Africa or Latin America (World Bank 1993: 29–31). Soon after the publication of that study, Alesina and Rodrik (1994: 478) confirmed on the basis of a broad set of international data that statistically speaking, 'the more unequal is the distribution of resources in society, the lower is the rate of economic growth'.

Development success in South-East Asia has been, in Widjojo's words (1995: 180), 'broad-based', involving little exacerbation of inequality. It has resulted not from the 'trickling down' of wealth derived from the rising incomes of an already prosperous few, but rather from simultaneous improvements in the productive and earning capacity of very large numbers of poor people. Hill (1997: 133) has identified 'equity' as one of three crucial factors – the others being 'macroeconomic orthodoxy' and 'openness' – that can be regarded on empirical grounds as belonging to the 'irreducible core' of any explanation for rapid growth in South-East Asia. In 1998 the charity Oxfam published a study entitled *Economic Growth with Equity* in which Suharto's Indonesia, on the face of it an unlikely object of admiration for such an organization, was held up as a model for equitable development (Watkins 1998).

In 2005, the World Bank devoted its annual *World Development Report* for 2006 to the theme of 'equity and development' and the proposition that 'equity is complementary, in some fundamental respects, to the pursuit of long-term prosperity' (World Bank 2005:

2). But despite the mounting statistical evidence to support this proposition, many remained sceptical. Collier and Dercon (2006: 226), criticizing the report, warned against any temptation to judge development and aid strategies 'in terms of whether they directly contribute to poverty reduction'. In their view this leads to short-sighted policies that 'redistribute both from the future and from the majority of the economy, to those who are currently poor'. Salutary examples of the consequences include the 'disastrous development cul-de-sacs' of Cuba and Venezuela (ibid.: 227, 228). Economic growth and poverty reduction are compatible only as joint outcomes of poli-cies designed exclusively to promote growth; policies which aim to combat poverty as such cannot be adopted without making growth less likely and risking diversion of the development trajectory into a Cuban cul-de-sac.

Similar opinions can be heard in Asia too. In 1990, Singaporean intellectual Kishore Mahbubani (1998: 189) included among his 'Ten Commandments for Developing Countries in the Nineties' the injunc-tion: 'Thou shalt not subsidise any products'. However, this is clearly *not* how successful Asian developmental states work in practice. In Mahbubani's own Singapore fully 86 per cent of all citizens live in housing built by the state, and although nowadays they mostly buy rather than rent their flats from the Housing Development Board, they do so at a much lower price than they would have to pay in a free market (Phang 2007). They are also assisted in this by Singapore's famous Central Provident Fund, a comprehensive national social security savings and insurance scheme based on compulsory contri-butions by both employees and employers (Vasoo and Lee 2001). Not for nothing has Singapore been characterized, along with Hong Kong, Taiwan and South Korea, as a 'Confucian welfare state' (Jones 1993).

What is true of these advanced developmental states is also true in lesser degree of the following wave of South-East Asian development success stories. Malaysia, as Collier (2007: 88) notes in *The Bottom Billion*, is 'a highly successful middle-income country' which is 'top of the league for investment inflows'. In 2008, Malaysia's ruling Barisan Nasional party won its twelfth consecutive election victory with a campaign concentrating not on the country's spectacular growth, but rather on its virtually free heathcare system and its price subsidies on flour, sugar, cooking oil and petrol. Key slogans included 'no more poverty', 'no-one left behind' and 'a place for all'. Although there is no unemployment benefit in Malaysia, and until recently no minimum wage, it is telling that the emblem of the Barisan is the weighing scale or *dacing*, symbolizing equity and justice. Malaysia is not the opposite of Cuba; it is Cuba *plus*, combining economic freedom and strong private sector development with a wide range of redistributive policies, and with the 'good social services' which Collier (ibid.: 12) concedes are a mitigating feature of the Cuban regime.

Long before socialist Vietnam embraced the market and launched its own Asian miracle under continued communist rule, all of the economically successful South-East Asian countries already had political systems with some more or less evidently socialist features. Singapore's ruling People's Action Party still officially describes its philosophy as one of 'socialist democracy' and was for many years a member of the Socialist International, from which it withdrew in 1976 after the Dutch Labour Party proposed to expel it. Although seldom recalled today, this event was important enough at the time to prompt the publication of a book, edited by later president of Singapore C. V. Devan Nair and entitled *Socialism that Works ... the Singapore Way* (1976), in which the PAP defended its socialist credentials with reference to public housing, state education, trade union representation in business and politics, and state-owned industrial enterprises.

In Indonesia under the New Order the word socialism was in itself anathema, the regime having its origins in a mass purge of Indonesia's communists in 1965. Nevertheless, many of the institutions of Suharto's developmental state were inherited from the 'Guided Democracy' of Suharto's predecessor Sukarno, established in 1959 following the breakdown of parliamentary democracy. The Guided Democracy regime incorporated the Indonesian Communist Party as a partner in power, and pursued socialist economic policies under the banner of a 'Guided Economy'. The New Order, it can almost be said, was Guided Democracy minus the communist party, plus economic freedom. Among the features which it inherited directly from its predecessor were its national constitution, its corporatist form of parliament, its ideological emphasis on *gotong royong* or mutual cooperation, and its 'government party' Golkar, an umbrella organization of non-communist labour unions, trade associations, youth, peasant, women's and veterans' groups (Reeve 1985). In some respects, there was continuity between the New Order and its predecessor even in the details of development policy. The main vehicle for disseminating Green Revolution technology in the early New Order period, the Bimas or 'Mass Guidance' agricultural extension programme, had its origins under Guided Democracy in 1963, before Suharto came to power (Rieffel 1969).

Throughout South-East Asia, pro-rural policies have reflected a pervasive concern with equity and redistribution as well as growth and modernization. Thailand is the South-East Asian country which has most clearly approximated a laissez-faire capitalist development path. For this it has paid a heavy price in the form of widening income inequality and an unstable polarization of political life between poor rural and rich urban interests, leading to the rise, fall, resurrection by proxy, second demise and second reincarnation (in 2011) of Thaksin Shinawatra's pro-rural Thai Rak Thai party. Yet even in Thailand the state has intervened to support smallholder farmers, particularly in the 1950s and 1960s by means of irrigation and infrastructure projects (Chapter 5), but also since 1970 by supporting rice prices, subsidizing fertilizer and providing cheap agricultural credit (Shigetomi 2004). Meanwhile King Bhumibol, the linchpin of Thai politics, has provided an ideological counterweight to market capitalism with his own crown-sponsored rural development projects, many of them initially built around cooperatives inspired by prototypes in Israel and China (Handley 2006: 241). A long-debated universal healthcare scheme for all Thais was finally introduced by the Thai Rak Thai party in 2002, in fulfilment of one of the election promises that had given it a landslide victory the previous year (Towse et al. 2004).

### Concluding observations and policy implications

Whatever is wrong with African governments, then, it is certainly not that they are too interested in redistribution from the rich to the poor. Nigeria has virtually no history of socialism, or of egalitarian political movements or impulses; in the following chapter it will be shown that Kenya, despite a certain amount of rhetorical 'African socialism' during the 1960s and 1970s, is in reality little different. Successful South-East Asian developmental states, by contrast, have shown consistent interest in including the poor in the development process. The political and historical reasons for this ideological contrast will be discussed in Chapter 7. For the moment, it is useful to conclude by summarizing the arguments made in the present chapter and briefly noting their policy implications.

Our opening comparison between Indonesia and Nigeria showed that agricultural and rural development, not export-oriented industrialization, was the key to initiating Indonesian economic growth and poverty reduction in the 1960s and 1970s; that state interventions and subsidies played a major part in bringing about the crucial transformation of the rural economy; and that despite the availability of ample financial resources, no comparable interventions took place in Nigeria, where the state had quite different development priorities. Marked differences also existed in the area of population policy, with Indonesia giving much higher priority to reducing the birth rate.

In Africa during the 1970s and 1980s, attempts by aid donors to promote 'integrated rural development' mostly met with limited enthusiasm from African governments, and consequently with limited success. However, in those cases where adequate cooperation was achieved, the results were sometimes encouraging. In Mali, the major irrigation project administered by the Office du Niger has enjoyed consistent support both from the national government and from international donors since 1978. Whereas at the beginning of the programme there was frequent hunger among local farmers, by 2008 the areal rice yield in the Office had risen more than sixfold. Poverty had declined sharply despite rapid immigration, and the area was a motor of economic growth. Mali was now self-sufficient in rice, with almost two-thirds of its production coming from the Office du Niger (Bais 2008: 278–82).

Potential for expansion of the area under irrigation, although often expensive to exploit, exists in many parts of Africa, particularly Nigeria (You et al. 2010: 28). Moreover, although the reasons for slow progress in African agriculture to date have been only partly technological, recent scientific advances are bringing an African counterpart of Asia's Green Revolution within closer reach. An example is the development in West Africa in the 1990s, under the direction of Sierra Leonean plant breeder Monty Jones, of an inter-species hybrid of Asian and African rice (*Oryza sativa* and *Oryza glaberrima* respectively) which combines Asian productivity with African resistance to drought and weeds: the 'New Rice for Africa', NERICA (Otsuka and Kalirajan 2006).

State-directed industrial development has almost as poor a performance record in South-East Asia as it does in Africa. When South-East Asian governments have attempted it, they have generally failed owing to control of the enterprises and institutions involved by political interest groups too strong to submit to imposed deadlines for exposure to international competition. An extreme example is the ill-fated Indonesian aerospace industry. Essentially the brainchild of one man, President Suharto's close protégé B. J. Habibie, this developed considerable technical expertise but because it could rely on virtually unlimited political support, it never achieved commercial viability, and did not survive Suharto's demise (Goldstein 2002; McKendrik 1992).

Indeed, with only a little stretching of the facts it is possible to argue that the less ideological and policy emphasis of any kind which South-East Asian governments have given to industrialization, the more likely they have been to industrialize. Of Thailand it has been said that 'it is not unreasonable to see the development of manufacturing exports during the 1970s as taking place in spite of official policy' (Dixon 1999: 104). Conversely, in Burma, by far the least industrialized of the major South-East Asian countries, the goal of industrialization has ironically been what Tin Maung Maung Than (2007: 3) describes as a 'fixation' of ruling elites from independence (1948) up to the present. There is a telling irony here: Burma, which set out single-mindedly to industrialize, failed to do so; whereas Thailand and Indonesia, which concentrated more strongly on the modernization of agriculture, succeeded in developing an internationally competitive industrial sector. Most African countries lie much closer on this spectrum to Burma than to Indonesia. While Suharto's technocrats were directing Indonesia's oil revenues into rural and agricultural development during the 1970s, their Nigerian counterparts, who for a time enjoyed similar power and autonomy, were squandering their country's oil windfall in the vain pursuit of what Collier and Gunning (2008: 211) describe as 'megalomanic industrial ambitions'.

Market-driven development of labour-intensive manufacturing by the private sector, on the other hand, is a different story. This kind of industrialization did eventually make a significant contribution to poverty reduction in Indonesia, where the garment industry alone employed almost a quarter of a million workers by 1990, and almost half a million by 2002 (Thee 2012: 251). Malaysia and Thailand too saw dramatic growth in exports of manufactured goods, mostly clothing and electronic products, in the 1980s, as has Vietnam more recently. South-East Asia's persistently labour-intensive manufacturing sector, often dominated (especially in Malaysia and Thailand) by foreign enterprise (Kimura 2004) and surprisingly weak in production linkages and technology transfer to domestic firms, has become a source of concern for many scholars of the region, who speak of 'technology-less industrialization' (Wade and Veneroso 1998: 9) and a 'middle-income trap' (Doner 2009: 276–80). But these concerns are surely of little relevance to Africa, where the achievement of middle-income status would universally be a cause for celebration. The South-East Asian evidence, moreover, suggests that this type of industrial development is not predicated on the completion of an earlier import-substituting phase driven by domestic demand.

If it was essentially misguided industrial policy, rather than the lack of a conducive agrarian setting, which limited the expansion of industrial employment in the first years of Indonesian growth, then why insist that agricultural development must take precedence over industrial development? Why should African governments not pursue liberal, pro-poor, export-oriented industrialization strategies immediately, as Collier proposes in *The Bottom Billion*, and tackle the problem of rural poverty by enabling the poor to move out of the agricultural sector? There is even some South-East Asian precedent for such an inverted sequence: in Cambodia during the late 1990s, more than 100,000 jobs were created by foreign investment in garment factories around Phnom Penh at a time when very little was being done by the Cambodian government to support agricultural or rural development (Bargawi 2005: 9).

One reason for continuing to insist on the paramount importance of agriculture is that the Cambodian sequence, as noted, is historically unusual, and that because of linkages involving stability, savings and investor confidence, export-oriented industry thrives better against the backdrop of a healthy rural economy even if it does not require domestic markets to prime it for international breakthrough. Even in Cambodia, with its precocious development of labour-intensive manufacturing, it is important to note that growth, and indeed industrialization, accelerated still further after premier Hun Sen initiated a new policy and spending commitment to rural and agricultural development in 2003 (Leliveld and Ten Brummelhuis 2013).

The most compelling reason for making smallholder agriculture the primary target of development policy in Africa, however, is the logic of numbers. In an underdeveloped economy dominated by peasant agriculture, simple arithmetic indicates that the most effective way to raise large numbers of incomes quickly is by making investments which enable smallholder farmers to raise their productivity and sell more of what they produce. 'Above all', as Widjojo straightforwardly put it in the First Five-Year Plan, 'agriculture has been selected because the greater part of the Indonesian people lives in this sector, working either as farmer producers or as farm laborers' (First Five-Year Development Plan 1969: 13). Formal sector manufacturing employment, if it can be provided on a large enough scale and in forms that are available to poor people without special skills or education, may be a useful complementary strategy. But only in a city-state like Singapore, where there is little or no agrarian hinterland, is industrialization likely to be feasible as a *primary* strategy for stimulating growth and fighting poverty. Elsewhere, it is agricultural development which has almost always had to play that role.

# 5 | VARIETIES OF RURAL BIAS

The previous chapter began by showing that Indonesia's achievements in sustained growth and mass poverty reduction during the 1970s and 1980s depended far more on agricultural and rural than on industrial and urban development, and that the most important single reason for the divergence between Indonesian and Nigerian development performances during the same period was Nigeria's failure to invest public resources in improving the productivity and incomes of smallholder farmers. In the present chapter, the same argument will be extended to the Malaysia–Kenya and Vietnam–Tanzania country comparisons. Whereas the pro-rural, pro-poor foundations of Indonesia's development success are partly recognized in existing literature (Timmer 2004, 2007; Watkins 1998), this is not so in the cases of Malaysia or Vietnam, which are often regarded as textbook examples of the export-oriented industrial development strategy, but which have hidden histories of pro-rural, pro-poor development. Kenya and Tanzania, conversely, are often regarded as two African countries which, in different ways, *have* given high priority to agriculture and the peasantry, yet without achieving the kind of developmental breakthrough seen in Malaysia and Vietnam. In what follows I will show that development strategies in Kenya and Tanzania were pro-rural only for short periods, and that even when they were pro-rural, they were far from being pro-poor. Some attention, finally, is also given to Thailand, as an additional and seldom acknowledged case of rural bias in South-East Asia.

## Malaysia: a forgotten case of rural bias

Malaysia has been cited as a classic example of the success of the industrial export-push strategy (World Bank 1993: 134–5). Today it is certainly a development success – almost the only country, among those which half a century ago belonged unambiguously to the 'Third World', that has very nearly succeeded in eliminating acute poverty. The contrast with Kenya (Chapter 1, Figure 1.5), which

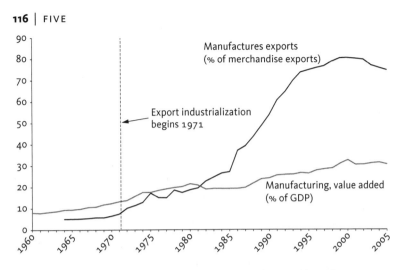

**5.1** Malaysia: industrialization, 1960–2005 (*source*: online World Development Indicators/World DataBank, World Bank)

saw only moderate per capita income growth in the 1960s and 1970s, and none at all in the 1980s and 1990s, is almost as dramatic as that between Indonesia and Nigeria. Malaysia is also a heavily industrialized country (Figure 5.1), its manufacturing sector accounting by the end of the twentieth century for three-quarters of its exports and 30 per cent of its GDP – figures similar to those of Germany. Its aspirations in the twenty-first century can be described as post-industrial: during the long premiership of prime minister Mahathir Mohamad (1981–2003), Malaysia became associated with a futuristic, urban and technological vision of development in which it and other poor countries would leap-frog the established rich nations into a new era of computers and biotechnology, far removed from the soil and toil of rural life.

Yet as in the case of Indonesia, the historical roots of Malaysian economic success lie in agricultural and rural development. Sustained economic growth in Malaysia began in 1958, immediately following the country's independence (as the Federation of Malaya) in 1957 and the ending of a military 'Emergency' during which the Communist Party of Malaya attempted to seize power from the waning British colonial regime by means of an armed insurgency in rural areas. The onset of growth coincided not with an industrial 'export push', but rather with the adoption of a strongly pro-agricultural, pro-rural, pro-poor development strategy. The most important architect of this strategy was deputy prime minister (and later prime minister) Tun Abdul Razak, who after his death in 1976 was officially awarded the title – as was Indonesia's Suharto in his own lifetime – of Bapa Pembangunan, the Father of Development. In 1959, Abdul Razak announced the nation's development priorities to its citizens in uncompromising terms.

> It is the declared policy of the Alliance Government to work for the prosperity and general well-being of the country and its people living both in the urban and the rural areas. With the progressive improvement of the Emergency situation, however, the Alliance Government decided to give top priority to the task of improving the lot of the rural inhabitants. [...] [T]he aim [...] will be to provide a sound economic foundation for peasant agriculture, to ensure that the man on the land receives the full reward for his work and enjoys the amenities of Malayan life in the same measure as his brother in the town. [...] In order that the aim may be achieved in the shortest possible time, it is the intention of the Government to marshal all available resources, and to deploy them with such determination and energy as were used to free the country from the menace of Communist terrorism. (Abdul Razak 1975: 5–6)

This emphasis on rural development was not quite as new as its propagandists claimed. In the last decade of the colonial regime there had already been considerable improvements to rural infrastructure, including irrigation facilities. The British authorities made these investments partly out of a concern that the country would soon be faced with food shortages due to population growth and political changes in Burma, Thailand and Vietnam, which for many years had provided Malaya with much of its rice (Draft Development Plan 1950: 38). Nevertheless, the general perception at the time of independence was one of 'a change from an unstated emphasis on urban development, or development for the modern sector, to a stated and actual emphasis on rural development, or development largely for the uplift of the Malays in the traditional sector' (Ness 1967: 89).

This perception was justified by a series of major new rural development initiatives in the period leading up to independence. In 1955, the year of the country's first general election, improved rice seeds were distributed free of charge for the first time to farmers, leading immediately to widespread increases in production per hectare (Lim 1967: 167). In the same year an existing pilot scheme of rubber-replanting grants, enabling rubber growers to replace ageing trees with new high-yielding stock, was greatly expanded, and its emphasis shifted from the estate to the smallholder sector (Rudner 1994: 136–8). Over the next two decades more than two-thirds of all small rubber holdings in the country would be rejuvenated with the aid of these grants, securing the incomes of about a million people (out of a national population of about ten million) for years to come (Barlow 1978: 87, 217, 233). The year 1956 saw the establishment of FELDA, the Federal Land Development Authority, the purpose of which was to open up frontier land for agricultural development and for the relocation of poor and landless rural people, and which was to become the most successful resettlement programme of its kind in the world (Sutton 1989).

To coordinate these and other rural development programmes, in 1959 the young national government created, alongside the existing ministries of agriculture, public works and so on, a new Ministry for Rural Development. This was an institution which had no direct parallel even in New Order Indonesia, and signified an even stronger commitment to the countryside as the main target of development strategy. Abdul Razak took the new portfolio himself alongside that of deputy prime minister, and directed the rural development effort from a military-style 'National Operations Room', the self-conscious efficiency of which seldom failed to impress visitors.

> The Minister, you feel, is on the bridge, or in the conning-tower; he has his hand on the controls; his work belongs to the era of the radar screen, the computer and the launching pad. This is no accident. The Ops. Room reflects the conscious determination of the Government, in this age of automation, to give both drive and the evidence of drive to economic development. (Moynihan 1964: 392)

Although it coordinated all aspects of rural development, including transport, health and education, its single most important objective was to raise the productivity of smallholder agriculture. During the 1960s this was pursued above all by further expanding the area under technical irrigation, enabling rice farmers to cultivate

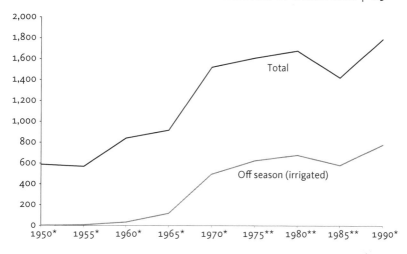

*Notes:* * = single agricultural year; ** = five-year moving average

**5.2** Peninsular Malaysia: rice production (thousand tonnes unhusked), 1950–90 (*source:* Courtenay 1995: 154)

two successive crops each year in place of one. In combination with improved, fast-growing rice varieties, irrigation made it possible for Malaysia's annual rice production to be tripled between 1955 and 1980 (Figure 5.2).

In peninsular Malaysia the area planted with modern rice breeds expanded by a factor of seven, and the area planted with two successive irrigated rice crops per year by a factor of five, between 1966 and 1977 alone (Courtenay 1995: 71, 153). In the early 1970s the goal of national rice self-sufficiency, a distant dream for colonial policy-makers two decades earlier, was very nearly achieved (Barker et al. 1985: 253). The single most important event here was the completion, in 1970, of the huge Muda irrigation scheme on the alluvial plain of north-west peninsular Malaysia, an area which even before the scheme had already produced almost half of the country's rice (Courtenay 1995: 74). The direct beneficiaries of the drive to improve rice agriculture were mostly peasant farmers: more than three-quarters of all rice farms in the country were under two hectares in area (Sivalingam 1993: 24), and in the most intensively cultivated areas, such as the Muda basin, most were under one hectare (Scott 1985: 69). As in Indonesia, the income gains which double cropping provided to small rice farmers ultimately served to invigorate the whole rural economy, including its non-agricultural sectors. Industry started to become important as a source of income for the Malaysian poor only after the opening of a number of industrial Free Trade Zones, designed to attract foreign investment in labour-intensive, export-oriented manufacturing activities, from 1972 onward (Rajah Rasiah 1993).

As in the case of Indonesia, then, economic growth was led by agricultural development, and preceded the industrial export push by more than a decade. It is true that, from the outset, the country also had an industrial development policy. Initially this was based on import substitution, and involved the protection of 'pioneer' or 'infant' industries in domestic markets (Second Five-Year Plan 1961: 19). It is also true that manufacturing industry, thanks to protection and inflated prices, had already begun to grow in the 1960s, before it became a significant producer of export goods. At this period, however, manufacturing still accounted for less than 15 per cent of GDP and less than 10 per cent of employment, compared to 33 and 50 per cent respectively for agriculture (Second Malaysia Plan 1971: 31, 98). Nor did the early development of import-substituting industry lay the foundations for the country's later export-oriented industrial growth. Malaysia's industrial export boom, as noted in the previous chapter, was led by the electronics sector, which was the result of new foreign direct investment and had no roots in the earlier import substitution phase.

In Malaysia, early industrial policy played only a marginal role in the development process, whether at that time or as a preparation for later events. This marginality was fully recognized by the planners. Under its first and second five-year plans (1956–60 and 1961–65), the government of Malaysia committed over twenty times more development funding to agriculture than to industry (Plan of Development 1956: viii; Second Five-Year Plan 1961: 29). Even as late as 1981–85, by which time Malaysia was already an industrialized country with a quarter of its workforce in manufacturing, the budgetary allocation to agriculture was still much higher than that to industry and commerce (Fourth Malaysia Plan 1981: 240–1). The national fascination with industry and technology was a later development, a phenomenon of the Mahathir era, by which time the country was perhaps beginning to be ready for such things. But the original architect of the

Malaysian development miracle was down-to-earth Abdul Razak in the 1950s, not flamboyant Dr Mahathir in the 1980s, and it is Abdul Razak's words and deeds which are today of greater relevance for the still-agrarian economies of Africa.

## The Malaysian development trajectory: sources of misunderstanding

There nevertheless remains a widespread belief, reflected in the existing Asia–Africa comparative literature (Kinuthia 2010; Nyagetera 2001), that it was the industrial export push of the 1970s and 1980s, in conjunction with the explicitly pro-Malay 'New Economic Policy' (NEP) adopted in 1970 following Malay–Chinese racial violence in 1969, which laid the real foundations for Malaysia's development success (Faaland 1990; Jesudason 1989; Peacock 1981). Some of the reasons for neglecting the significance of what happened before the NEP are ideological, having to do with the instincts and interests of the modern Malaysian political establishment. Others, however, have to do with the opacity, in some respects, of the relevant historical record.

Although sustained growth in Malaysia dates from 1958, first of all, it did accelerate in the early 1970s – and would become faster still (albeit less continuous) in the 1980s and 1990s (Chapter 1, Figure 1.5). Secondly, the time lag between the onset of sustained growth (1958) and that of export-oriented industrialization (1972) is shorter in the Malaysian than in the Indonesian case (Chapter 4), obscuring to some extent the lack of association between these two turning points. Thirdly, the effects of Malaysia's pre-1970 development efforts in the specific and crucial area of poverty reduction are obscured by two circumstances. One is that the earliest available poverty statistics at national level date only from 1970, which makes it convenient to use that year as the automatic starting point of any development narrative. Progress in poverty reduction after that date was certainly rapid (Chapter 1, Table 1.1). The other confusing circumstance is that the fragmentary Malaysian poverty data which we do have from before 1970 indicate that progress against poverty in the 1950s and 1960s was much less impressive than in the 1970s and 1980s.

According to the results of a stratified sample of 26,310 households surveyed in the wake of the 1970 census, the overall number of Malaysian households living below the national poverty line was

791,800, or 49 per cent of the total. Extending the same poverty line backwards (allowing for inflation) to a much smaller household budget survey (2,760 families) carried out following the 1957 census suggests that in 1957 there were 623,000 poor households in the country (Othman 1984: 87), corresponding to 56 per cent of the then smaller population (Lee 1976: 4). The proportion of Malaysians living in poverty, then, declined only by a few percentage points between 1957 and 1970, and the absolute number increased. The poorest 30–40 per cent of households, moreover, appear to have suffered an actual decline in income in that period (Peacock 1981: 640; Snodgrass 1980: 81). The prevailing view in the late 1960s, correspondingly, was that the rural development effort was failing, and failing in particular to benefit poor Malay farmers (Rudner 1994: 113). Although the race rioting of 1969 was primarily an urban affair, the role played in that traumatic event by Malay economic frustrations seems to support the idea that Malaysia's real developmental turning point took place with the adoption, in the wake of the riots, of the NEP in 1970.

Against this evidence that the pro-rural development policies of the 1950s and 1960s were unsuccessful, however, two countervailing observations need to be made. First, there was no sudden or radical switch to an urban-industrial strategy in 1970. Agriculture and the countryside continued to dominate development spending during the first decade of the NEP (see Table 5.1 below), and in absoute terms the scale of rural public spending actually increased. All of the major rural programmes dating from before 1970 were continued and extended: rural road building and electrification (begun on a large scale in the 1950s), the rubber replanting scheme (1952/1955), free distribution of improved rice seeds (1955), selective fertilizer subsidies (1955), FELDA (1956), the major irrigation projects (1960s), family planning (1966), and the Malaysian Agricultural Bank (1969). Sometimes there was now a sharper focus on the very poor: the rice support price (Chapter 3), for instance, was raised. But in the field of rural development, there was a high degree of continuity between the 1960s and the 1970s.

The second and more important argument against dismissing the early pro-rural development effort as ineffective is that most of those Malaysians disimpoverished during the 1970s were rice or rubber farmers, and there is good reason to think that most of them were reaping the delayed benefits of rural public investments dating

TABLE 5.1 Proportion of national development budget allocated to agriculture  (per cent), Malaysia and Kenya, 1956–90

| Malaysia | | Kenya | |
|---|---|---|---|
| First Five-Year Development Plan, 1956–60[1] | 25.9 | Development Programme, 1957–60 (pre-independence)[2] | 36.3 |
| Second Five-Year Plan, 1961–65[3] | 25.4 | Development Programme, 1960–63 (pre-independence)[4] | 27.5 |
| First Malaysia Plan, 1966–70[5] | 23.9 | First Development Plan, 1964–70[6] | 28.8 |
| Second Malaysia Plan, 1971–75[7] | 26.5 | Second Development Plan, 1970–74[8] | 12.8 |
| Third Malaysia Plan, 1976–80[9] | 25.5 | Third Development Plan, 1974–78[10] | 15.3 |
| Fourth Malaysia Plan, 1981–85[11] | 21.3 | Fourth Development Plan, 1979–83[12] | 18.7 |
| Fifth Malaysia Plan, 1986–90[13] | 17.1 | Fifth Development Plan, 1984–88[14] | 11.5 |

*Notes:* 1. Plan of Development 1956: viii; 2. Development Programme 1957: 60; 3. Second Five-Year Plan 1961: 29–30; 4. Development Programme 1960: 22; 5. First Malaysia Plan 1965: 69 (includes forestry and fisheries); 6. Development Plan 1964: 121; 7. Second Malaysia Plan 1971: 68 (includes forestry and fisheries); 8. Development Plan 1969: 148–50; 9. Third Malaysia Plan 1976: 240 (includes forestry and fisheries); 10. Development Plan 1974: 173, 202; 11. Fourth Malaysia Plan 1981: 240 (includes forestry and fisheries); 12. Development Plan 1979: 119, 225; 13. Fifth Malaysia Plan 1986: 246 (includes 'rural development'); 14. Development Plan 1984: 88.

from much earlier (Othman 1984: 211, 276). Although domestically developed new rice varieties played a role in Malaysia's agricultural development, compared to Indonesia's slightly later Green Revolution, which was heavily based on the 'quick fix' of 'miracle' HYV seed/fertilizer technology devised at the International Rice Research Institute in the Philippines during the 1960s, Malaysia's rural transformation was a slower process, involving public investments on which the returns were substantially *delayed*.

Figure 5.2 shows that most of the huge increase in national rice production which took place between 1955 and 1980 came not from rising single-harvest yields, but from double cropping: that is, the cultivation of an additional crop in the dry season. The technical irrigation projects which made this possible took time to complete, and their benefits (in terms of income gains from double cropping) were not fully realized until the 1970s. The crucial Muda scheme, for instance, was conceived in 1960, designed from 1961 to 1964, and approved in 1965; construction began in 1966, but the first irrigation water did not start to flow until 1970, and the whole scheme was not fully completed until 1973. Yet the benefits of the scheme, when they came, were dramatic: in the years 1969–74, rice production in the Muda area doubled, and farm incomes rose by an average of 80 per cent (World Bank 1975: 1–3, Annex 3, Fig. 1, Annex 5, p. 6). Of all those Malaysians who rose out of poverty between 1970 and 1980, 32 per cent were rice farmers (Othman 1984: 211).

A similar structural time lag between public investments and private returns was also present in the rubber sector. Although rubber smallholders steadily increased their output and productivity from the 1950s onward, this process was slowed by the six-year maturation period which newly planted rubber trees require before coming into production. In this sector, additional delay was caused by the misfortune that the international price of rubber fell by 40 per cent between 1957 and 1970 (Lee 1976: 14) before rebounding by more than 130 per cent between 1970 and 1980 (Othman 1984: 208). If more than 60 per cent of all smallholder rubber had not already been rejuvenated under the replanting scheme before 1970 (Lee 1976: 27), smallholders would not have been able to cash in on the subsequent boom. Of all those Malaysians who rose out of poverty between 1970 and 1980, 40 per cent were rubber smallholders (Othman 1984: 211).

In the short term, the results of Razak's decision in 1959 to commit 'all available reources' to bringing about rural development 'in the shortest possible time' clearly failed to meet the high expectations which it generated. A close look at the Malaysian evidence as a whole, nevertheless, indicates that in longer perspective Razak's strategy of starting by putting all eggs in the rural basket was in fact successful, and that Malaysia's route to development has been far more similar to Indonesia's than a superficial comparison would suggest.

A final factor worth mentioning here is that from 1950 to 1965, development efforts in Malaysia struggled to keep pace with an annual population growth rate that was consistently above 3 per cent. By 1975, however, population growth, thanks (as in Indonesia) to a combination of socio-economic change and officially sponsored family planning (Nai Peng Tey 2007), had slowed to 2.5 per cent, enabling rural anti-poverty programmes to make more headway (Snodgrass 1980: 263).

**Kenya: a rare case of rural bias in Africa?**

Like Malaysia, Kenya appears at first sight to challenge the proposition that 'pro-poor, pro-rural public spending' (Chapter 1) is the key to achieving sustained growth with mass poverty reduction. Kenya is usually thought of as one African country which, unlike most, *did* invest in smallholder agriculture rather than 'squeezing' it for the benefit of urban and industrial interests. Robert Bates (1989: 1) wrote of a 'Kenyan exceptionalism' in this respect. A biographical study of four 'public managers of Kenyan rural development' by David Leonard (1991) is provocatively entitled *African Successes*. The paradox that this alleged success did not result in poverty reduction on an Asian scale is the more striking since our two other proposed preconditions for developmental success, macroeconomic stability and economic freedom, have also been more nearly met for longer periods in Kenya than in most African countries – although not, it bears repeating, as thoroughly met as in Malaysia (Chapter 3).

At first glance, Kenyan planning documents support the view that Kenya was always an exception to the African pattern of urban-industrial development bias. Some passages from Kenya's first national development plan (1964–70), particularly in its revised and definitive 1966 version, could easily have been written by a Malaysian or Indonesian technocrat of the same period.

> During the Plan period the Government will emphasize the development of agriculture and in particular the expansion of output, productivity and employment on small farms. [...] Growth in agriculture will establish the basis for a much broader development throughout the economy. It will also serve as a brake on the flow of people into towns [...]. (Development Plan 1966: 62, 64)

In a contemporary article entitled 'Kenya's cautious development plan', economist Judith Heyer (1966: 5) described the Kenyan strategy as 'surprising' in its prescription of 'continuing predominance for agriculture' and its 'lack of emphasis on industrial expansion'. The primacy of rural development was to remain a theme of every subsequent Kenyan development plan throughout the 1970s and 1980s.

A key question here, however, is to what extent the frequently expressed Kenyan commitment to agriculture was reflected in practical policy choices and spending priorities. As in our Indonesia–Nigeria comparison (Chapter 4), the proportion of the national development budget allocated to agriculture may once again serve as a (very rough) index of the real level of rural emphasis in development strategy (Table 5.1, page 123).

In all of its national plans of the period from 1956 to 1980, the Malaysian government devoted an impressive 23–26 per cent of its development budget to the agricultural sector – although the actually disbursed proportions were sometimes slightly lower (Rudner 1994: 114). In Kenya an even higher proportion was allocated to agriculture during the last few years of British rule (when total development spending was, however, very small), and in the first few years of independence (1964–70). But whereas much conventional wisdom attributes the subsequent slackening of Kenyan rural development efforts to the 'structural adjustment' forced on the country during the fiscal crisis of the 1980s, the figures in Table 5.1 show that in reality the initially strong focus on agriculture was already lost in the 1970s, when government finances were still relatively healthy (Chapter 3). In the 1980s, in fact, the agricultural focus was partly (but temporarily) regained – although by then, funding to back it up was limited.

Both the budgetary concentration on agriculture in the 1960s, and its subsequent decline, would appear even greater if the costs of resettling 30,000 African farmers on land previously held by European immigrants in the highlands of Kenya were included in the category of agricultural expenditure. In 1966–70 almost 20 per cent of the entire development budget was devoted to this 'Million Acre Settlement Scheme', above and beyond the 28 per cent earmarked for general agricultural development (Henley 2012: 236). The purpose of the scheme was political: to end the control of Kenya's most productive farmland by a small number of white settlers, and to ease the tensions caused by overcrowding and landlessness in the adjacent areas of African peasant farming. This was in essence a redistributive endeavour: almost half of the money involved was used simply to purchase the land from its previous owners, and another 22 per cent to pay administrative costs (Von Haugwitz and Thorwart 1972: 77). Poverty alleviation was at most a secondary objective: in a contemporary official publication the Scheme is revealingly described as 'a bold large-scale scheme for the transfer of land ownership from Europeans to Africans which would, *incidentally*, in the course of time, help to absorb many of the unemployed' (Nottidge and Goldsack 1966: 1; emphasis added). Malaysia too spent substantial sums on farmer resettlement, but the Malaysian FELDA projects differed from the Million Acre Scheme in using unoccupied rather than redistributed land, and in featuring much higher levels of developmental investment; more on this below.

The agricultural budget shares shown in Table 5.1, then, exclude the costs of land settlement. On this basis the high point of rural bias in Kenya was actually reached in the late 1950s, when over a third of all development funding was devoted to agriculture. As in Malaysia, pro-rural public spending in Kenya originated towards the end of the colonial period, when political pressure (in this case from the Mau Mau uprising or 'emergency', the same term being used in both colonies) led the British authorities to pay unprecedented attention to indigenous, popular interests in the countryside. In Kenya the state's shift away from its traditional focus on European business and settler interests was marked by the adoption in 1954 of the 'Swynnerton Plan', officially entitled *A Plan to Intensify the Development of African Agriculture in Kenya* (Swynnerton 1954). But whereas Malaysia's budgetary commitment to rural development was sustained and strengthened after independence, Kenya's was not.

Rural bias in Kenya, then, was essentially a colonial phenomenon associated with two British policy responses to anti-colonial unrest, the Swynnerton Plan and the Million Acre Scheme. After independence, it persisted only for a few years before agricultural spending fell to proportional levels well below Malaysia's. Arthur Hazlewood, in his textbook on the Kenyan economy in the Kenyatta era, judged that agricultural services were already being 'neglected' in the 1960s (Hazlewood 1979: 143). It is telling that official propaganda from that period directed at the Kenyan public, rather than at an international or academic audience, presents education, not agriculture, as the centrepiece of national planning, appealing to the popular dream of escape from farming into a world of desk jobs, 'highly skilled people' and 'modern living' (Towards a Better Future 1966: 11). Although education consumed a smaller proportion of the development budget – 7.8 per cent of the plan total in 1964–70 (Development Plan 1964: 122) – it was a very large item of recurrent expenditure, and educational expansion in the early years of independence was dramatic. Enrolment in primary schools grew by a factor of more than three, and in secondary schools by a factor of almost eight, between 1963 and 1975 (Eshiwani 1990: 21).

Also interesting to note is that the temporary resurgence of agricultural spending which took place in the name of a new 'Basic Needs Strategy' under the fourth development plan was inspired by an influential report on employment, incomes and equality in Kenya which was produced by foreign consultants for the International Labour Office (ILO 1972). After much procrastination, some (not all) of the recommendations in this report, which proposed a comprehensively pro-poor approach to development, were rather reluctantly accepted by the Kenyan government (Ergas 1982: 60). This sequence of events reinforces the impression that rural bias was a foreign priority running against the grain of indigenous concerns. In Malaysia, by contrast, the sustained emphasis on rural development after 1957 owed little or nothing to foreign influence.

## Rural bias without pro-poor bias

It cannot be denied that even when the great land redistribution of the 1960s is left out of consideration, agricultural development spending in Kenya was still proportionally higher in the period from 1957 to 1970 (although not, to repeat, in later years) than anything seen in Malaysia. But there is another respect, too, in which the Kenyan commitment to the agricultural sector differed from its Malaysian counterpart: a critical lack of focus on the problem of rural *poverty*.

Kenya's short-lived rural bias, as noted, had its origins in the Swynnerton Plan of 1954. A look at the text of this seminal document already helps to explain why, even when it was pro-rural, Kenyan development policy was seldom pro-poor. In Kenya, development was seen from the outset as an intrinsically and inevitably *inequitable* process.

> In the past Government policy has been to maintain the tribal system of tenure so that all the people have had bits of land [...].
> In future, if these recommendations are accepted, former Government policy will be reversed and able, energetic or rich Africans will be able to acquire more land and bad or poor farmers less, creating a landed and a landless class. This is a normal step in the evolution of a country. (Swynnerton 1954: 10)

Despite the Kenyatta government's rhetoric of 'African socialism', this elitist view of the driving forces behind development was to remain an important feature of Kenyan planning after independence. Until deep into the 1970s, Kenyan rural development projects continued to distinguish explicitly between 'progressive' well-to-do smallholders, who could be relied on to spearhead change for the better, and poorer 'laggards', whose conservatism and aversity to risk made them slow to adopt productivity-enhancing innovations (Ergas 1982: 53; Leo 1978: 637). When it came to practical spending choices, the tendency of the planners was to put their money on the already well-to-do, who they believed would make the most productive use of it, rather than on the poor who had the greatest need of it. Announcing the country's first major public credit programme for smallholder agriculture, Kenya's first national development plan was explicit that credit would initially be provided only to an elite group of prosperous, progressive smallholders.

> Ambitious as it is, this programme will benefit only about 3 per cent of Kenya's land-owning peasantry (excluding pastoralists); the 3 per cent comprising, moreover, relatively progressive smallholders who are by definition already much better off than the rest. Thus, the programme is only a first step in Kenya's agrarian revolution. (Development Plan 1966: 133)

Remarkably given its minuscule outreach, farm credit was to account during the plan period for almost a quarter of all agricultural development spending (ibid.: 127–8). Fertilizer, too, was quite generously subsidized in Kenya from 1963 onward, but again it was only the rich who benefited. Eighty per cent of the subsidized fertilizer was consumed on fewer than three thousand large farms and estates, leading the authors of the above-mentioned ILO report (1972: 158, 433) to recommend that the subsidy be either abolished, or redirected so as to encourage supply via rural retailers in small packages suitable for use by peasant maize growers.

Kenya's strategy of betting on the rich, and deliberately promoting inequality on the assumption that the poor would ultimately also benefit from the dynamism of the 'progressive' elements in rural society, was questioned at the time not only by critical and radical scholars (Leys 1975; Wasserman 1973), but also by more moderate commentators like Heyer.

Altogether 59 per cent of the small-farm development expenditure
is directly allocable to the high-potential areas, a large part of it to
the more progressive farmers in these areas [...]. The programme
is very unequal in its distribution. There is some justification
for this if it is felt that Kenya cannot afford to be egalitarian
at present, and the bulk of the resources must go to areas of
high-potential where the returns are likely to be high [...]. The
major failure of the agricultural programme is in its neglect of
the famine problem. The famine areas, primarily the marginal
agricultural areas which are heavily populated, get no specific
allocation of funds, and there are no proposals for the alleviation
of their problems. (Heyer 1966: 7)

In Malaysia the most important developmental intervention in
agriculture – irrigation for double cropping – was likewise concentrated in high-potential areas. But it was never focused only on a few
'progressive farmers' and its effect, at least in the short term, was to
promote the development of owner-occupied household farms and
reduce the size of the 'landless class' – the same class the growth of
which Swynnerton regarded as an inevitable concomitant of successful development in Kenya (Wong 1987: 10–12). State fertilizer subsidies
in Malaysia, meanwhile, were for many years directed exclusively to
farmers living in areas of *low* production potential – that is, in those
places where their effect on yields was *least* strong – as compensation
for the fact that investment in irrigation was concentrated elsewhere
(Brown 1973: 165).

Besides being consistent with the general elitism of Kenyan development strategy, the indifference to food security noted by Heyer
also reflects a second, related contrast between agricultural development policy in Kenya and Malaysia: a greater emphasis in Kenya on
export crops relative to food crops. In the 1950s, the improvement
of African agriculture was treated as synonymous with the cultivation by African farmers of cash crops for export. In the Swynnerton
Plan almost nothing was said about food crops, except that for the
moment these should continue to be grown on a subsistence basis
'to assure the people's food supplies until such time as they win a
big enough return from their cash crops' (Swynnerton 1954: 13). In
the 1960s, Kenya's first national development plan was still explicit

that efforts to increase agricultural productivity should focus in the first place on export crops. The reasons for this choice had more to do with macroeconomic strategy and foreign exchange management than with poverty alleviation, or even with rural development in general.

> It has been decided that increases in agricultural output will be intended primarily for export markets, but that increases in manufacturing output will be more heavily directed towards satisfying domestic demands, largely through import substitution. Development in agriculture, therefore, will tend to increase Kenya's foreign exchange, while industrial development will aid in conserving it for those goods most urgently needed. (Development Plan 1964: 34)

Official neglect of food crop agriculture continued well into the 1970s. In the Third Development Plan (1974–78), a document of more than five hundred pages, less than two pages of text is devoted to the country's staple food, maize, and less than 10 per cent of projected agricultural research expenditure is allocated to this crop (Development Plan 1974: 208, 233–4). Not until the advent of the Basic Needs Strategy under the fourth plan (1979–83), in which it was acknowledged for the first time that malnutrition was widespread among Kenyan children and that there were 'places and times when food is short' (Development Plan 1979: 146), did the improvement of food production acquire any priority even in rhetorical terms. Kenya's persistent indifference towards what Heyer called the 'famine problem' contrasted sharply with the contemporary Malaysian concern with food security.

### A case study of divergent priorities: FELDA and the Million Acre Scheme

Although their primary policy focus was on food crops, the South-East Asian countries did not neglect export agriculture. The importance of smallholder rubber as an object of developmental intervention in Malaysia has already been mentioned. The Malaysian FELDA land settlement programme concentrated exclusively on the production of export crops (initially rubber, later palm oil), and as a flagship rural development programme it was in this respect unusual in the South-East Asian context. But in other respects, few things better illustrate the persistent contrasts between South-East Asian and African approaches to rural development than does a comparison between FELDA and the 'Million Acre Settlement Scheme' that accounted for such a large proportion of the development budget in Kenya during the 1960s.

The Million Acre Scheme was designed in the first place to solve a political problem, not to alleviate poverty. Its beneficiaries, in fact, included rich as well as poor farmers. An elite 15 per cent of the settlers placed under the scheme paid substantial deposits to acquire large plots in special low-density settlement zones which occupied some of the best land, and where access to support services was better than elsewhere (Leo 1978: 623–9; Von Haugwitz and Thorwart 1972: 12–18). Subdivided in turn into a standard low-density category and an even more privileged 'yeoman' class, these were the 'progressive' farmers whose efficiency was expected to ensure that the scheme did not lead to a drop in agricultural production or export earnings. Even within the standard high-density areas, there were from the outset three different categories of plot, differentiated by size and 'target income'. As the scheme proceeded, additional large parcels within the high-density zones were sold to individual buyers in order to take advantage of 'the growing demand from men with capital and ability for larger units with a higher income potential' (Nottidge and Goldsack 1966: 22). Even as it redistributed from Europeans to Africans, then, the Million Acre Scheme deliberately created an elaborate system of stratification among its African beneficiaries.

In Malaysia, by contrast, FELDA drew its settlers almost exclusively from the ranks of the very poor (landless, or owning less than 0.8 hectare of land), and the new communities in which it placed them were by design egalitarian (Robertson 1975). Unlike the Million Acre Scheme, FELDA did not simply redistribute already occupied and developed agricultural land. Its new settlements were located in previously uninhabited frontier areas which were not suitable for traditional rice-based peasant farming, but which, once identified, cleared of forest and made accessible by road, could be planted with commercial tree crops. FELDA's goal, as laid out at its inaugural meeting in 1956, was to identify 'good land' and 'good people to develop it', and to 'bring the best of each together to produce the maximum wealth for Malaya's future' (Shamsul Bahrin and Perera 1977: 5). Transforming remote, uninhabited rainforest into productive commercial farms for people with no capital of their own to bring to the task was a costly undertaking, and one that called for intensive, sustained support to the settlers during the establishment phase. In 1967, Abdul Razak explained to a foreign audience what it entailed:

> Many of our rural people are either landless or land hungry. [...] To leave such a man to his own resources, to give him ten acres of jungle and tell him to start a new life, simply does not work. He starts off without the reserves of money, knowledge or sheer human spirit to undertake such a formidable task. [...] Our method is different. First we send in the surveyors armed with a soil map to find a suitable patch of jungle where rubber or oil palm or some other crop can be grown successfully. Then the bulldozers move in to clear the jungle, and roads are laid on, with piped water and in some cases electricity as well. Good wooden houses are built according to a village plan, with a school, a community centre and a place of worship. Then the settlers move in together with a village administrator and they begin to cultivate high quality rubber or oil palm under the supervision of experts. While the rubber is growing they receive a small monthly allowance from the government [...]. After six years, when the rubber is ready for tapping, the village becomes a thriving community. [...] Every settler has ten acres which he cannot sell or subdivide [...]. (Shaw 1976: 135)

Accordingly, the Malaysian state invested heavily in FELDA in material as well as ideological terms. Between 1960 and 1975, FELDA resettled 33,706 families at a total cost of 1,147 million Malaysian dollars – about US$11,300 per family at then current prices (Shamsul Bahrin and Perera 1977: 62, 133, 137, 144). Between 1960 and 1968 the Million Acre Scheme in Kenya resettled 31,081 families at a cost of 24.5 million Kenyan pounds, or about US$2,250 per family (Von Haugwitz and Thorwart 1972: 12, 77). Almost half of the Kenyan expenditure, moreover, served simply to buy the land from its previous owners, an outlay which was not required in the Malaysian case. Excluding land purchase, the investment per family in Kenya was only US$1,200. Malaysia, in other words, was investing almost ten times more than Kenya in the future of each of its rural settlers. When it is also remembered that all of the Malaysian settlers were initially poor, whereas the Kenyan scheme included a substantial non-poor component, it becomes clear that the comparison strongly confirms our general conclusion: Kenyan rhetoric notwithstanding, Malaysia in this period displayed a far more serious pro-poor, pro-rural bias in its development efforts.

### Choices or constraints?

There are, of course, environmental differences between South-East Asia and sub-Saharan Africa which have a bearing on development strategies and outcomes. Unlike Malaysia, Kenya did not possess extensive rainforests waiting to be transformed into oil palm plantations. Its food crop farming systems were also less amenable to smallholder-focused technological improvement than the intensive rice agriculture which was at the centre of the Green Revolution in Asia. In wet rice cultivation, economies of scale and mechanization are intrinsically limited, making production on very small holdings relatively efficient (Bray 1986). This does not mean, however, that the Kenyan predilection for large holdings was a rational or inevitable one given its very different context of un-irrigated mixed farming under semi-arid conditions. In the Million Acre Scheme, as noted, some of the best land was reserved for low-density settlement by large-scale farmers on the assumption that these would use it most efficiently. But in practice the small high-density farms proved to be no less productive than the large ones (Von Haugwitz and Thorwart 1972: 42; Leo 1978: 634), and in the national plan for 1974–78 it was noted that 'most farm products can be produced very successfully on small-scale farms' (Development Plan 1974: 199). Technical considerations, then, provide at most a partial explanation for Kenyan planners' prejudice against smallholder agriculture in the 1960s and 1970s.

The success of Malaysia's agricultural revolution depended heavily on the dramatic production gains made possible by year-round irrigation, the Kenyan potential for which is more limited. On the other hand, only a small fraction of that potential has ever been exploited (Blank et al. 2002: 36; National Irrigation and Drainage Policy 2009: 2). In addition, much greater increases in unirrigated food crop produc-

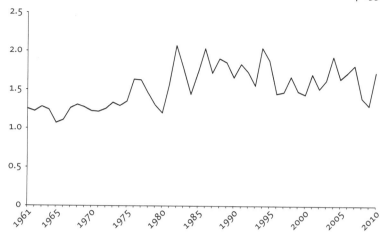

**5.3** Kenya: average maize yield (tonnes per hectare), 1961–2010 (*source*: FAOSTAT online)

tion would have been possible in Kenya if the use of fertilizer had become more widespread. Although improved maize varieties became widely available in Kenya during the 1980s, the yield obtained from them was very sensitive to adequate fertilizer application. Failure to achieve this, together with weak production incentives due to poor rural roads and marketing facilities, goes a long way towards explaining why maize yields in Kenya have risen only slowly and haltingly since 1960 (Figure 5.3).

In the 1990s, yields from improved maize grown on small farms in the less fertile areas were typically between 25 and 50 per cent below potentially achievable levels, mainly because fertilizer was hardly used owing to expense or unavailability (Hassan and Karanja 1997: 84–5). A critical constraint here was lack of credit: fewer than 1 per cent of rural households had access to formal credit from the government's Agricultural Finance Corporation (Oluoch-Kosura and Karugia 2005: 187). Only 1 per cent of all AFC credit, conversely, went to small farmers (De Groote et al. 2005: 35) – another example of the extreme and persistent elitism of Kenya's agricultural development strategy. In the same period, the official Kenya Agricultural Research Institute (KARI) was described by one close observer as 'an elitist institute, with many of its staff despising the peasantry and its poverty [...]; in and around KARI there was no idea that Kenya needed a food-oriented, farmer-first strategy connected to massive poverty alleviation' (Ton Dietz, personal communication, 30 July 2012).

Environmental contrasts are not the only possible reason why Kenyan planners might have been more constrained in their policy choices than their Malaysian counterparts. Another important contrast concerns the quantity of financial resources available for developmental investment in the two countries. In the late 1950s, Malaysia was already between two and three times more prosperous than Kenya on a per capita basis (Chapter 1, Figure 1.5), giving it a much larger domestic revenue base. In the 1970s, total (and per capita) development spending (in US dollar terms) was more than six times higher, on average, in Malaysia than in Kenya (Kinuthia 2013: 60, 72). It has been argued that if the Kenyan state had enjoyed oil revenues on a scale comparable to Malaysia's during the 1980s, it could have avoided the debt crisis, and the even tighter budgetary constraints, to which it was subject in those years (Van Donge 2012: 64). Kinuthia (2013: 207) suggests that the difference in overall development expenditure between the two countries is in itself sufficient to 'explain the differences in development outcomes'.

Whether or not this is true is ultimately a matter of conjecture. It must be stressed, however, that whatever the absolute expenditure figures, the proportional allocation of public spending (in particular the development budget) to different sectors and activities remains important as an indication of the level of priority given to each type of intervention. What is certain is that in the past, pro-poor, pro-rural development has not enjoyed any kind of priority from Kenyan governments, which have never attempted to promote the productivity and profitability of smallholder agriculture with anything like the same determination as their Malaysian counterparts. In the following chapter it will be argued that the same indifference towards peasant agriculture continues in Kenya today; and also that in developing-country contexts, high political priority, even more than availability of development funding, tends to be a *sine qua non* of effective development policy.

### Vietnam: more than the market

Vietnam's astonishing development performance over the last twenty-five years (Chapter 1, Figure 1.6 and Table 1.1) is usually discussed in terms of the success of the liberalizing, market-oriented economic reforms that were initiated on a partly informal basis in the early 1980s, and formalized with the adoption of the national Doi Moi or 'renovation' strategy in 1986. The view that Vietnam has succeeded only to the extent that it has liberalized and privatized (Dapice 2003; Wolff 1999) has not gone unchallenged. Brian van Arkadie and Do Duc Dinh (2004), in their comparative commentary on economic reform in Tanzania and Vietnam, argue that Vietnam's concern to preserve partial state ownership in some sectors has been beneficial compared to Tanzania's donor-driven rush to privatize, and also that certain successful public investments of the pre-reform era, notably in education and health care, enabled Vietnam to seize subsequent economic opportunities more effectively than Tanzania. In what follows I will argue that the importance of public investment was particularly marked in the agricultural sector, specifically food crop (rice) agriculture, which played as crucial a role in Vietnam's developmental take-off during the 1990s as it had in the transformation of Malaysia and Indonesia during the 1970s.

In the thirteen years between 1978 and 1991, rice production in Vietnam doubled, eliminating food shortages, raising many millions of rural incomes, and enabling the country to begin exporting rice for the first time in decades. There is little doubt that this would not have been possible without the well-known market-oriented reforms of that period: the decollectivization of agriculture, and the progressive deregulation of markets for agricultural products and inputs (Chapter 3). Another very important and much less widely appreciated factor, however, was the expansion of irrigation infrastructure. Figure 5.4 shows the changing seasonal composition of rice production, comprising the main rainy-season harvest, obtainable without technical irrigation, and two types of off- or dry-season crop, known as spring and summer rice. As in the Malaysian case, it is clear that most of the growth in rice production achieved during this take-off period of economic growth derived from a dramatic increase in supplementary, off-season production.

This increase in cropping intensity was made possible by year-round irrigation. Between 1976 and 1995 Vietnam's total irrigated area increased almost threefold, from about 900 to about 2,400 square kilometres (Young et al. 2002: 11–12). The most rapid expansion of

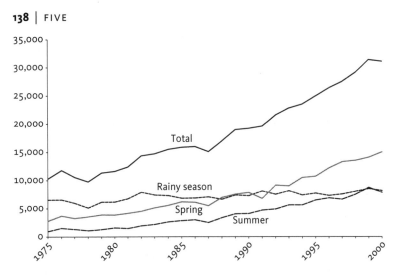

**5.4** Vietnam: rice production (thousand tonnes unhusked), 1975–2000 (*sources*: General Statistical Office 2000: 190; Young et al. 2002: 9)

all took place in the country's most important rice-producing area, the Mekong Delta of South Vietnam, in the years immediately following national unification in 1975. In 1976, 44 per cent of the area of the Mekong Delta was under irrigation; just four years later in 1980, thanks to a vigorous programme of canal building, a reported 72 per cent (Pingali and Xuan 1992: 711). Double cropping became common during this period, and by 1990 had completely replaced single cropping in many Delta villages (Kono 2001: 74, 79). Ironically, it may even have been the resulting boom in surplus rice production which, by creating additional political pressure to deregulate rice markets (Kerkvliet 2005), sparked off the great liberalization of Doi Moi, rather than vice versa.

> Another question is why did farmers rush to adopt double cropping of rice even during the socialist economy period, when the incentive to increase rice production is thought to have been small. One possible answer is as follows. Doi moi was initiated in the Mekong Delta. Introduction of market price policy in Long An province in 1985 is said to have been the first step [...]. Long An province is located at the periphery of the delta, and the land and water conditions are suitable for intensive rice cultivation. [...] Increase of rice productivity may be one of the driving forces

toward doi moi. Farmers' demands for free sale of rice may have led to modification of the socialist economy. (Kono 2001: 84)

A further irony here, notes Kono Yasuyuki (ibid.: 83), is that the rapid construction of irrigation infrastructure was greatly facilitated by the fact that 'villagers had to follow the instructions of the local authority' and 'could not reject the government's plans for new canal construction'. Landowners were obliged to give up land for new canals without compensation, and the canals were constructed using compulsory ('community') labour. In this way state socialism, by making possible surplus production, paved the way for the market economy that would replace it. 'While the socialist economy reduced the cost of canal development and consequently provided a chance for all farmers to increase rice production, this achievement led to modification of the socialist economy and the introduction of a market economy' (ibid.: 84).

Whether or not Kono's account is fully correct as an analysis of the causal chain of events leading to the creation of a market economy in Vietnam, it is clear that Vietnam's successful rural development, like that of Malaysia and Indonesia, was based on a combination of individual economic freedom and large collective investments in public infrastructure. In the years following Doi Moi, irrigation continued to be the largest single category of public investment outlay. In the period 1986–90, it is also interesting to note, fully half of irrigation spending was paid for by foreign aid (Young et al. 2002: 11).

A final point to be stressed here is that, unlike many other states inspired by Marxism, communist Vietnam, at least after 1975, gave high priority to agricultural development, not only as a source of surplus for investment in other sectors, but also as an instrument of development in its own right, and particularly as a source of food. The effort to develop irrigation, then, was part of a more general pro-agricultural strategy. At the Fourth National Congress of the Vietnam Communist Party in 1976, prime minister and politburo member Pham Van Dong put this in clear terms.

The most important task is to concentrate all our vigour and resources on developing agriculture comprehensively, strongly and stably in order to satisfy strongly the country's food needs [...]. To mobilise existing and establish new industrial units, especially mechanical engineering ones, in order to serve first of all agriculture [...]. (Tran 1998: 7)

At the following congress in 1981, general secretary Le Duan reiterated that during the 1980s it would be 'necessary to concentrate on a vigorous development of agriculture, to regard it as a top priority'. And although in practice the industrial sector always absorbed a somewhat greater share of public investment, proportional development budget allocations to agriculture during the late pre-reform period were substantial: 20.0 per cent in 1976, 19.0 per cent in 1980, and 18.6 per cent in 1985 (ibid.: 7, 8).

### Tanzania: flawed vision

Like Kenya, Tanzania in the 1960s gave relatively high priority, by African standards, to rural development. Unlike Kenya, it did so partly out of an ideological commitment to egalitarian, socialist ideals. Those same ideals also inclined it towards statist and collectivist development models, the influence of which increased rapidly in the years immediately following independence in 1961. In 1967, President Julius Nyerere's ruling party TANU (Tanganyika African National Union) committed itself and the country to a fully socialist development strategy, inspired by the principle of *ujamaa* or 'familyhood', in which the state would have control over the principal means of both production and distribution.

Introducing Tanzania's Second Five-Year Plan in 1969, Nyerere stressed that the move to 'African socialism' did not mean a change of sectoral priorities. On the contrary, like contemporary leaders in Indonesia and Malaysia, he was at pains to stress that the accelerated pursuit of rural development would mean cutting back on investment in the industrial and urban spheres.

Industrialization [...] was not the central element in the First Plan any more than it is in the Second. We did then, as we do now, recognize that the basis for our development in the near future must be agriculture. [...] The decision to give top priority to rural development does not only affect what is done in the rural areas; it also has implications for every other aspect of the Development Plan. Thus, for example, it means that there is less money and less manpower which can be devoted to improving conditions in the urban areas. In this Second Plan period it is therefore necessary to put a limit [...] on urban infrastructure expenditure [...]. (Second Five-Year Plan 1969: xvi–xvii)

The social dislocation and economic stagnation (Chapter 3) which resulted from Nyerere's attempt to collectivize agriculture and replace private trade by state and cooperative institutions quickly went down in the annals of scholarship as an object lesson in how not to pursue development (Coulson 1979; Von Freyhold 1979). It has been argued that because the price policies and agricultural marketing systems of the period favoured state employees and urban and industrial consumers to the detriment of peasants, *ujamaa* was also far less pro-rural, even by design, than official rhetoric suggested (Ellis 1983). Nevertheless, there is no doubt that the collectivization effort, and the associated policy of forcibly regrouping scattered populations into new nuclear villages, reflected a genuine commitment on the part of the Tanzanian leaders to the task of improving the living conditions of the peasant masses.

People who are farming together can obtain the economic advantages of large-scale farming, in the better utilization of machinery, purchase of supplies, marketing of crops [...]. It becomes easier to supply technical advice through agricultural extension and supervisory officers, who can teach a group more easily in one place, rather than travelling from one small shamba [farmstead] to another. It is also easier to provide social facilities like water supplies, medical and educational services [...]. (People's Plan for Progress 1969: 32)

The pattern of public spending was certainly pro-rural, with 25.7 per cent of the development buget in the first five-year plan (1964–69), and 23.1 per cent in the second (post-Arusha) plan (1969–74), dedicated to agriculture (Five-Year Plan 1964, I: 92; Second Five-Year Plan 1969, I: 211). And in terms of infrastructure and public service provision (schooling, piped water, agricultural extension), the rural development efforts of the period do seem to have had some success (Collier et al. 1986: 110).

On the face of it, then, what happened in Tanzania in the 1970s was that the potential benefits of Nyerere's rural development bias were cancelled out, and obscured to subsequent generations of Tanzanians, by his failure to appreciate that competitive markets and individual enterprise are also essential ingredients of development success. Particularly unfortunate, given the centrality of irrigation to the Asian development experience, was that the most substantial irrigation schemes developed in Tanzania under *ujamaa* were designed as large-scale state farms (Second Five-Year Plan 1969, I: 48).

Yet there is arguably also a second respect in which the Tanzanian development vision of the 1960s and 1970s was flawed, and which may help to explain why the ultimate legacy of that period, and the developmental outcome following the restoration of economic freedom in the 1990s, was less positive than in the case of Vietnam. Tanzania's rural development strategy prior to the Arusha Declaration may be described, despite Nyerere's socialism, as an elitist strategy, although in a different way from Kenya's. It featured two discrete components, an 'improvement approach', based on low-cost agricultural extension services to peasant communities *in situ*, and an expensive 'transformation approach', based on new, purpose-built, nuclear villages anticipating in many ways the '*ujamaa villages*' of the 1970s.

> The transformation approach involves the re-grouping and re-settling of farmers on the most favourable soil available, installing there a system of private or collective ownership and the introducing of supervised crop rotation and mixed farming that conduces towards the maintenance of soil fertility. (Five-Year Plan 1964: 27)

Official expectations for the gradualist, *in situ* 'improvement' approach were never high. As in Kenya, traditional peasant smallholders were thought too conservative, their holdings too small and their methods too inefficient, to be worth investing much public money in. What was assumed to be needed was a wholesale *transformation* of the peasantry, or at least of a fortunate few peasants, into sophisticated, large-scale, modern farmers, and it was this which the state was prepared to invest in. In Nyerere's own words:

> Almost all the help which Government can give in the way of tractors, improved houses, and rural water supplies, will be con-

centrated on these new Village Settlement Schemes. Volunteers coming to these new areas will be becoming modern farmers in every sense; they will use machinery and perhaps irrigation because the land tenure will be such as to ensure areas permanently large enough to justify the investment; they will have to follow laid-down crop rotations; and they will live in villages, going daily to their shambas. (Ibid.: x)

Although not explicitly conceived as an extension of the 'transformation approach', in reality *ujamaa* was to a large extent an attempt to expand that method, previously reserved for an elite of progressive volunteers, to the whole of the rural population. As before, the transformation was to take place under close bureaucratic supervision, the importance attached to which reflected a pervasive lack of trust in the knowledge and judgement of the uneducated Tanzanian peasant. The perception of rural development as a cultural and pedagogic challenge, as well as an economic process, has been present in South-East Asia too: in Malaysia, for instance, the FELDA scheme was seen partly as a means of creating a 'new kind of Malaysian', intermediate between peasant and city dweller, en route to modernity (Robertson 1975). Nevertheless, the assumption that development is in the first place a matter of cultural and technological modernization, rather than simply a matter of making poor people less poor, tends to be stronger in Africa than in South-East Asia, with pernicious consequences for African policy choices. More will be said about this, and about the greater faith placed by South-East Asian planners in the ability of their peasant compatriots to make their own economic choices, in the following chapter.

### Conclusion

In the previous chapter, an Indonesia–Nigeria comparison was used to introduce the argument that pro-poor, pro-rural public spending is an essential element of South-East Asian development success. This chapter has broadened that argument to encompass the Malaysia–Kenya and Vietnam–Tanzania country pairs. Kenyan development strategy was pro-agricultural and pro-rural only for the first few years after independence, and then only ambivalently so. More importantly, it was never pro-poor; rich, 'progressive' farmers were always the main focus. Tanzania pursued a consciously pro-rural strategy in the 1960s and 1970s, and in the decade following the Arusha Declaration (1967) there was undoubtedly also a strong pro-poor intent. However, because markets were seen as part of the cause of the poverty problem rather than part of its solution, the principle of economic freedom was not respected, with the result that outcomes were poor. There are also signs of a lack of respect for the peasantry itself, and of a counterproductive desire to do away with existing rural ways of life rather than simply make them more profitable. By contrast both Malaysia and Vietnam, despite appearances to the contrary, fit squarely into the Indonesian pattern whereby industrialization is preceded by strong agricultural and rural growth, based on massive rural public spending for the benefit of small farmers.

It may come as a surprise to some readers that the same pattern can also be found in another highly successful, and today highly industrialized, South-East Asian country, Thailand. Unlike Malaysia and Indonesia, from the 1950s to the 1970s Thailand effectively suppressed the domestic price of food, to the disadvantage of farmers and the benefit of urban consumers, by imposing a substantial tax on the export of rice, which (again in contrast to the situation in Malaysia and Indonesia) was the country's most important export product as well as its staple food (Muscat 1994: 75–7). Because of this tax burden upon peasant agriculture, Thailand has often been portrayed as a classic example of urban, not rural, development bias (Bello et al. 1998: 38; Dixon 1999: 143, 242; Siriprachai 2007: 140).

The ways in which tax revenues were spent, however, displayed anything but urban bias. Rural public spending in Thailand began to accelerate in the early 1950s (Suwannathat-Pian 1995: 151), and received strong new impetus under the military government of Sarit Thanarat, which seized power in 1957.

> The Sarit government's commitment to development could soon claim substantial accomplishments. More than any previous government, it attended to rural needs through highway construction, irrigation, rural electrification, and agricultural research and extension work. Particular attention was paid to the most densely populated and poorest regions of the country [...]. (Wyatt 2003: 272)

In Thailand's first national development plan (1961–66), 21.8 per cent of the development budget went to agriculture, and another 28.6 per cent to transport and communications (Evaluation of the First Six-Year Plan 1967: 13). Sarit's successor, Field Marshal Thanom Kittikachorn, was able to claim in his preface to the second national plan (1967–71) that '75 to 80 percent of the entire development budget represents investment expenditures for various projects designed specifically to yield benefits to the rural communities' (Second National Economic and Social Development Plan 1967: i).

As elsewhere in South-East Asia, the results of this pro-rural strategy were impressive. Between 1950 and 1970 the total area under technical irrigation tripled, causing average rice yields to rise by almost 50 per cent, and the total length of surfaced roads grew almost by a factor of ten, enabling the total area under cultivation to be expanded by more than 50 per cent (Ingram 1971: 238, 239, 276, 277). In the early 1950s, 'after a century of zero growth of output per head of population' (Warr 1993: 1), per capita income began to rise at a steadily increasing rate. Between 1963 and 1976, the percentage of the population living below the national poverty line fell from 57 to 33 per cent; by 1981, it was down to 24 per cent (Rigg 2003: 99). Throughout this period, agriculture was the leading sector in the Thai economy and the main source of economic growth. As in Indonesia, manufacturing did not take over that role until the 1980s. Even then, Thailand continued to stand out as an unusually rural country relative to its level of per capita income, which was now more than three times what it had been in 1950. In 1990 the urban population was only 23 per cent of the total, and 70 per cent of the population still worked in agriculture (Siamwalla et al. 1993: 81; Warr 1993: 4, 36).

The policy contrasts between Asian and African countries with respect to rural development were influenced to some extent by differences in environmental and social conditions. We have noted the crucial importance of dry-season irrigation in all our Asian case studies. Indeed, it has been argued that technical irrigation has been a vital motor of early growth in *all* the successful developing economies of 'Monsoon Asia', enabling them to make use of the huge labour reserves previously wasted during the dry season, when the possibilities for agricultural production were limited (Oshima

1987: 47–71). The choice to invest in irrigation was of course facilitated by the fact that seasonal wet rice cultivation was already the
mainstay of peasant agriculture, so that the extension to year-round
cropping did not involve radical change. The fact that existing patterns of landownership in South-East Asia (except the Philippines)
were relatively egalitarian was also an advantage (Hayami 2001). In
Indonesia and Malaysia, finally, the fact that rice had long had to
be imported to meet domestic demand served to focus the minds
of policy-makers on food crop agriculture, which was also the key
to poverty reduction.

On each of these points, however, there are important qualifications to be made. Rice may have been the mainstay of agricultural
development in South-East Asia, but it was not the whole story.
The significance of smallholder rubber as a target of developmental
intervention in Malaysia has already been noted, and newly propa-
gated varieties of maize, kenaf and cassava played important roles,
alongside rice, in Thai agricultural growth during the 1960s and 1970s
(Siamwalla et al. 1993: 82–5). South-East Asian planners may have
been well served by the fact that most farms in their countries were
small, but in Kenya and Tanzania, as we have seen, it was precisely
the lack of large-scale farms which was perceived as the greatest
*impediment* to agricultural development. And if the policy focus on
agriculture in Indonesia, Malaysia and Vietnam had to do with the
absence of national food self-sufficiency, this was certainly not true
of Thailand, where even experts have sometimes been puzzled by
the scale of rural public investment in the post-war period.

> Before 1980, probably the largest impact of government action
> on agricultural production occurred through its decisions on
> irrigation investments. The objectives of the Thai government
> in making these investments are far from clear. As an exporter
> of rice, the government certainly had little drive to attain self-
> sufficiency [...]. (Ibid.: 110)

The following chapter will elaborate on a simple solution to this
puzzle: in Thailand, as in other South-East Asian countries, development policies were seriously intended to reduce poverty. In Africa,
by and large, they were not.

# 6 | ELEMENTS OF THE DEVELOPMENTAL MINDSET

The previous two chapters were devoted to arguing that in South-East Asia the transition to sustained economic growth with mass poverty reduction was based in the first place on rural and agricultural development, and that this development resulted directly from vigorous measures taken by governments to promote it – most importantly, pro-agricultural, pro-rural and pro-poor public spending, in combination with economic stabilization and (where necessary) market deregulation.

The argument was based mainly on the evidence of our three country pairs, but there are reasons to think that it is much more widely valid. As Shenggen Fan and colleagues at the International Food Policy Research Institute have shown using a database which includes China and India as well as most South-East Asian countries, the biggest and most consistent differences in public spending patterns between developing Asia (in 1980) and underdeveloped Africa (in 1980 and 2005) lie in the degree of priority given to two sectors (Table 6.1). The first is agriculture, and the second is transport and communications, a sector also intimately connected to rural development.

TABLE 6.1 Composition of total public spending (per cent), Africa and Asia, 1980 and 2005

|  | Africa 1980 | Africa 2005 | Asia 1980 | Asia 2005 |
|---|---|---|---|---|
| Agriculture | 6.4 | 5.0 | 14.9 | 6.5 |
| Education | 12.2 | 17.9 | 13.8 | 17.9 |
| Health | 3.7 | 6.5 | 5.3 | 5.4 |
| Transport and communications | 6.3 | 3.7 | 11.7 | 4.5 |
| Social security | 5.7 | 5.6 | 1.9 | 8.7 |
| Defence | 14.6 | 8.1 | 17.6 | 7.9 |
| Other | 51.0 | 53.1 | 34.8 | 49.1 |

*Source*: Fan 2008: 25.

Athough spending priorities among African governments in 2005 were not markedly different from those found in (by then increasingly prosperous) Asia at the same date, with respect to agriculture and transport they remained in clear contrast to the priorities observed in Asia at the time when many Asian countries were still as poor as Africa, but already in the process of successful developmental take-off, around 1980.

The present chapter is an attempt to identify certain deeper principles and assumptions underlying the characteristic South-East Asian choice of pro-poor but economically liberal developmental strategies – elements, we might say, of the South-East Asian developmental 'mindset'. My analysis here is more concrete and specific than the existing (and useful) discourse of 'shared growth' outlined in Chapter 2, but also broader and more amenable to generalization than the policy-prescriptive emphasis on three preconditions for developmental take-off (macroeconomic stability, economic freedom and pro-rural public spending) which has informed this book so far.

This broadening of the analysis has several aspects. First, the following discussion is no longer restricted entirely to issues of policy choice, but also touches on the themes of good governance and effective policy *implementation* which have been more or less absent in earlier chapters. Secondly, the principles of successful development strategy identified below apply not only to the primary sphere of rural and agricultural development, but also to certain later, secondary, supplementary, but nevertheless successful, initiatives taken by South-East Asian governments to promote development in the industrial sector. By the same token, the analysis here also aspires to wider geographical validity: whereas our three policy preconditions apply specifically to countries with a large agrarian hinterland, the principles identified below should also be applicable to a city-state such as Singapore, or to the management of urban development within a specific city.

Three deeper principles, I will argue, can be said to underlie both the choice of successful policies, and their successful implementation, in South-East Asia. The first is the principle of *outreach*, or: 'quantity, not quality'. The primary criterion by which policies and interventions are selected in successful developmental states is the *number of people* to whom they provide direct material benefit. The second is the principle of *urgency*. At least at the beginning of the development process, at the point of transition from persistent poverty to sustained growth, successful development strategies do not involve meticulous long-term planning based on what is desirable in the future. They involve establishing clear priorities based on what is *un*desirable in the present, and acting on those priorities quickly using the resources immediately to hand. The third principle is that of *expediency*, or: 'results, not rules'. In successful developmental states, legal principles, administrative procedures, ideological precepts and ethical considerations (other than poverty reduction itself) all take second place to the goal of improving the living conditions of as many people as possible, as quickly as possible. Achieving that goal may involve tolerating corruption, bending rules and infringing rights.

Unsuccessful development strategies in Africa, by contrast, are typically characterized by an emphasis on qualitative issues such as value added, technology transfer and human capital rather than on mass impact; on long-term aspirations rather than on immediate needs; and on rules, laws and principles rather than on efficacy. These points are illustrated below with particular reference to Malaysia, Kenya, Indonesia, Nigeria, Vietnam and Tanzania.

### Outreach: quantity, not quality

In successful development strategies, the key criterion by which interventions are selected is the *number of people* they can reach and benefit in economic terms. They are not selected according to the size or type of benefit they bring to each individual beneficiary, and certainly not according to theoretical elegance, technical sophistication or aesthetic appeal. Malaysia, the most celebrated (after Singapore) of South-East Asia's development success stories, provides a first illustration. Since the 1980s, Malaysia has been associated with a futuristic, technological vision of development in which skills, knowledge and science bring developed-country status within reach. As we saw in the previous chapter, however, the Malaysian development miracle began not in the 1980s but in the 1950s, when the initial transition to sustained per capita income growth took place. At that time, development in Malaysia was perceived very differently from today: not in terms of a beckoning future of technology and prosperity, but as a desperate race against the rising numbers, falling incomes and mounting anger of the rural poor. The first five-year development plan for the Federation of Malaya, written in 1956, begins its discussion of policy priorities with a grim synopsis of the problems facing the country.

> Of these the rapid increase in population – one of the highest in the world – is the most outstanding. [...] [T]he Government may have 5 years, but not more, in which to promote an expansion in the country's economy sufficient to absorb a rapidly rising labour force in the sixties. [...] [T]he Federation [...] must not merely provide expanding opportunities for productive jobs, but must do so in ways which will reduce the pressure of population on the land and yet raise the standard of living in the farming community nearer to those levels enjoyed in other sectors of the economy. For any widening of the existing gap will generate social and racial tensions [...]. (Plan of Development 1956: 30)

'Added to the demands imposed on the economy by rapid population growth', echoed the Second Five-Year Plan in 1961, 'is the further problem of the depressed situation and land hunger of large numbers of people in the rural areas. [...] Without a vigorous and widespread rural development effort on many fronts, the rural situation can only continue to deteriorate' (Second Five-Year Plan 1961: 14–15).

Against this backdrop of what was perceived as impending catastrophe, the policies adopted by the government of the newly independent nation were designed with one thing above all in mind: the need to provide income and employment for as many very poor people as possible, as quickly as possible. One such policy was directed at the rubber industry, in which hundreds of thousands of people were employed as smallholder producers as well as plantation labourers. In the 1950s, Malaysian rubber producers faced a double challenge of declining productivity due to ageing trees, and growing international competition from synthetic rubber. The threat from synthetic rubber could be met with the help of improved varieties of natural rubber, but only if planters could be persuaded to cut down their old stands and forgo years of income while newly planted high-yielding trees grew to maturity. In 1955 the federal government started to provide a substantial grant, equivalent to about US$4,000 at today's prices, for every hectare of land cleared and replanted. Smallholder rubber planters did not have to repay this grant, although they helped to finance it via a tax on exported rubber. By 1973 over half a million hectares of small rubber holdings, two-thirds of the national total, had been rejuvenated in this way, securing the incomes of more than a quarter of a million smallholders for many years to come. Including dependants, the number of people directly helped by the replanting policy in the smallholder sector alone from 1955 to 1973 was probably about one million (Barlow 1978: 87, 217, 233).

In the 1960s the focus of Malaysian development policy shifted from rubber to rice, and to the improvement of rice production by means of year-round irrigation. The single most important irrigation project was the Muda scheme, located on the coastal plain of north-western peninsular Malaysia in the states of Perlis and Kedah. This area produced 40 per cent of the country's domestic rice crop and was home to well over half a million people, most of them dependent on rice farming and many of them poor and landless. The irrigation project, begun in 1966 and completed in 1973, transformed the economy of this rice-bowl region in a few short years by enabling almost all of its farmers to double their rice production by growing two crops each year instead of one. The resulting increases in income supply and labour demand brought prosperity to what had been one of the poorer parts of Malaysia. Permanent indebtedness almost disappeared, the rate of infant mortality was cut by half, and poverty-driven emigration from the region was replaced by opportunity-driven immigration (Scott 1985: 63–8). Besides its half-million direct beneficiaries, together with other irrigation schemes around the country the Muda project also helped Malaysia as a whole to reduce its vulnerability to international trade disturbances by becoming virtually self-sufficient in rice for the first time in centuries.

In the 1970s, manufacturing industry began for the first time to play an important role in Malaysia's development. Earlier attempts to promote import-substituting manufactures for the domestic market had failed to generate substantial employment for the poor, so now the government turned to a new strategy of encouraging foreign investment in export-oriented manufacturing industry. A key tactic here was the opening of Free Trade Zones, beginning with Bayan

Lepas on Penang island in 1972. These FTZs were industrial estates designed to attract transnational investment by means of good infrastructure and tax exemptions, as well as low wages and freedom from customs duty on imports and exports. They proved very popular with electronics, electrical, textile and garment manufacturers seeking to shift labour-intensive operations away from the high-wage economies of North America, Europe and Japan. By 1984, 80,000 people were directly employed by manufacturing firms in Malaysia's ten FTZs (Rajah Rasiah 1993: 134). Although many of the employees were young women, including dependants the total number of beneficiaries can still reasonably be estimated at a quarter of a million.

In what we might call qualitative terms, serious doubts can be raised about all three of these interventions. Rubber replanting was never going to produce a structural transformation of the Malaysian economy, only give a new lease of life to an already old industry. Technical irrigation, although it helped the very poor as well as the less poor, also widened the income gap between poorer and richer farmers, and within a decade its initial positive effect on wages for landless labourers was being eroded by the introduction of tractors and combine harvesters on the larger holdings (Ramli 1988: 210; Scott 1985: 75–6). The jobs created in the FTZs were mostly unskilled, sometimes dangerous, and other than labour the foreign companies involved purchased almost nothing from Malaysian suppliers, so that there were no significant economic linkages or technology transfers (Rajah Rasiah 1993: 134–40).

The key thing to note about these early Malaysian interventions, however, is their sheer scale, their efficiency in reaching very large numbers of people by direct and simple means. Rubber replanting: a once-off grant scheme, relatively easy to administer and monitor – one million people helped (although as noted in Chapter 5, a serious slump in the price of rubber during the 1960s meant that the benefits were not reaped until after 1970). The Muda irrigation scheme: two big dams, seven years, and half a million incomes are raised. Free Trade Zones: a little infrastructure, some clever public relations overseas, and a quarter of a million people benefit. And all this in a country with a total population, in the 1960s, of less than ten million. The leading principle here was: quantity, not quality.

In neighbouring Indonesia, ten times larger than Malaysia in population, the same problems were faced, and the same kinds of solution applied, on a scale that was greater still. The leading figure among the 'technocrats' who shaped Indonesia's spectacular economic transformation after 1965 was Widjojo Nitisastro, who headed Bappenas, the National Planning Agency, from 1967 to 1983. As noted in Chapter 4, an important fact about Widjojo is that he was initially more a demographer than an economist. This made him acutely aware of what rapid population growth could mean for the economic condition of the Indonesian people. His 1961 Berkeley doctoral dissertation dealt with the relationship between demography and economic development, and his book *Population Trends in Indonesia*, published in 1970, consisted of an annotated set of long-term demographic reconstructions and projections for the period 1775–1991. Very much a work of empirical scholarship rather than a policy document, in its last paragraph this book nevertheless concludes with a sharp warning about the implications of demographic change for Indonesia's economic future.

> Thus, the high rate of population increase, the large burden of child dependency, the rapid process of urban growth, the heavy concentration of the population on a relatively small island, and the radical rejuvenation of the working-age population, all point sharply to the need for a massive development effort to create expanding employment opportunities, accompanied by a rapid spread of fertility control. (Widjojo 1970: 238)

Under the direction of Widjojo and his colleagues, such a 'massive development effort' was duly launched. As in Malaysia it came in two distinct stages, both of them involving rapid growth in labour-intensive economic sectors: first, from 1967, a productivity revolution in smallholder agriculture based on public investments and subsidies; and later, beginning in 1983, a complementary expansion of export-oriented manufacturing industry, based on economic de-regulation and private investment (Widjojo 1995: 177). In the Indonesian case the agricultural revolution relied heavily on the new high-yielding, fertilizer-responsive rice breeds developed in the Philippines in the 1960s, and was driven by a combination of improved extension services and heavy fertilizer subsidies. It affected many millions of peasant farmers: by 1985, 80 per cent of all rice land in the country was planted with improved varieties and farmed by intensified methods, as a result of which national rice production had doubled (Hill 2000b: 132, 135). Since more than half of the national workforce was employed in agriculture, mostly in rice farming, the impact on poverty was swift and dramatic. Between 1970 and 1985 the proportion of the population living below the national poverty line fell from 60 to 20 per cent (Figure 4.2, page 88), meaning that in that fifteen-year period more than fifty million Indonesians had escaped for the first time from absolute poverty.

In Indonesia's first five-year development plan, written in 1969, Widjojo explained that the decision to concentrate all efforts on the agricultural sector was in the first place a straightforward matter of arithmetic: the central aim was simply to benefit as many Indonesians as possible.

> Above all, agriculture has been selected because the greater part of the Indonesian people lives in this sector, working either as farmer producers or as farm laborers. Agricultural development increases the earnings of the majority of the Indonesian people and thus increases national income. (First Five-Year Development Plan 1969: 13)

In Africa, by comparison, the emphasis on scale and numbers in development strategy has been much less strong. While Indonesia was spending its windfall oil revenues on labour-intensive peasant agriculture in the 1970s, another giant, military-ruled, oil-producing country, Nigeria, was spending its own oil windfall on capital-intensive industrial projects, including a massive steelworks that never produced any steel. Even when they did function, the new Nigerian industries employed very few people. In theory they were eventually supposed to create wider income and employment growth by stimulating other sectors of the economy. But in practice, as the leading Nigerian planner of the period, Alison Ayida, once admitted in an unguarded moment, nobody expected this to happen any time soon.

> The FMG [Federal Military Government], he [Ayida] acknowledged with disarming frankness, knows perfectly well that its development policies are contributing to an exacerbation of income

disparities in Nigeria, but accepts this as part of the price of rapid development. The next generation, he added, will have to deal with the consequences.[1]

In the 1980s it was still not the spectacular success of Indonesia's agriculture-led development which inspired Nigerian policy-makers, but rather the 'military-industrial complex' of Brazil, a country of gross inequality and, by that time, increasingly sluggish growth (Africa Confidential 1985: 2).

In Kenya, where the agricultural sector was not neglected to the same extent as in Nigeria, development efforts were nevertheless hampered by a similarly elitist vision of the development process. In this vision a small group of 'progressive' well-to-do smallholders, who could be relied on to spearhead change for the better, was distinguished from a much larger group of poorer 'laggards', whose conservatism and aversity to risk supposedly made them slow to adopt productivity-enhancing innovations. When it came to practical spending choices, the instinct of the Kenyan policy-makers was to put their money on the few already prosperous farmers, who they believed would make the best use of it, rather than on the mass of poor farmers who had the greatest need of it (Chapter 5). Time and again the leading principle seems to have been: quality, not quantity. Attention was paid not to the most land and the most farmers, but to the best land and the best farmers.

Despite equally rapid population growth and equally massive rural poverty, the sense of urgency and foreboding which inspired Indonesian and Malaysian leaders to make scale and outreach their first priorities in development policy has been all but absent in Kenya. In so far as Kenyan policy-makers have had any development priority which involves mass outreach, it is not agriculture, but education. The impressive effort made in this area in the 1960s and 1970s was undoubtedly in line with popular as well as elite aspirations. 'Perhaps the outstanding fact about education in Kenya', notes one source from 1974, 'has been that everyone has wanted it and wanted it more than any other single thing' (Court and Ghai 1974: 10). But

---

1 Draft paper by staff of the US embassy, Lagos, 6 December 1973, in the National Archives of the UK, FCO 65/1529. I am grateful to Stephen Ellis for providing me with this quotation.

at another level the national obsession with education reflects the same elitism, and the same emphasis on qualitative rather than quantitative change, which has made Kenyan agricultural development strategy so narrow and ineffective. The underlying assumption is that development depends on the qualitative improvement of Kenya's human resources; and the obverse side of that assumption is a pervasive contempt for the abilities of the uneducated peasant, sometimes even when it comes to his own profession of farming.

In Tanzania under Nyerere, despite a much stronger pro-poor focus in development planning, an in some ways even more pronounced version of the same condescension was pervasive in policy-making circles. Not only were existing peasant skills deemed more or less irrelevant to modern agriculture; peasants were also thought to be without material aspirations, which would therefore have to be deliberately inculcated in them before they could play their role in a modern economy.

> Eighty-five per cent of Tanganyikan consumers are peasant farmers and it is their effective demand for consumer and producer goods which [...] sets the pace for the expansion of the non-agricultural sectors. By diversifying the material needs of the peasant farmer through influencing his aspiration and will and that of his family to attain a higher standard of living [...], a rapid development of the domestic market will be made possible. [...] The Government has therefore decided to attach special priority to community development action the essential purpose of which will be by adult education, exhortation and example, to enlighten both men and women on possibilities of attaining a different, higher and more satisfying standard of living. (Five-Year Plan 1964: 12)

Nyerere's attempt after 1967 to rely on the coercive power of the state for developmental purposes was inspired not only by socialist ideology, but also by an assumption that the peasantry (at least in its current condition) was more or less indifferent to economic incentives. There was also a persistent and revealing tendency to blame peasant ignorance, rather than the shortcomings of the command economy, for development failures. Looking back in 1977 on ten years of *ujamaa*, Nyerere declared:

The [...] peasants of Tanzania [...] have worked hard. But they have worked without sufficient knowledge and understanding of improved husbandry [...]. More effort on small-scale irrigation and the building of dams could at least reduce the loss imposed by rain shortage. And we must also stress the importance of planting, weeding and harvesting at the right times, as well as proper spacing; for these do not cost anything but can result in a greatly increased harvest. (Nyerere 1979: 54)

In South-East Asia the theory of economic 'dualism', contrasting the allegedly conservative, culturally predetermined, unscientific and economically irrational behaviour of peasants with the rationality and dynamism of modern economic actors, was highly developed in colonial academic literature and remained influential well into the post-war period (Boeke 1953; Parkinson 1967). Yet Malaysian and Indonesian policy-makers of the 1960s and 1970s, while believing in the value of (especially primary) education and the need for agricultural extension services, also tended to trust in the wisdom and judgement of peasant farmers, even with respect to radical innovations in agricultural technology.

Professor Widjojo [...] had great faith in farmers. He felt strongly that they were both more responsive and responsible than was generally thought to be the case – especially by economists who had worked in and on Indonesia, *the* key case country for much of the development literature on dualism. (Falcon 2007: 27–8)

This faith was to prove justified. In Indonesia, the rapid spread of fertilizer use and improved rice breeds took place only partly through the official agricultural extension channels; much of the dissemination process was based on free markets and on word of mouth (Booth 1988: 148–9). In Malaysia, seeds of an experimental rice variety not yet scheduled for public release were at one point actually stolen from a research station in the Muda area by impatient farmers. Within two years of the theft, two-thirds of the Muda plain were reportedly planted with the new variety, which had also spread to all other major rice-bowl areas in the country (Jenkins and Lai 1989: 46).

In recent years, no development strategy has generated as much enthusiasm and optimism as microfinance. In Africa the microfinance scene, while lively and innovative, is characterized by small, diverse institutions with limited individual or collective outreach, many of them based on initiatives by foreign donors but designed with idealistic principles of local ownership and participatory management in mind (Ouédraogo and Gentil 2008; UNHSP 2005). In South-East Asia, microfinance is characterized by monolithic state-owned banks with massive outreach. Of the top six countries in the world in terms of microfinance penetration rates (measured by borrowing clients as a percentage of population) at the beginning of the present century, four – Indonesia, Thailand, Vietnam and Cambodia – were in South-East Asia. In Indonesia a single state-owned bank, the Indonesian People's Bank, was serving one quarter of all Indonesian households, comprising more than fifty million people. In Vietnam, three state-owned microfinance institutions reached between them almost half of all rural households in the country. In Thailand, the state microfinance Bank for Agriculture and Agricultural Cooperatives (BAAC) even claimed to be reaching 90 per cent of all rural households – 70 per cent directly, and another 20 per cent indirectly via cooperative societies (Henley and Goenka 2010: 5–6).

A final example of Africa's orientation towards quality rather than quantity in development strategy concerns the persistent emphasis placed by African planners, and their foreign advisers, on 'capturing value added' and 'moving up the value chain' into more technologically sophisticated production activities. Kenya's *Vision 2030* long-term planning document, published in 2007, gives high priority to the goals of 'moving the economy up the value chain', 'exploiting opportunities in value addition to local agricultural produce', and 'adding value to intermediate imports and capturing the "last step" of value addition [...] in metals and plastics' (Kenya Vision 2007: ix–x). In the past, this kind of strategy has often led in Africa to projects which create only very limited employment and income for the poor, and at worst to projects which actually reduce the incomes of peasant farmers and poor consumers by forcing them to sell to monopsonistic processors and buy from monopolistic manufacturers (Chapter 3). While it is conceivable that future applications of the 'value added' strategy might be less damaging to the interests of the poor, this is not a strategy which played a central role in the transition to sustained growth and poverty reduction in South-East Asia. In Malaysia and

Indonesia, economic growth was initially based largely on increased production of unprocessed rice, and later on the electronics and textile industries, neither of which made use of local raw materials which they could add value to – or indeed of any local inputs at all, other than very large quantities of cheap labour.

That the 'quantity, not quality' formula still works under today's conditions is demonstrated by the case of late developer Vietnam. Using a characteristically South-East Asian combination of rigorous market liberalization and heavy public investment in land settlement, irrigation, farm credit and rural infrastructure, Vietnam has risen from nowhere to become the world's second-largest producer of coffee after Brazil, as well as to overtake Thailand as an exporter of rice. Almost all Vietnamese coffee is robusta coffee, the second-rate variety used to make instant coffee, and it is frequently disparaged for its poor quality even by robusta standards. Most of it is exported in unprocessed form as green beans. Vietnamese rice is likewise a second-grade product, worth much less than Thai rice on international markets. The Vietnamese export manufacturing sector specializes in very cheap clothing and shoes. Vietnam has succeeded in becoming a major exporter of all these products not by looking for innovative product niches, or exploiting new technology or moving up the value chain. Like its predecessors, it succeeded by moving in at the bottom end of the market, exploiting a massive international demand for cheap, simple products.

So far the principle of outreach has been discussed entirely in the context of pro-poor, pro-agricultural public spending, but in South-East Asia it has also explicitly informed the fulfilment of another key condition for sustained growth with poverty reduction, macroeconomic stability. For the Indonesian technocrats, as noted in Chapter 4, controlling inflation and maintaining a competitive exchange rate were not matters of ideological principle, nor even policy objectives in their own right, but rather preconditions for mass poverty reduction. The 1978 devaluation of the rupiah, which has been called 'one of the boldest and wisest macro-policy decisions made in the post World War II period' (Falcon 2007: 30), has also been described as 'a payoff from the corporatist nature of the Indonesian state' (Wing Thye Woo 1988: 347), in the sense that, as a measure designed to benefit smallholder producers of export crops, it reflected the New Order's desire to include the rural poor as well as the urban rich in the development process. Likewise, the technocrats' commitment to deregulation in most sectors of the economy was pragmatic rather than ideological in nature (Chapter 3), the higher goal which it served being that of broad-based, inclusive development.

## Urgency: priorities, not plans

As in the Malaysian and Indonesian cases, Vietnam's more recent development achievements have been driven by an acute awareness among the country's leaders both of the scale of the challenge facing them, and of its urgency.

> More important to the Communist Party than economic dogma is self-preservation. Everything else: growth, poverty reduction, regional equality, media freedom, environmental protection – everything – is subordinate to that basic instinct. To survive, the Party knows it has to match a simple, but terrifying, figure: one million jobs a year. Every year Vietnam's schools produce a million new peasants and proletarians, the product of a huge post-war baby boom which is showing little sign of slowing down despite an intense 'two-child' policy. Growth is vital, but not at the expense of creating too much inequality. So is reducing poverty, but not at the expense of impeding growth too much. Over the past 30 years policy has swung back and forth, sometimes favouring growth, sometimes stability. The beneficiaries have been the peasants and proletarians. (Hayton 2010: 3)

It is often assumed that economic success in South-East Asia owes much to meticulous planning and long-term vision. But this is only very partly true. Asked to explain the 'Thai vision of development', a senior Dutch diplomat in Thailand once replied drily: 'I have never met a Thai with vision.'[2] Even in Singapore, regarded today as the epitome of planning, development efforts in the early years of independence were characterized less by measure and foresight than by the dogged, desperate courting of any investor willing to employ substantial numbers of Singaporeans. As a former official (later chairman) of Singapore's powerful Economic Development Board recalled:

---

2 With thanks to Roel van der Veen for this anecdote.

The goal was to create jobs, more jobs, and still more jobs, and the system was to make calls on any and all companies who could be contacted – high tech, low tech, whatever tech ... For every one hundred calls you might get ten responses, and from those ten responses you might get two visits, and from those two visits you might get one 'yes'. (Schein 1996: 60)

Not until 200,000 people, out of a total population of just over two million, were already employed in (mostly labour-intensive) manufacturing, and unemployment had been almost eliminated, did Singapore start to concern itself with selectively favouring high value-added industries or training its workforce in the skills necessary to attract and retain them (ibid.: 77).

In the Indonesian case it is true that national planning played an important role in development from the beginning, and that the planners acted on the assumption that political stability would enable their current plans to form the basis for further development in the future. But if we look at Indonesia's development plans, particularly those covering the transition to sustained growth and the period of mass poverty reduction in the 1970s and 1980s, we find that they are surprisingly sketchy, not only about long-term goals, but even about events during the five-year periods to which they refer. The crucial first plan, covering the period 1969–74, contains no macroeconomic framework and none of the customary projections of economic growth, savings and investment. Instead it simply sets out a list of sectoral priorities, and prescribes a series of policy measures with respect to each one of them. These priorities are determined not by long-term goals, but by immediate needs.

If the Indonesian technocrats were not much concerned with the technicalities of economic planning, they were very much concerned with establishing priorities and sticking to them. The first important set of policy advice which they presented to the New Order government, adopted as state policy in 1966 amid a crisis of falling incomes and hyperinflation, had at its core a simple 'scale of national priorities'. In the short term, the top three were: (a) bringing inflation under control; (b) meeting food needs; and (c) rehabilitating the economic infrastructure. In the longer term, the priorities were declared to be: (a) agricultural development; (b) infrastructural development; and (c) the development of industry, mining and oil production (Widjojo 2010: 91, 95). Once inflation had been duly reduced by balancing the state's finances through a combination of spending cuts and foreign aid, it was agriculture which became, in the words of Widjojo in the first five-year plan, 'the central arena in which all efforts are concentrated and results expected' (First Five-Year Development Plan 1969: 11).

Because agricultural development inevitably took longer to achieve than macroeconomic stability, this priority was maintained long after the crisis in which the New Order was born had passed. Agriculture remained the largest item on the development budget for the next two decades, above transport and industry, ahead too of the health, education and other social investment which has figured so strongly in African development efforts. Such was the priority accorded to agricultural development that the national goal of rice self-sufficiency, which was achieved in 1984, was described as 'Indonesia's equivalent of America's Apollo mission to the moon' (Prawiro 1998: 131). Urban problems and interests were entirely subordinated to the rural development effort. 'Any effort to overcome the problems of the urban areas', declared Widjojo, 'will always be defeated if the rural areas themselves are unable to solve the unemployment problem' (First Five-Year Development Plan 1969: 105–6). Industrialization, in the words of another leading technocrat, 'was not considered desirable' on the grounds that it 'would mainly benefit the large urban centres' (Salim 1997: 57).

In Malaysia too the policies associated with economic take-off were not policies of long-term industrial vision, but policies of rural crisis containment, and they were pursued with equal single-mindedness. As we have seen, the onset of sustained growth in Malaysia coincided not with an industrial 'export push' of the type highlighted by the World Bank's interpretation of the 'East Asian Miracle', but rather with the adoption of a strongly pro-rural, pro-poor development strategy. The foremost architect of this strategy was deputy prime minister, minister of rural development and later prime minister Abdul Razak, Malaysia's 'Father of Development', who in 1959 announced his government's determination to 'give top priority to the task of improving the lot of the rural inhabitant' and to 'marshal all available resources' to that end (Chapter 5).

In the Federation of Malaya's national development plan for 1961–65, co-authored by Razak and the first to be drawn up after independence, the first objective of the plan is specified as: 'To provide facilities and opportunities for the rural population to improve its levels of economic and social well-being'. The urban areas are not mentioned at all until the fifth and last objective, which includes a commitment 'to extend the public health services over a wider coverage of the rural as well as urban population' and 'to provide more adequately for rural and urban utilities'. Under the 1961–65 plan, the Malaysian government committed twenty times more development funding to agriculture than to industry (Second Five Year Plan 1961: 16, 29). As in Indonesia, the bias towards agriculture was maintained consistently for many years: as late as 1981–85, by which time Malaysia was already an industrialized country with a quarter of its workforce in manufacturing, the budgetary allocation to agriculture was still much higher than that to industry and commerce (Fourth Malaysia Plan 1981: 240–1).

African development planners, by contrast, have had a much greater inclination to spread their eggs over a large number of different baskets. In Kenya there was thought to be a need for 'rural–urban balance', entailing *coordination* of rural and urban development rather than the establishment of a clear order of priority.

> [A] careful balance must be maintained between them. If rural development lags behind, people will migrate to the urban areas [...]. If urban development proceeds too slowly, the rural areas will suffer from lack of access to supplies and a weak demand for their products [...]. (Development Plan 1979: 45)

In Nigeria the watchword was 'diversification', which meant reducing the country's economic dependency not only on the oil sector, but also on agriculture (Third National Development Plan 1975, I: 31). In the 1970s, Nigeria pursued diversification partly by pumping state money into capital-intensive manufacturing projects: cement, steel, machine tools, motor vehicles (Chapter 4). It has been suggested that 'the *raison d'être* of most of these projects was blatant corruption' (Thorbecke 1998: 133), and large import-substituting industrial projects undoubtedly provided more scope for illicit kickbacks than did (for instance) agricultural extension services or Free Trade Zones.

But corruption was not the whole story here: the 1970s saw the high point of technocratic power and autonomy in Nigeria, when planners enjoyed more freedom from this kind of pressure than at any other time (Collier and Gunning 2008: 211). The industrialization drive also reflected the fact that Nigerian technocrats like Ayida had a vision of the development process which was simply very diffferent from that of their Indonesian or Malaysian counterparts.

The essence of this difference in vision, I would suggest, is that whereas the South-East Asians saw development as an incremental (albeit potentially rapid) process whereby poor people become richer, the Africans saw it more as a transformative process whereby poor countries acquire various things which rich countries have, and poor ones do not. At some risk of oversimplification, we can say that heavy industry was favoured in Nigeria in the 1970s essentially because Nigerians saw that it was one of those things (others included higher education) which their country did not yet have, but which developed countries did have, and which it was therefore thought necessary to have in order to develop. Their reference point, in other words, was an idealized state of industrial modernity, the desired *end point* of the development process. In Indonesia in the 1970s and Malaysia in the 1960s, by contrast, the reference point was an immediate and grim reality of rural poverty, the *un*desired *starting point* of the development process. This was a reality which could be changed only by tackling the problems at root using whatever resources lay immediately to hand: not by planning for the future, but by establishing immediate priorities and acting on them. There was a constant sense of acute, energizing urgency: faced with any kind of bureaucratic obstruction or inertia, Abdul Razak liked to chastise those responsible by quoting the Chinese proverb which notes that 'it is impossible to buy an inch of time with an inch of gold' (Shaw 1976: 133).

Today in Africa, steelworks and universities have been replaced as perceived hallmarks of development by new symbols of modernity: computers, supermarkets, accountability, human rights. But the underlying vision of development as a matter of acquiring certain attributes of developed status is still very pervasive. Nigeria's 2004 *National Economic Empowerment and Development Strategy*, for instance, contains almost as much text on information technology, the financial services sector and indeed the film industry as it does on agriculture – and considerably more on education, human rights and the administration of justice than it does on agriculture (NEEDS 2004: 34–8, 68–70, 73–6). A 2008 academic volume entitled *Economic Policy Options for a Prosperous Nigeria*, containing work by more than thirty authors and boasting Paul Collier and Chukwuma Soludo among its editors, contains nothing at all on agriculture, although readers are referred to an online contribution on 'Agricultural export potential in Nigeria', which somehow never made it into the printed version of the book (Collier et al. 2008: 8). Nigeria's most recent national development strategy document, covering the period 2011–15, is entitled *The Transformation Agenda* and continues to prioritize the creation of non-agricultural employment, in particular for the benefit of 'school leavers with senior secondary qualifications and graduates of tertiary institutions' (Transformation Agenda 2011: 8). At a Tracking Development conference in The Hague in 2012, Nigerian minister of agriculture Akinwumi Adesina denied that Africa has failed to appreciate the developmental importance of the farm sector, and announced that his own government intended to make Nigeria 'a power-house of food production and export' – only to confess, when pressed for details, that at present only 3 per cent of Nigerian public spending is dedicated to agriculture (Vlasblom 2013: 38).

Kenya's long-term national plan *Kenya Vision 2030*, from 2007, is a striking example of a development plan inspired above all by fantasies of modernity. Its pages gleam with motorways and skyscrapers, and its economic platform begins not with agriculture, the sector in which the bulk of the nation's workforce is employed, but with tourism – in relation to which the plan, reading more like a travel brochure, promises that Kenya will provide 'a high-end, diverse, and distinctive visitor experience' (p. ix). After a cursory look at agriculture, with an emphasis on export crops and value addition, *Kenya Vision 2030* then moves on to the third sectoral priority, wholesale and retail trading. Here again the 'overall strategy' is a characteristically elitist one: to 'increase formal market share in the country' (p. 59) – for instance, by supporting the expansion of supermarket chains, almost inevitably at the expense of informal employment in the sector.

Like not a few other recent African planning documents, *Kenya Vision 2030* is apparently inspired partly by Malaysia's earlier *Vision 2020* development concept. The problem, however, is that in terms of national income and economic structure, Kenya today is still decades behind where Malaysia was in 1991 when its then prime minister, Mahathir Mohamad, announced *Vision 2020*. By that stage, Malaysia already had more than thirty years of sustained growth and poverty reduction behind it – achievements made possible not by tourism, supermarkets and value-added products, but by rubber, rice and low-wage, labour-intensive manufacturing employment.

Another telling example of Africa's determination to misunderstand the development lessons of Asia can be found in the text of an interview with former deputy prime minister of Malaysia (1981–86) Tun Musa Hitam, published in *New African* magazine in 2011. Asked to explain 'the secret of the Malaysian success', Musa replies that the first step was to develop agriculture, and the second to provide low-wage manufacturing employment in factories built by foreign companies.

> *Musa Hitam*: A lot of foreign investors came. We said: 'Come to us, open your factories, give jobs to our people.' The salaries were low, but it was better than having no jobs. Our people got the jobs. So they were able to support themselves. That was the second stage. [...]
>
> *Interviewer*: It was strategic planning, wasn't it?
>
> *Musa Hitam*: Yes. First, we had five-year plans, and we implemented them diligently. Five years, five years, five years at a time.
>
> (Yaïche 2011: 24)

The persistent impression in this interview is one of a conversation at cross-purposes. Passing over Musa's point about the need for rapid employment expansion at all costs, the interviewer presses for confirmation of his own conviction that 'strategic planning' is crucial to development success. Musa agrees, but stresses that the time span that really mattered to Malaysian planners was a short one: 'five years, five years at a time'. Again the point is lost on his interlocutor, who then switches to another characteristic African preoccupation, the unwillingness of foreign investors to contribute to the public purse. But the Malaysian sticks to his guns: foreign industrial concerns were not invited into the country in order to pay taxes, only to provide jobs.

> *Interviewer*: Many companies hate paying tax, they fly away from countries where the tax regime is stiff. How did you solve this problem?

*Musa Hitam:* Very simple, in order to attract foreign investors to Malaysia, we exempted them from paying taxes for the first 10 years. We wanted them to come here as our priority was providing jobs to the people. That was number one. (Ibid.: 24)

Musa's choice of words here is telling: not only does he specify the necessary strategy, he also speaks the language of *priority*, of identifying a clear 'number one', of making a painful but ultimately *simple* choice to pursue one goal *and not another*. Successful development planners not only avoid trying to think too far ahead; they also avoid trying to do too many different things at once.

In countries where the machinery of government is weak, inefficient or corrupt, getting the policy priorities right is particularly important. Even the most underpaid, most incompetent civil servants, as anyone knows who has witnessed a presidential or ministerial visit to a backwater province in South-East Asia, tend to be capable of amazing feats of efficiency and discipline when they suddenly feel the heat of power and the danger of displeasing the seriously powerful. But as soon as that danger is no longer acute, discipline quickly lapses. By the same token, only those policies which are known to enjoy the highest priority in the highest political circles have much chance of being implemented efficiently. In addition, high political priority serves to protect key policies from dilution as a result of pressure from competing interest groups or competing ideas on development strategy.

In terms of sectoral priorities, Professor Widjojo was clear from the outset that the overwhelming emphasis should be on agriculture. [...] This absolute priority for agriculture was [...] useful in fending off overly ambitious proposals from other sectors. In responding to requests from Bappenas for proposed activities to be included in the new plan, many agencies found it easier and more compelling to pull out old projects proposals that had been formulated but never approved for funding in previous years. Often these were ambitious, capital-intensive undertakings that had limited economic justification under the prevailing circumstances. Bappenas, under Professor Widjojo's leadership, kept pressing the ministries and departments to focus on less glamorous activities that were likely to yield more immediate benefits at much lower cost. (Cole 2007: 126–7)

In a powerful 1994 retrospective on his country's development achievements, Widjojo emphasized that the first precondition for successful poverty reduction is 'true commitment to achieving it'.

> What lessons can be drawn from Indonesia's experience in achieving a rapid reduction of poverty? First and foremost is the need for a true commitment to achieving it. It has to be a true commitment as opposed to adhering passively to [...] fashions in the development debate. Such a commitment has to be translated into operational policies and programs to be implemented in a consistent manner. These policies and programs have to be internally designed and self-imposed rather than being parts of conditions attached to loans or grants. The test of a true commitment arrives when the availability of resources is rapidly declining: whether to forgo other claims or to yield to pressures and sacrifice the poverty-reduction programs. (Widjojo 1995: 180)

The issue of commitment, and its translation into policies which give absolute priority to poverty alleviation, is logically prior to the questions of policy *implementation* and 'good governance' which currently preoccupy many commentators on Africa's problems. Particularly in a context of *poor* governance, political commitment at the highest level is itself a large part of the key to effective policy implementation; and effective implementation of policies which do *not* reflect commitment to poverty alleviation will not help anyway. In Kenya and Nigeria, that commitment seems in general to have been absent among policy-making elites (although no doubt there were many individual exceptions). 'Lip-service', lamented one observer in Kenya in the 1970s, 'is being paid to rural development, but it has no political backing. [...] There is no initiative coming from the high-level political organs' (Heyer 1976: 29–30). In Malaysia and Indonesia, by contrast, rural development was the personal concern and responsibility of (respectively) Razak and Suharto, who both staked their own political reputation on its success, and so could not afford to allow it to fail.

The personal backing of a head of state, however, is not in itself sufficient to ensure that pro-poor agricultural development becomes a reality. To make a difference, the pro-poor vision must be shared among a substantial section of the political elite. In 2005, Tanzania looked set to break the African mould of urban-biased development when its government announced plans for a massive fourfold expansion of the land area under irrigation within five years, and for substantial tariff protection of the domestic rice market in the interests of farmer income and national food self-sufficiency. But the practical outcomes of Tanzania's Agricultural Sector Development Policy (ASDP) have been very mixed, with rice smuggling widely tolerated, and implementation of the irrigation schemes marred by inadequate provision for system operation and maintenance. The main reason for this does not seem to be any intrinsic weakness in the implementing institutions, but rather the fact that the policies in question resulted from a surprise personal initiative by the (in 2005) president-in-waiting Jakaya Kikwete, and were neither supported by, nor even discussed with, any other members of the policy-making elite – technocrats and aid donors included.

> There is no indication that the decision [...] was in any way prepared. Indeed, senior technical staff involved with irrigation had not been consulted and were taken by surprise. The president's decision came out of the blue, as one of them said. Staff did not consider the target to be a credible commitment, but no one questioned it openly. The technocrats were simply bypassed. So were the donors – and they were sceptical. [...] Apart from the president's personal intervention to push for a major public investment programme in irrigation, it is difficult to detect any fingerprints of other prominent members of the ruling coalition in the design of the ASDP. [...] [N] either the agricultural ministers nor the permanent secretaries seem to have played active roles [...]. (Therkildsen 2011: 16–18)

The motives behind Kikwete's quixotic order to invest in rice agriculture, moreover, throw further light both on the poor practical outcomes of the ASDP, and on the persistent underlying contrasts between African and South-East Asian development strategies, even in those rare cases where they appear at first sight to be similar. The president's decision was based not in the first place on the potential of wet rice farming to reduce mass poverty, but rather on a desire to 'transform', 'modernize', even 'revolutionize' Tanzanian agriculture by means of a dramatic state-led development initiative. Therkildsen (ibid.: 34) describes it as reflecting an 'ideological legacy of party-driven modernisation of agriculture' inherited from the socialist period.

> [T]he push for a huge irrigation construction programme seems driven by the new president's desire to signal decisiveness and by the repeated party emphasis on the need to revolutionise agriculture. There is a long tradition for this type of party-led 'we must run while others walk' policy making in Tanzania [...]. In [...] past efforts to transform agriculture (none of which achieved much), the state has always been central. The irrigation component clearly fits that tradition despite ASDP's explicit references to market driven agricultural development and to the importance of the private sector. (Ibid.: 35)

Despite appearances, then, Tanzania's recent irrigation initiative – half-hearted as it is – remains at root more akin to the excesses of Nyerere's *ujamaa* project than to the successes of Vietnam's agricultural development policy since liberalization. Unlike its South-East Asian counterparts, it is not based on a desire to reduce poverty on as large a scale as possible, with the greatest possible urgency, and by the most practical available means. On the contrary, it reflects precisely the mistaken priorities that have so often been fatal for African development endeavours in the past: ambitious plans rather than practical exigencies, end points rather than starting points, transformation rather than incremental change, and a 'cargo cult' conception of the development process in which progress is measured by technical attributes of modernity acquired, not by poor people made richer.

### Expediency: results, not rules

We have seen that in their commitment to market-friendly development strategies, Widjojo and his colleagues were no neoliberal ideologues; their self-professed guideline was 'pragmatism, that is, the principle that what is good is what works' (Sadli 1997: 243). When drastically devaluing the rupiah against the US dollar in 1978, for instance, they broke with all liberal orthodoxy by temporarily imposing coercive price controls to prevent domestic retailers from responding by immediately raising their prices, which would have caused the benefits of the devaluation to be lost.

The irrational rise in prices was rolled back [...] by sheer force – and all the more effectively. Then, when the inflationary momentum had been broken, firms were gradually allowed to reflect increased costs in their prices; later, still gradually, but actually quite fast, price controls were altogether lifted. [...] Many an orthodox practitioner of economic liberalism is horrified by this story. Price controls have a well-deserved reputation for being ineffective. And indeed they generally are, in the long run [...]. In this case, they worked because they were a temporary counter to a temporary panic [...]. Exchange controls and price controls: the firm and lasting abandonment of one, and later recourse to the other, illustrate a seemingly contradictory attitude to economic orthodoxy. But there is no contradiction; in reality, they show up a fundamental characteristic of Indonesian economic policy, a deep distrust of labels and policy categories, complete dedication to pragmatism. (Baneth 1997: 286)

The same kind of willingness to sacrifice principles for the sake of performance (or perhaps: lower principles for the sake of higher principles) is evident in the loud silence of the Indonesian technocrats on the subject of corruption. Widjojo himself is said to have been personally incorruptible (Keyfitz 2007: 37; De Pourtales 2007: 288), raising chickens at home to supplement his family's diet although he 'could have become rich by simply stretching out his hand and acccepting a payoff from one of the many opportunists seeking concessions from his government' (Tolbert 2007: 235). Yet his 'deep sense of political reality – of what is possible and what is not' (Masters 2007: 68) prevented him and his colleagues from jeopardizing the development endeavour by publicly criticizing the corrupt behaviour of powerful others.

Indonesia is well known for having combined rapid growth and poverty reduction with a very high level of corruption (Chapter 7). The rule of law has never had much significance there even at an ideological level, and in day-to-day practice it hardly exists at all. A common estimate is that during the Suharto era, 30 per cent of all development loans to the Indonesian government disappeared into private pockets (Harahap 1999: 3). It is often said that Suharto tolerated and even encouraged corruption among lower officials in order to defuse criticism of his own transgressions. But there was also another, less sinister aspect of the New Order's indifference to leakages of public money: its focus was not on obedience to rules, but on the achievement of results.

The fact that a proportion of development funds could be misappropriated with impunity does not mean that that there was no institutional control on how those funds were spent. The corruption of the Suharto period was a managed form of corruption.[3] Even at village and district level, three distinct monitoring and auditing mechanisms were at work. The first was the Inspectorate of Finance and Development (BPKP), a branch of the national Ministry of Finance. The second was the Provincial Inspectorate (IWiProp), under the provincial government. And the third was the regional branch of the state political party Golkar, to which all civil servants belonged, and which was always under strong pressure to deliver convincing victories in the managed national elections which the New Order staged every five years, and in which two 'opposition' parties – albeit tame, carefully controlled ones – also participated alongside Golkar.

It was this multiple system of institutional checks, rather than any cultural norm with regard to an 'acceptable' level of corruption, which ensured that the level of abuse remained within predictable limits. The partial breakdown of these checks since the end of the New Order also explains why today, now that organized corruption has given way to disorganized corruption, abuses are frequently more serious and less predictable. But the crucial point to note is that the auditing agencies of the Suharto period were not much interested in inspecting account books, which of course always balanced perfectly anyway, or in interviewing contractors in relation to prices and tendering procedures. The main thing they wanted to see was that the concrete investments for which funds had been designated – be they irrigation canals, feeder roads or school buildings – were present, complete and functional. Their inspection reports included photographs and assessments by technical consultants (BPKP 1985: 4, 23–4, 27). It was because of this orientation towards concrete results

---

3 The following account is largely based on an interview with economist Ari Kuncoro at the Economic and Social Research Institute (LPEM), Economics Faculty, University of Indonesia, Jakarta, on 24 March 2010. I am grateful to him for sharing his knowledge and insights on this topic.

that the national auditing authority at local level was called not the Inspectorate of Finance, but the Inspectorate of Finance *and Development*. Its inspectors were on the hunt not in the first place for stolen funds, but rather for what they called 'fictitious projects'. If they found one, the official involved would typically be sacked and replaced without any possibility of legal recourse.

There was another way, too, in which the developmental state in Indonesia minimized the impact of corruption without actually trying to prevent it: by keeping to a minimum the number of institutions and transactions involved in the implementation of development projects and the disbursement of development funds. Indonesian planners knew that the more hands the money had to pass through before it reached its intended destination, the more of it would inevitably disappear en route. Disbursement mechanisms therefore had to be simple, and this meant in the first place a high degree of centralization, with little devolution of public spending responsibilities. Three-quarters of the development budget, and 80 per cent of total public spending, was controlled and spent directly by the central government and its sectoral agencies without ever passing through lower levels of the state bureaucracy (Morfit 1986: 63–5).

Of the 25 per cent of development funds which did go to the regional and local authorities, almost all was delivered directly from Jakarta to the authority in question, without passing through intermediate levels of administration, in the form of Inpres or 'Presidential Instruction' grants. In the early years of the New Order these Inpres grants, which were made automatically on an annual basis and did not have to be applied for or justified in advance, went almost exclusively to the most local units of government, the village and the district, which were allowed a high degree of discretion regarding how to spend them. In the sense that spending decisions were delegated to village level, this was a rare piece of decentralization in the Indonesian context. But by bypassing all intermediate tiers of administration, of which there were three between the village and the central government, it eliminated all the leakages which corruption at those levels would otherwise have entailed. Assuming that the rate of illicit appropriation at each level of disbursement was 15 per cent, this meant that 85 per cent of the village Inpres funds were used productively, as opposed to little more than half if all levels of the bureaucracy had been involved.

Another example of how the New Order used its concentrated power to deal with corruption is provided by its decision in 1985 to replace the whole of the national customs service, the illicit activities of which had become a serious impediment to the new national strategy of export-oriented industrialization, with the services of a private Swiss company contracted to take over its functions. Such was the success of this measure that clearance costs for imported and exported goods dropped immediately by 80 per cent (Dick 1985: 10). It was a decade before the administration of customs duties was returned to public sector hands.

In Malaysia, corruption as such was a much less widespread problem than in Indonesia. But in implementing development policy there was still a strong need for simplification in order to minimize bureaucratic delay and inefficiency. One way in which this was tackled was by replacing written communication at the lower levels of the bureaucracy by more frequent face-to-face meetings, thereby 'transforming communications from a predominantly paper process to a predominantly oral process' (Ness 1967: 171). More serious problems were faced at higher levels owing to the fact that Malaysia, unlike Indonesia, was a federal state with an in some ways cumbersome administrative structure. The function of the new Ministry of Rural Development created in 1959 was partly to bypass the state authorities and enable the central government to intervene directly to promote rural development at the district and village levels (to which levels, as in Indonesia, considerable planning and spending authority was devolved). In pursuing this goal of linking the villages directly to the ministry, Abdul Razak was not squeamish about using all the means at his disposal.

> The power of procedural rules in the bureaucracy gave administrators at all levels some insulation against the power of the new ministry. [...] Legal forms of insulation derived largely from Malaya's federal structure. [...] In breaking through these forms of insulation, the Minister of Rural Development used his wide range of powers in the state. [...] As Deputy Prime Minister he was second in command of the ruling Alliance party, the super-bureaucratic decision-making body. [...] In addition, the Malayanization of the bureaucracy was moving ahead at a rapid

pace, giving the Minister opportunities to advance rapidly then men who performed according to his wishes. (Ibid.: 160–2)

Like Suharto in Indonesia in the 1970s and 1980s, and Hun Sen in Cambodia today, Abdul Razak did not hesitate to use special discretionary powers and funds to associate himself in a very personal way with the rural development campaign and its benefits.

> The minister himself [...] travels indefatigably [...]. On the ground he will open a new lock or visit a new school or travel over a new road. He will meet local representatives, and hear their views. [...] If he is then shown a footbridge which the old have difficulty in crossing, or a local school that is too small, he will be in the mood to listen and may sanction improvements there and then. [...] To make such on-the-spot sanction possible the Minister secured from the Treasury a Minor Rural Development Schemes Fund [...]. (Moynihan 1964: 401)

This and other expediently direct forms of central government intervention at local level were possible thanks not only to the personal power of Abdul Razak, but also to the rigorous national priority accorded to rural development efforts in Malaysia.

In another federal state, Nigeria, any attempt by the federal government to circumvent the authority of the state governments, particularly where money is involved, tends to lead to acute political struggles, including legal actions in the Supreme Court (Suberu 2008). At least until Indonesia's dramatic political liberalization and decentralization following the fall of Suharto in 1998, far greater value was attached to regional autonomy and decentralization in Africa than in South-East Asia. The effects of this difference on economic development in Africa were seldom positive. One predictable result of Nigeria's jealously guarded political decentralization is that endemic corruption, being replicated and multiplied at every level of the system, has a much more serious negative effect on the implementation of development policies than it did in Indonesia under Suharto's centralized regime.

> In essence, the Nigerian revenue-sharing system has promoted truly monumental levels of corruption and predation at all tiers of the federal system, leading to dysfunctional governance, anti-

developmental outcomes, social frustrations, political agitation and violence. (Suberu 2009: 82)

Of course, the characteristic African enthusiasm for local rights reflects real configurations of political power, and to interpret it purely as an ideological phenomenon would be naive. Nevertheless, it is hard not to see in it an echo of the same legalistic way of thinking which inspires Africans time and again to support 'anti-corruption' campaigns that in reality are little more than vendettas against political rivals of incumbent rulers, and which bring no benefit in terms of economic development. Indeed, one (of course by no means the only) cause of 'capital flight' in Africa is that so many rich Africans prefer to invest their money overseas, where it is relatively safe in the event of attempts to prosecute them for corruption. In Suharto's Indonesia, by contrast, ill-gotten gains were mostly invested domestically, where they benefited the economy as a whole, on the assumption that no serious attempt would ever be made to recover them – and indeed, on the whole none was, not even after the fall of the dictatorship.

The negative effects of legalistic thinking on development policy in Africa also extend to the financial sphere, where policy-makers, encouraged by foreign donors and advisers, have put their faith in the idea that the way to make credit available to the poor is to have bureaucrats and lawyers issue them with formal titles to their land which they can use as collateral when applying for loans (Deininger 2003; De Soto 2000). This approach is based purely on an exaggerated view of the importance of the rule of law to economic growth in developed countries, and lacks any basis in real experience with microfinance programmes in today's developing countries. In South-East Asia, which along with Bangladesh boasts the most successful microfinance schemes in the world, land titles almost never play a significant role – not least because when this was tried in the past, it tended to result in massive appropriation of peasant land by moneylenders. Instead, loan security is based not on collateral but on very small, very regular repayment schedules, and on graduated credit systems in which the initial loan is very small and the ability to borrow more depends on successful repayment of the earlier credit (Henley and Goenka 2010).

The importance of valuing results more highly than rules is nowhere clearer than in the case of Vietnam, where economic growth and poverty reduction have depended heavily on liberalizing the country's chronically over-regulated socialist economy. Much of this liberalization has been achieved not by means of formal deregulation, but simply by tolerating illegality and corruption. This is known as *pha rao*, 'fence-breaking', the constructive bending of rules in order to get useful things done.

> Take the current President, for example – Nguyen Minh Triet. President Triet rose to power through the structures of Binh Duong province, just outside Ho Chi Minh City. He helped to turn it into an economic powerhouse, attracting huge amounts of foreign investment, providing hundreds of thousands of jobs and contributing a significant proportion of the national budget. He did so by bending the rules, *breaking fences*, to please investors. He cut through planning regulations to get industrial sites built, he did deals over taxation to attract foreign companies and gave state enterprises a helping hand when they needed it. The reward for his success was promotion within the Party, first to boss of Ho Chi Minh city and then to head of state. But his base is still Binh Duong province and it's now a family fiefdom. His nephew has taken over as the provincial boss and his family control many of its administrative structures. Vietnamese talk about being under someone's 'umbrella'. Triet's 'umbrella' shelters his family and network in Binh Duong just as his colleagues' umbrellas shelter theirs in other places. This shelter gives provinces, state-owned enterprises and, increasingly, the individuals in charge of them leeway to bend and break rules, knowing they are 'protected' from the law. (Hayton 2010: 20–1)

One thing which often strikes Asianists when talking with Africans and Africa specialists is the importance which the latter typically attach to the rule of law and the eradication of corruption as pre-conditions for development. While South-East Asians are generally also in favour of law and against corruption, in view of the Indonesian and Vietnamese experiences they are much less convinced of the connection between these things and development performance. In successful developmental states, legal principles, administrative procedures and political rights all take second place to the goal of improving the material living conditions of as many people as possible, as quickly as possible. Achieving that goal may involve tolerating corruption, bending rules and infringing rights. It is the end that counts, not the means.

## Conclusion

This chapter has tried to clarify what it is that successful development strategies aim to do: to alleviate poverty on a massive *scale* (outreach), with great *speed* (urgency), and with a pragmatic and sometimes ruthless eye for *simplicity* (expediency). In the process it has challenged some important misconceptions about what it takes to be a successful developmental state. One such misconception is that corruption and the resulting failures of policy implementation (as opposed to policy formulation) are primary reasons for failures in development. This idea remains a central pillar of international policy advice to poor countries in Africa and elsewhere (McNeil and Malena 2010; Nabli 2008; World Bank 2010), even though in academic circles it is increasingly questioned (Andrews 2008; Booth 2012; Khan 2007; Rodrik 2008; Wedeman 2002). Another misconception, as yet perhaps less frequently questioned, is the idea that forward planning and long time horizons are essential for development success, and that the lack of them is a critical problem in Africa (Kelsall 2013; Lewis 2007).

What remains to be explained is why some leaders choose to pursue poverty reduction by all available means, and others do not. Under what specific conditions do regimes emerge that are likely to commit themselves to the principles of outreach, urgency and expediency, and therefore to prioritize pro-poor, pro-rural public spending in combination with economic freedom and macroeconomic stability? The concluding chapter will attempt to address this question.

# 7 | ORIGINS OF THE DIVERGENCE

The previous chapters have laid out a theory of developmental success in which developmental *intent*, not institutional constraint or other forms of 'path dependency', is the key to bringing about sustained growth with simultaneous mass poverty reduction. Where this has not happened in our African case studies, it has been because policy-makers and decision-makers at the apex of the national political system have not seriously tried to make it happen. At one level, what is necessary to make development work is to choose the right poli-cies: that is, policies which simultaneously ensure macroeconomic stability, economic freedom and substantial public investment in rural infrastructure and smallholder agriculture. At a deeper level, both the selection and the effective implementation of these policies in South-East Asia reflected an implicit adherence among both plan-ners and political leaders to three underlying principles or goals of development strategy: mass outreach, rapid impact, and flexibility or expediency with respect to the means by which outreach and impact were achieved.

This concluding chapter begins by reiterating and highlighting the virtues of an intentional, rather than an institutional, approach to the explanation of development success and failure in the case of our canonical Indonesia–Nigeria comparison. It then goes on to explore, partly on a biographical basis, why the intentions of Indonesian and Nigerian leaders differed. An important part of the answer is found to lie in contrasting ideas not only regarding how development can be achieved, but also regarding what development actually consists of. These differences in how development is under-stood are not limited to Indonesia and Nigeria, but appear to exist rather consistently between the two regions of South-East Asia and sub-Saharan Africa. An investigation of their origins leads after all to a consideration of 'initial conditions' in the form of history, and of how contrasting historical experiences have shaped the world-views of today's African and South-East Asian elites. A concluding section on the prospects for an end to the developmental divergence between the two regions notes that world-views, however deeply rooted in history, may nevertheless be easier to change than political systems, and that the practical value of comparing Asian and African development trajectories lies in the potential contribution of such comparisons to the task of changing those aspects of African leaders' world-views which are obstacles to development.

### Nigeria and Indonesia: roving versus stationary bandits?

One influential view of Nigeria's failure to translate its oil wealth into national prosperity blames that failure on the country's institutional fragmentation. As already noted in Chapter 2, this view is cogently argued by Peter Lewis in his twin-country comparative study *Growing Apart; oil, politics, and economic change in Indonesia and Nigeria* (2007).

> The failure of Nigerian development stems above all from the absence of a political and institutional center to serve as a principal of economic change. Nigeria's elites, divided along communal and factional lines, have not consolidated stable political regimes or fostered capable state organizations. [...] Nigeria embodies a striking absence of central authority, whether arising from a strong leader, a governing party, the military, or the bureaucracy, to furnish public goods and enforce institutional prerogatives. [...] Nigeria's poor economic performance is linked to this central problem of collective action. (Ibid.: 77–8)

In the absence of a durable political consensus, uncertainty about the future means that the political calculus of each new government is 'shaped by the short-term exigencies of regime survival' (ibid.: 280). Under these conditions any policy aimed at generating shared growth is quickly subverted by corruption as those people who have the most immediate access to development funds reason – correctly – that if they do not steal those funds themselves, others will. Economic life becomes a 'tragedy of the commons' (Hardin 1968), its protagonists 'rational fools' (Sen 1977) whose logic of self-interest leads them to bankrupt their own common future.

In Indonesia under the New Order, by contrast, the uncontested sway of President Suharto over a period of thirty-two years (1966–98) made him what Mancur Olson (2000: 6) described as a 'stationary bandit', a predatory ruler with a rational interest in promoting national growth in order to maximize his own future pickings. Suharto's Indonesia, in this view, enjoyed 'a better class of corruption' (McLeod 2000) thanks to the fact that his regime, although very corrupt, was also both very stable and very centralized. These characteristics gave power-holders incentives to moderate their predatory demands on economic producers with a view to ensuring that the same producers remained able to produce further revenue for the same power-holders in the future (Macintyre 2000, 2001). As a result, stable, cooperative relations emerged between political and economic elites (Braadbaart 1996; Khan and Jomo 2000). Suharto's benevolence during his long sway as Indonesia's great stationary bandit, according to the Lewis argument, stands in readily comprehensible antithesis to the behaviour of Nigeria's many 'roving bandits', whose only interest during their short spells in power has been to plunder and run.

Looking at Nigeria's three discrete civilian republics interspersed by two periods of military rule, its six successful and three failed *coups d'état*, its political assassinations and incarcerations, and its periodically multiplying and shrinking semi-autonomous constituent states, it is impossible to deny that, compared with Indonesia, the country has lacked stability and consolidation. Nevertheless, there are also reasons to think that institutional shortcomings are only part of the story of Nigeria's economic failure.

On close inspection, the institutional incapacity which is supposed to result from the country's political instability and fragmentation proves surprisingly selective. State-owned steelworks and oil refineries may fail to produce any steel or fuel, but at the same time Nigeria has succeeded in planning and building, over a period spanning several regime changes and the national economic collapse of the 1980s, a completely new and rather efficient capital city. The Nigerian military, meanwhile, remained a capable force, able to mount sustained operations outside the country's borders. Even the seriousness of Nigeria's political instability at the national level should not be exaggerated. Since the end of the civil war in 1970, Nigeria has in fact been just as successful as Indonesia in maintaining national unity in the face of formidable ethnic diversity. And as Akinyoade (2008) has pointed out, the characteristically short terms of tenure seen in ministerial and other public appointments in Nigeria often result from a system whereby official positions are allocated in a rotational way as part of a political 'reward system' designed to keep competing ethnic and other interests in balance. Frequent changes of incumbent, in other words, are not a reflection of instability, but precisely a system for safeguarding stability.

Even the impact of regime change itself is often less serious than might be assumed, thanks to the pervasive Nigerian phenomenon of 'godfatherism' whereby individuals who do not (or no longer) occupy formal positions of power nevertheless continue to wield power from behind the scenes (Albert 2005). The newcomer to the literature is in fact struck less by the bloodiness and instability of Nigerian politics than by the underlying continuity and even coherence of the country's political elite, divisions among whom often prove disconcertingly shallow and temporary. In his arresting book *This House Has Fallen*, journalist Karl Maier described former general and president Ibrahim Badamasi Babangida ('IBB') in 1998 as 'a major player in the country's political scene for the past two decades, nearly half of Nigeria's entire independence' (Maier 2000: 44). Babangida was at the centre of the military coup which ended the Second Republic in 1983; from 1985 to 1993 he was himself head of state; and his presidential successors, the generals Sani Abacha and Abdulsalami Abubakar, were both his close associates.

> By now IBB had been out of the presidency for more than half a decade, but his close personal ties to the width and breadth of the Nigerian elite, military and civilian alike, together with a war chest believed to total billions of dollars, ensured his continued influence. Abacha had been his deputy when he was in power, and with his successor Abubakar Babangida maintained a friendship that had begun in boyhood. (Ibid.: 43)

Abubakar's elected successor, former general Olusegun Obasanjo, was the same man who had led the country as military ruler from 1976 to 1979, and under whose regime Babangida had served as a member of the Supreme Military Council. Babangida himself was reportedly a major financier of Obasanjo's 1999 election campaign (ibid.: 74). Babangida's sustained influence, as supreme godfather of Nigerian politics in the late twentieth century, is hard to reconcile with the idea of the Nigerian economy as little more than the battleground and booty of roving bandits.

As evidence for the institutional origins of Indonesia's development success, then, the Nigerian comparison is a good deal less conclusive than Lewis and others would have us believe. Further doubts emerge from a closer look at New Order Indonesia itself. In retrospect it may seem obvious that Suharto's rule was destined to last, and that he, his military barons, his business cronies and his economic advisers could afford to plan with confidence for the future. At the time, however, this was far from clear. Although stability was always a central objective of the New Order, the contemporary perception was seldom that the survival of the regime could be taken for granted. Born in an anti-communist bloodbath in 1965, it subsequently enjoyed only a few years of uncontested consolidation before facing a series of challenges from dissident generals, students and Muslim leaders. Elson (2001: 203), in his biography of Suharto, describes the decade 1973–83 as 'a long period of bitter domestic political strife' and 'except for the period of his downfall, the most critical, difficult and dangerous stage of his long reign'.

Even in the late 1980s and early 1990s, Suharto was still obliged to reposition his regime on shifting and dangerous political sands, seeking a new civilian and Islamic support base as his original military and secular allies became disillusioned with him. In the most authoritative single account of the New Order, Michael Vatikiotis's *Indonesian Politics under Suharto* (1993), the concluding chapter is tellingly entitled 'The fragile state'. Especially in the early years of the regime, as we saw in Chapter 6 of the present book, even Suharto's politically insulated technocratic economic planners typically worked with short, not long, time frames. Far from being a handicap, as the institutional theory would indicate, this orientation towards short-term goals was in fact an important reason for their spectacular success.

Another reason to question the institutional explanation for Indonesian success proposed by Lewis is that it is more or less directly contradicted by a different institutionalist argument advanced by specialists on another South-East Asian country, Thailand, to explain the success of Thai industrial development since the 1970s. In the Indonesian literature, as noted, competitive (as opposed to monopolistic) corruption is viewed as a dangerous development pitfall to be avoided at all costs. In the literature on Thailand, however, 'competitive clientelism' appears as the saving grace of the country's corrupt system of government–business relations, serving to ensure healthy competition, and hence efficiency and international competitiveness, in sectors which under more centralized political conditions would have become the stagnant monopolies of politically connected crony capitalists (Doner 2009: 101, 149, 192; Unger 1998: 125).

> In addition to protecting property rights, clientelism contributed to competition by lowering entry barriers for new entrants into the textile industry. Competition among factions in the political elite gave textile entrepreneurs choices of patrons. Instead of 'monopoly clientelism', which forces entrepreneurs to establish links with a single dominant patron and often leads to the suppression of competition, Thailand's 'competitive clientelism' allowed a number of competing firms to emerge. (Doner and Ramsay 2000: 158–9)

Theoretically, it might be possible to reconcile this with the Lewis argument by looking more closely at the Thai system and investigating why Thai political patrons, despite their inability to monopolize any business sector, are nevertheless apparently able to protect their own clients from predation by rival patrons, whereas in Nigeria this is not always the case. A more straightforward conclusion, however, is that developmental states can in fact emerge and succeed in a variety of institutional settings. This proposition is supported by the observation that under the democratically elected government of Thaksin Shinawatra (2001–06), Thailand once again acquired many of the characteristics of a developmental state (Phongpaichit and Baker 2009: 355) despite institutional conditions quite different from those found under the authoritarian and semi-authoritarian developmental regimes of the past. There is, in any case, a simpler explanation for divergent developmental performances in the Indonesian and Nigerian cases: that success depends on the *intentions* of the governments concerned, as expressed in policy choices.

### The primacy of policy

One key advantage of Indonesia's political stability under the New Order regime, according to the institutional model, was that it enabled a group of economic experts, the 'technocrats', to direct the course of development fairly consistently for a period of three decades. The role of Indonesia's technocrats in the making of the country's economic miracle has become legendary. Under Suharto a so-called 'Berkeley mafia' of economists trained in the United States – Widjojo Nitisastro, Mohamad Sadli, Ali Wardhana, Emil Salim – together with others such as the Dutch-trained economists Sumitro Djojohadikusumo and Radius Prawiro, occupied key ministerial posts and were shielded by presidential power from political pressures that might otherwise have interfered with their plans (Bresnan 1993: 51–85; Thee 2003: 21–38).

Nigeria, however, has had its technocrats too. Under the military regime led by Yakubu Gowon which came to power in 1966, a group of experts trained in economics, including Allison Ayida, Philip Asiodu, Oletunji Aboyade and Olu Falae, acquired great influence and autonomy.

> The executive devolved strategic policy responsibilities to a coterie of senior civil servants who became known as the 'super' permanent secretaries, more commonly super permsecs. The super permsecs occupied key positions in the Ministries of Finance, Economic Development, Petroleum, Defense, Industry, and Trade, and they became de facto powers behind the throne in matters of economic policy. This small group embodied a technocratic clique who steered the country through a dramatic shift in economic strategy and policy. (Lewis 2007: 134–5)

The heyday of the Nigerian technocrats, as Lewis stresses, was short compared to that of their Indonesian counterparts, ending not long after the fall of the Gowon regime to a *coup d'état* in 1975. Ayida, Permanent Secretary at the Ministry of Economic Development from 1963 onward, retired under political pressure in 1977 (Kayode and Otobo 2004: 38, 130). Three circumstances, nevertheless, make it worth taking the role of the technocrats in Nigeria's economic history seriously.

First, their key ideas and assumptions were widely shared in Nigeria and continued to influence national policy under subsequent governments. Falae remained a Permanent Secretary until 1981 and was reappointed in 1986 by Babangida, under whom he went on to serve as Minister of Finance and Economic Development in 1989–90 (Falae 2004: 21–2). University of Ibadan economics professor Oletunji Aboyade, who as technical adviser to the Ministry of Economic Development worked under Ayida on the Second National Development Plan (1970–74), was also chairman of Babangida's Presidential Advisory Committee from 1985 to 1992 (Olaopa 1997: 187–223). Secondly, the period at which the power of the technocrats was at its height in the early 1970s was precisely the period in which Nigerian and Indonesian development trajectories began their fatal divergence. And thirdly, the direction of the 'dramatic shift' which Lewis notes the Nigerian technocrats brought about in development strategy from 1970 onward was in crucial ways different from the one followed at the same period by their Indonesian counterparts.

The most important difference, as we have repeatedly seen, lay in the level of emphasis accorded to rural development, and especially to agriculture. 'Even in the most intoxicating moments of the oil boom', as Radius Prawiro (1998: 145) put it, 'the [Indonesian] government never lost sight of the importance of agriculture.' In Nigeria, by stark contrast, the technocrats' response to the oil windfall of the 1970s was to indulge their industrial ambitions, at the expense of rural and agricultural development (Chapter 4).

> In effect, the oil boom provided the resources to implement the civil servants' industrial vision. That the technocrats could realize their megalomanic industrial ambitions reflects Nigeria's political economy at that time. The position of civil servants was unusually strong since they were shielded by the military from control by politicians. [...] Hence the bureaucrats enjoyed a period of unconstrained power at the very time when the resources were available to implement their vision. (Collier and Gunning 2008: 211)

This vision of development was not inspired by a concern with providing mass industrial employment for the poor – nor even, apparently, by a faith in the 'spillover' or 'growth pole' effects of industrial development on those parts of the economy which did benefit the poor. Instead, the issues which interested the Nigerian technocrats most were more technical and elitist in character: value added, skill acquisition, technology transfer, indigenous ownership and regional equity.

We must aim for the most rapid increase in the volume and diversity of manufacturing activity. There are however other objectives equally important: Large increases in value added and the retained portion of value added; manpower development and a significant transfer of technology; greater Nigerian ownership of industrial investment and a greater dispersal of new investments taking into full account the criterion of viability. (Asiodu 1971: 193)

In its lack of concern with the articulation (if any) between industrialization and poverty reduction, Nigeria's urban-industrial planning bias was symptomatic of a deeper malaise: a failure even seriously to aim for, let alone to achieve, what the World Bank, in its report on the 'East Asian Miracle', called 'shared growth' (World Bank 1993: 13). 'At no time', note Bevan, Collier and Gunning (1999: 382) in the comparison of Nigerian and Indonesian political economies which they authored for the World Bank, 'did the Nigerian government implement a program focused directly on the poor.'

Similar policy contrasts, as we have seen, existed with respect to our two other basic preconditions for sustained growth and rapid poverty reduction: economic freedom, and macroeconomic stability (Chapter 3). Although liberal and orthodox in economic orientation by the African standards of their day, the Nigerian technocrats of the 1970s were still more inclined to interfere in the free operation of markets than were their Indonesian counterparts. Their obsession with indigenous ownership made them, in contrast to the leading members of the 'Berkeley mafia', hostile to foreign investment and prone to industrial protectionism. In order to counterbalance the power of foreign interests in the private sector, they believed, for the time being the state itself would need to control the 'commanding heights' of the national economy (Kayode and Otobo 2004: 193; Olaopa 1997: 118).

Turning to macroeconomic management, although the Nigerian planners understood the importance of controlling inflation, their exchange rate policies were influenced by the same defensive, elitist form of nationalism which informed their industrial policy. By refusing – unlike their Indonesian counterparts – to devalue the naira against the dollar during the oil boom, they caused lasting damage to Nigeria's agricultural and non-oil export sectors, as well as contributing to the acute inflationary crisis following the massive emergency devaluation which eventually became unavoidable in 1986. In their own thinking, their insistence on maintaining a strong naira was linked to nationalism and national prestige. But the national constituency which they primarily had in mind here consisted of urban consumers of imported goods (Ayida 1987: 223); the collateral damage done by overvaluation to the interests of ordinary Nigerian farmers hardly seems to have been considered. By contrast the Indonesian devaluations – particularly the first of them in 1978, which took place at a time when industrial exports were still a thing of the future – were designed specifically to benefit smallholder producers of export crops (Wing 1988: 347).

These multiple, systematic differences in strategy between Indonesian and Nigerian planners make it highly unlikely that the only reason why the Nigerian technocratic plans failed was that they were not properly implemented. Even if Ayida and his colleagues had continued to determine economic policy for longer, it is very hard to believe that they would have engineered a Nigerian economic miracle to match that of Indonesia. What explains the surprisingly consistent differences in approach between the two groups of technocrats? The following sections briefly explore six areas of difference in which answers may lie: differences in intellectual background, in personal experience of economic management and mismanagement, in political interests and incentives, in political ideology and experience, in social origins, and in culturally embedded attitudes to community, modernity and the developed world.

### Intellectual influences on developmental visions

To what extent did the contrasting visions of Indonesian and Nigerian planners reflect differences in educational experience and intellectual background? The Indonesian technocrats were not all educated exclusively in economics. Sadli trained initially as an engineer, while Widjojo, at least in his published work, was always more a demographer than an economist. But all did have a formal training in economics, and most also had an intellectual orientation which can be described as technical and practical rather than polemical and philosophical. Their thinking was guided to a large extent by 'pragmatism, that is, the principle that what is good is what works' (Sadli 1997: 243). The empirical, policy-oriented mindset of the Indonesian technocrats undoubtedly had something to do with the fact that most of them had studied economics in the United States. Emil Salim (1997: 55) later wrote that while Dutch professors in Jakarta had given him 'an understanding of the philosophical aspects of economics', it was from his teachers at Berkeley that he had 'learned about economic policy tools'.

Although the Nigerian technocrats also included trained economists, their intellectual background was somewhat different. Ayida and Asiodu both studied Politics, Philosophy and Economics (PPE) at Oxford – traditionally a preparation for a career in public life, and as much a breeding ground for charismatic leaders as for technocrats: well-known PPE graduates include Benazir Bhutto and Aung San Suu Kyi. This background in 'political economy', rather than economics *pur sang*, may have encouraged Ayida and Asiodu in their conviction that development must involve using state power to change established structures of ownership and patterns of behaviour. Onaolopo Soleye, the finance minister who resisted devaluation in the early 1980s, was trained at the London School of Economics and Political Science (LSE) and referred to himself as a sociologist rather than an economist. He believed that it was sometimes right, as well as expedient, for political considerations to take precedence over issues of 'economic viability' when it came to the formulation of development policy (interview with Ahmad Helmy Fuady, 12 May 2009).

Others, such as Aboyade and Falae, had more conventional disciplinary backgrounds in economics. But it is interesting to note that Aboyade's 'greatest influence' during his student years in Hull was the British Marxist historian John Saville (Olaopa 1997: 46), and that Falae, in a recent publication (2004: 93), prominently quotes British socialist intellectual Harold Laski (1893–1950). In the 1950s and 1960s Laski's inconsistent ideas were an important influence behind the unsuccessful *dirigiste* development strategies of many newly independent countries – notably India, where there was said to be 'a vacant chair at every Cabinet meeting [...] reserved for the ghost of Professor Harold Laski' (Kramnick and Sheerman 1993: 589).

Similar influences, on the other hand, were part of the background of the Indonesian technocrats too. Their founding father was Rotterdam-trained economics professor Sumitro Djojohadikusumo

(1917–2001), who mentored most of them at the University of Indonesia in the 1950s, and who himself held ministerial positions under Suharto from 1968 to 1978. Having been 'greatly impressed by Harold Laski's socialist ideas' as a student (Thee 2001: 176), Sumitro initially sought to establish an affiliation programme with the LSE, where Laski had taught, before eventually developing instead the link with the University of California which led to the creation of the Berkeley mafia. According to Thee Kian Wie (ibid.: 176), it was only with reluctance that Sumitro turned to the Americans since 'as a socialist he was less attracted to America's capitalist system'.

Sumitro's father had been a protégé of Dutch Indonesianist J. H. Boeke, whose influential theory of economic dualism has been described as 'a sort of dependency theory *avant la lettre*' (Schmit 1991: 64), and although Sumitro did not share the pessimism of Boeke or the dependency theorists proper, he did believe in the need for strong state intervention to overcome structural constraints on development, particularly in the industrial sphere (Thee 2001: 178). In the 1950s he argued in a public debate with Bank of Indonesia president Sjafruddin Prawiranegara, who already favoured a strong emphasis on agriculture, that Indonesia would only become a rich nation if it 'industrialised as rapidly as possible' (Sumitro 1986: 36). Sadli, too, was at this period still a believer in state-led industrialization along socialist lines.

> The prevailing ideology throughout this period was certainly not an adherence to the free market; rather it was a belief in planning and a strong role for government in promoting economic development and controlling the commanding heights of the economy. There was an attraction to the Indian model of planning, along the lines of Mahalanobis. The [...] problem was seen in terms of mobilising the required capital funds. It was only at a much later date that we discovered the importance of markets. (Sadli 1993: 38)

Even during their study in the USA, the later Berkeley mafia continued to be exposed to diverse schools of economic thought. Salim studied under institutional economist Harvey Leibenstein and wrote his thesis on Egypt, by his own account 'because it was a socialist rather than a capitalist-oriented country' (Salim 1997: 54). Head of the School of Economics at Berkeley from 1956 to 1959, ironically, was Andreas Papandreou, later twice socialist prime minister of Greece and not a man remembered either for his management of the Greek economy, or for his love of American capitalism. 'Reagan would probably have a heart attack', Sumitro was later to remark, 'if he knew one of the main reasons for the creation of the Berkeley Mafia in Jakarta was Papandreou!' (Sumitro 1986: 33). The content of what Indonesia's Berkeley economics graduates were taught there, then, cannot in itself explain why they later opted so strongly for a development strategy which was at once liberal and rural in its orientation.

### The role of lessons from experience

At least as important as the intellectual background of the Indonesian technocrats was their practical experience of Indonesia's dramatic economic decline in the decade preceding the rise of the New Order in 1965. Under Suharto's predecesor, Sukarno, the nationalist, interventionist impulses displayed by the Nigerian technocrats had already been given free rein to a degree never matched in Nigeria, and with disastrous consequences. Import licensing regulations, the nationalization of foreign enterprises, and persistent government overspending, combined with underinvestment in public services and infrastructure, and exacerbated by political instability and population growth, had by 1965 reduced the country to chronic poverty and indebtedness. The rupiah was ten times overvalued (Thorbecke 1998: 119). Relief was provided only by black markets, smuggling and a level of corruption that made Indonesia, in the words of a local wit, 'the most *laisser faire* socialist economy in the world' (Arndt 1984: 29). In 1965 the budget deficit exceeded 50 per cent of government expenditures, inflation exceeded 650 per cent, hunger was widespread, the country was the world's biggest importer of rice, per capita income was lower than it had been in 1930, and Indonesia had become 'the number one economic failure among the major underdeveloped countries' (Higgins 1968: 679).

During the ten years which it took for this crisis to develop, many of the principles which would later guide New Order policy were established through pragmatic observation of what was going wrong. Sumitro, for instance, was obliged to witness at first hand the disadvantages of foreign exchange controls.

Turning to foreign exchange policies – if you look at my writings in 1954/5, I was a strong protagonist of foreign exchange control. [...] Then I saw what happened under [...] Soekarno. In 1983 there was a movement toward the reimposition of exchange controls. I went to the President and argued strongly against it. I know how easy it is to smuggle goods and I know that those who are close to the sources of power will get their hands on the foreign exchange. (Sumitro 1986: 38–9)

Likewise, to the extent that Sumitro became a supporter of free trade, it was because he 'saw how much harm was done, what chaos the uncertainty created in the business world' when the import licensing system was abused for political purposes in the 1950s (ibid.: 37). The same practical learning process is also evident in the writings of the younger future technocrats. In 1960, Sadli wrote a critical article on Indonesia's increasingly numerous and powerful public enterprises, particularly industrial enterprises, pointing to structural problems in the areas of finance, management and efficiency (Sadli 1960). In the same year, Widjojo published a critique of investment-based growth models which he opened with a quotation from arch-enemy of economic planning Friedrich von Hayek: 'I am profoundly convinced that we should be doing more good to the underdeveloped countries if we succeeded in spreading the understanding of elementary economics than by elaborating sophisticated theories of economic growth' (Widjojo 1960: 499).

In Chapter 1 it was mentioned that there is a saying in Indonesian economic circles, sometimes known as Sadli's Law, that bad times produce good policies, and good times bad policies (Hill and Thee 2008: 154). Certainly this principle is applicable to many aspects of the Indonesian development story. Even the fundamental New Order policy focus on agriculture had much to do with the traumatic experience of rice shortages towards the end of the Sukarno regime and in the first years of the New Order, as vividly recalled by a US food policy adviser of that period:

My overwhelming first memory of the time was of [...] an incredibly intense small group poring over the rice data in the most *minute* detail. Dr. Widjojo and Dr. Saleh Afiff [...] were worrying about each rain, each inbound ship, and almost literally, each grain of rice that existed or might exist in the next few months. Food security issues dominated the talk of Government and of the entire country [...]. (Falcon 2007: 26)

Part of the explanation for Nigeria's very different policy direction in the 1970s is that despite the civil war (1967–70), Nigeria had not previously experienced an economic crisis of similar magnitude to drive home – or, as arguably happened in Indonesia, fortuitously exaggerate – valuable policy lessons. Exchange rate overvaluation and crop marketing interventions had been costly to exporters, and tariff protection in the interests of import-substituting industrialization costly to consumers; but with distortions at more moderate and consistent levels than in Indonesia, and in the absence of forced expropriations, persistent budget deficits, or massive neglect of infrastructure, as yet the consequences caused little alarm. Indeed, in 1969 the impressive recent growth of the manufacturing sector – albeit powered by tariff-inflated, monopoly-ridden prices – still seemed to the Nigerian planners to bode well for the future.

In the light of the achievements of the past, continued progress even during the crisis and the projects indicated by various detailed studies, the prospects for rapid post-war development are bright. The strategy should essentially be to base our industrial development on the Nigerian internal market and to expand rapidly the sectors where rapid growth is possible [...]. Given our resources it should not be difficult to achieve over the next seven years an average growth rate in industry of about 15 per cent. (Asiodu 1971: 200)

When the growth collapse eventually came at the beginning of the 1980s, it was blamed more on 'Dutch disease', the volatility of oil prices, corruption and the heavy public spending of the late 1970s than on the policies which had made Nigeria, in contrast to Indonesia, unable to overcome the so-called 'resource curse' and sustain development spending in the face of reduced oil revenues. Decades later the Nigerian public was still largely convinced that good policies had been undermined by bad luck and weak implementation, and the authors of the policies in question were still essentially unrepentant (Kayode and Otobo 2004: 44; Olaopa 1997: 123).

If Nigerians by and large failed to draw useful conclusions from the economic crisis of the early 1980s, Indonesians definitely recognized the policy lessons to be drawn from their own rather different crisis in the early 1960s. With respect to Indonesia's abandonment of regulatory nationalism in favour of pragmatic liberalism, in fact, 'Sadli's Law', that bad times produce good policies, seems to go a long way towards explaining the policy shift which paved the way for sustained growth after 1967.

## Political incentives and developmental intent

With respect to the adoption at the same period of strongly pro-rural, pro-poor development policies, a different kind of crisis arguably played the same cathartic role in the Indonesian (and wider South-East Asian) case: a political crisis caused by the threat of communist revolution, a threat nourished by rural poverty and deprivation. The Indonesian New Order was born in the violent destruction of the Indonesian Communist Party in 1965, and its pro-poor development priorities reflected its concern to prevent a resurgence of agrarian radicalism. Some authors even see a connection with an older tradition of millenarian peasant revolt stretching back to the Java War (1825–30) and beyond.

> Millenarianism, in the guise of Communism, may be what the Soeharto government is really afraid of or perhaps the official attitude toward the countryside is based on the fear of the proletarianization of the peasants if they moved to the cities. In any case, regardless of whether it is communism or millenarianism or proletarianization, the correct *political* response is to raise the standard of living in the rural areas. (Wing 1988: 340–1)

In Nigeria this perceived political *imperative* to reduce rural poverty was absent. With the political scene fragmented along regional lines and no significant party representing rural or peasant interests, the rural population was considered to 'operate outside the public realm' (Osaghae et al. 1998: 24). Here Nigeria conforms to a more general African pattern whereby the primary threat to the power of a government is perceived to come from urban unrest and intra-elite rivalry, typically culminating in a military coup.

African elites have implemented policies to favor the urban sector over the rural sector, because the immediate constituencies for African rulers are civil servants, members of the armed forces, and workers organized in trade unions (and frequently employed in the public sector). (Bienen and Gersovitz 1985: 741)

The idea that the origins of the successful Asian developmental states lay in their 'systemic vulnerability' (Doner et al. 2005) to comprehensive destruction as a result of impending peasant revolution – and/or foreign invasion – is an influential one in the literature (Campos and Root 1996; Slater 2010; Van der Veen 2010). More effectively than electoral vulnerability or the danger of an intra-elite coup, proponents of this view argue, systemic threats to the interests of existing elites forced the regimes which faced them to take the interests of the non-elite masses seriously. The communist danger also encouraged habitually fractious elements of the national political establishment to unite in support of an (often military-led) regime which could protect their common interests.

Some writers have extended this line of explanation in a geographical and structural direction by linking the comparative lack of mass political mobilization of the rural poor in Africa with the generally greater ethnic fragmentation of African countries, or with their lower rural population densities (Bezemer and Headey 2008: 1348; Birner and Resnick 2010: 1446). A more obvious factor is South-East Asia's proximity to communist China, and its more direct involvement in the Cold War and the superpower conflicts of the mid-twentieth century.

There is no doubt that the adoption of pro-poor development strategies in South-East Asia was connected with the radical, violent and regime-threatening 'contentious politics' (Slater 2010) which swept the region in the decades between 1950 and 1980 as the result of communist movements and communist propaganda. 'If stomachs are full people do not turn to communism', as a deputy prime minister of Thailand straightforwardly put it in 1966 (Dixon 1999: 85). Or as Prime Minister Lee Kuan Yew put it in the urban context of Singapore: 'the best way to fight communism was by providing people jobs and housing' (Schein 1996: 31).

The alliances and strategies underpinning shared growth were

often counter-revolutionary in inspiration. Pro-poor policies remin-
iscent in many ways of socialist states (Chapter 4) were imitated by
capitalist governments in order to help defeat communist threats;
or, in the more recent converse case of Vietnam, capitalist policies
were adopted by a socialist government, partly in order to pre-empt
the threat of popular discontent (Chapter 6). In Indonesia, it is no
coincidence that the emblem of the New Order state party Golkar
incorporated symbols of basic material welfare, in the form of rice
and cotton panicles, which recalled communist banners. In Malaysia,
the most important and effective anti-poverty programmes were initiated while the country was facing an armed communist insurgency
within its own borders (1948–60). Thailand, which faced not only
a domestic communist insurgency (1959–83) but also a perceived
external military threat from communist Vietnam, appears an even
better fit with the 'systemic vulnerability' model (Warr 1993: 29).

The anti-communist struggle, of course, had international as well
as national aspects, South-East Asia being the hottest and bloodiest
theatre, after Korea, of the so-called Cold War. The Green Revolution
in rice farming, for example, was made possible by the International
Rice Research Institute (IRRI) established in the Philippines in 1960
by the American Ford and Rockefeller Foundations, and the term
'Green Revolution' itself was coined by USAID director William Gaud
in 1968 to contrast capitalist Asia's reliance on peaceful progress with
the violent 'Red Revolution' of the Soviets.

In their origins, then, the successful developmental states of
South-East Asia were either counter-revolutionary states facing, or
recently having faced, a serious communist threat (Thailand, Malaysia, Indonesia), or liberalizing post-revolutionary states concerned
to avoid alienating their mass support base (Vietnam). In Vietnam,
where the communists succeeded in coming to power, they were
ultimately obliged to deliver some of the benefits they had promised
to the poor, even if this meant abandoning a large part of their
original anti-capitalist ideology. In fact it can almost be said that
in South-East Asia there are just two species of successful developmental state: the counter-revolutionary state, and the liberalizing
post-revolutionary state.

On this analysis, the key to the emergence of a successful developmental state would appear to be a national history of revolutionary

socialism. In most African countries socialism has been either completely absent, as in Nigeria, or present only in nationalist rhetoric, as in the case of Kenya with its vaguely conceived, market-conforming 'African Socialism'. In Tanzania, by way of exception, socialism has been present and important – but only in a state-led, bureaucratic form. Tanzanian socialism never took the form of a revolutionary threat to an existing regime, as it did in Malaysia or Indonesia, still less the form of a successful popular revolution held ultimately to economic account, as it arguably was in Vietnam, by the expectations which it had created among millions of people who had suffered for the sake of its success.

Before closing the case on the relationship between revolutionary socialism and the developmental state, however, we must note that political exigency was not the only driving force behind the strong developmental intent in South-East Asia. In the case of Indonesia, there is no doubt that the political calculus of the early New Order did favour rural bias: in the 1960s and 1970s, Suharto's closest political advisers were in 'unanimous agreement' on 'the need to give priority to agricultural development' (Salim 1997: 58). However, there is considerable doubt as to whether the same calculus was prominent in the minds of his *economic* advisers, who were equally in agreement with the strategy. In recent interviews key technocrats of the period have strenuously denied this, insisting that the communist threat was already eliminated in 1965 and that their subsequent decision to focus on agriculture was simply a matter of economic rationality, and indeed common sense, given that most Indonesians lived in the countryside and depended, directly or indirectly, on the agricultural sector (interviews, Ali Wardhana, 28 December 2008; Subroto, 21 August 2008). Here the technocrats echo more or less exactly the words of their de facto leader, Widjojo, when he wrote in the text of the First Five-Year Plan (1969–74) that 'agriculture has been selected because the greater part of the Indonesian people lives in this sector', and because agricultural development 'increases the earnings of the majority of the Indonesian people' (Chapter 6, page 154).

Former Nigerian technocrats, not surprisingly, are even more reluctant to accept that their own neglect of rural development had to do with the demands of urban political constituencies. Their typical reaction to this suggestion, indeed, is first to deny any such neglect;

then, confronted by evidence from plans and budgets, to assert that primary responsibility for agricultural development lay with the constituent states rather than the federal government; and finally to express doubt as to whether a greater policy emphasis on agriculture at any level of government would have made any difference anyway.

Unlike the Indonesian technocrats, who were all professional academics turned policy-makers, most of the Nigerians were already civil servants before they were sent abroad for higher education. Conceivably this meant that they enjoyed somewhat less mental distance from the bureaucratic elite to which they belonged, and somewhat less objectivity, than did the Indonesians. Nevertheless, it bears repeating that the major policy divergence took place during the 1970s at the high point of technocratic autonomy in both countries, and that the Nigerian industrialization drive has been described as one of the few instances in post-colonial Africa in which 'public spending was driven by a (technocratic) economic vision, rather than by the self-interest of the regime' (Collier and Gunning 2008: 211). Neither the Nigerian nor the Indonesian technocrats, of course, were blind to political realities. But if their fundamental preferences regarding sectoral priorities and levels of regulation were influenced by political interests, it was probably only in an indirect, even subconscious way.

A glance at Malaysia confirms that communism and anti-communism are not the whole story behind the choice of inclusive development strategies in South-East Asia. Communism in Malaysia was almost entirely an affair of the ethnic Chinese minority in that country. Yet both the intended and the actual beneficiaries of the rural development effort of the 1960s and 1970s were Malays, who showed almost no sign of being attracted to communism anyway. One factor here, it has been suggested, was the existence of a tacit 'quid pro quo' agreement by which economic progress for poor Malays would be the price of their consent to Chinese participation in the Alliance government (Rudner 1994: 101). But this does not seem enough to explain why rural development was pursued, in Razak's words, 'with such determination and energy as were used to free the country from the menace of Communist terrorism' (Abdul Razak 1975: 6). Even without the rural development effort, the Alliance would already have been able to take credit for defeating the Chinese-dominated Malayan

Communist Party (MCP), thereby averting a much greater threat to Malay political dominance.

Dan Slater, applying the 'systemic vulnerability' argument to Malaysia, attributes the elite 'protection pact' underpinning Malaysia's developmental state more to the threat of radical Chinese and Malay communalism in the 1960s and 1970s than to the communist threat of the 1950s (Slater 2010: 92–3, 116–24). But the intercommunal crisis and race riots of 1969 clearly cannot explain the country's earlier and wholehearted drive for rural development (Chapter 5), conceived as a continuation of the anti-communist struggle (Chapter 6) and couched in a military language of 'Operations Rooms' and 'Red Books' (Ness 1967: 142–55), yet targeting a rural Malay population whose distrust of the Chinese already made them all but immune to communist propaganda, and by whom 'the MCP was generally considered a mortal enemy' (Slater 2010: 84).

In the case of contemporary Vietnam, finally, we may ask whether it really makes sense to see 'self-preservation' as the Communist Party's foremost incentive to deliver inclusive development, as Hayton (2010: 3) claims. Is it not more likely, given the complete absence of organized political opposition in Vietnam, that Vietnamese leaders are holding *themselves* to account for their country's development performance, than that they are being obliged to do so by any sense of 'systemic vulnerability'? If the interpretation in terms of self-accountability is even partly correct, then clearly we need to look beyond political incentives, at least as narrowly understood, if we are fully to understand the Asia–Africa development divergence.

### Nationalism and political ideology

Earlier in this chapter (and in Chapter 3) we saw that although nationalism was an important source of motivation for policy-makers in both Nigeria and Indonesia, the nationalist impulses involved took significantly different forms. In Nigeria, the economic policies of the 1960s, 1970s and 1980s were shaped by a 'bourgeois nationalism' which focused defensively on the relationship between Nigeria and the outside world, particularly the developed countries. The exchange rate parity of the naira with the US dollar, for instance, was jealously defended, and every effort made to promote Nigerian ownership of business and capital at the expense of foreign interests.

Solidarity between Nigerian elites and the Nigerian poor, on the other hand, was virtually absent. In Indonesia, by contrast, the national interest, at least after 1965, was understood in much more inclusive terms, and more in relation to the challenge of improving domestic conditions over time than in terms of comparisons or relations with other countries.

The technocrats of the Indonesian New Order have been described by one of their number as 'having the interest of the whole country at heart' (Sadli 1997: 243). In a tribute to Widjojo a former Dutch ambassador to Indonesia has expressed this benevolent aspect of the regime and its leadership in even stronger terms.

> Both President Soeharto and Prof. Widjojo are compassionate
> men: the welfare of the people comes first in their mind. I cannot
> recall meeting with the President or Prof. Widjojo without the
> conversation at one point turning to the Javanese farmer or
> the urban poor and the need for grass-root development. (Van
> Gorkom 2007: 182)

Fear of a possible revolt of the masses does not in itself seem enough to account for this paradox of 'compassionate' dictatorship. Suharto's pro-poor policies also bore the stamp of a society united, at least in principle, by an inclusive sense of nationhood forged in a violent anti-colonial struggle in which part of the national elite, including Suharto himself, retreated to the countryside and lived alongside a peasantry on which it depended for support and survival. Widjojo, too, was among those for whom this was a formative experience. In 1945, when the future Nigerian technocrats were enjoying dances, debates and 'elite cultural activities' in Lagos (Fuady 2012: 119), Widjojo, at the age of eighteen, joined a student militia which participated in the guerrilla war against the Dutch in the countryside of East Java (Harun Zain 2008: 169). Fifteen years later in California, he and his colleagues of the future 'Berkeley mafia' were to impress their teachers with their quiet determination to use the knowledge they were acquiring not just for their personal advancement, but for the good of their country.

> I often had the feeling that our Indonesian friends [...] yearned to
> return to the tropics and sometimes suffered from homesickness

– not unusual emotions among foreign students. But this group was more mature than our average graduate students: many were veterans of Indonesia's War of Liberation; some were married; all had a strong sense of duty. For them the study of economics and especially economic development were not matters of theoretical niceties. (Rosovsky 2007: 41)

The Indonesian army which came to power in 1965, as Bevan, Collier and Gunning (1999: 419) point out, had its origins in the struggle for independence and was originally a mass, people's army with a political as well as a military function. While the Sukarno regime which preceded the New Order was hamstrung by its regulatory impulses and not strong on rural public spending, its populist, quasi-socialist ideology and its incorporation of the Indonesian Communist Party did give it at least the serious aspiration to include the poor in the development process.

Even to the extent that the Suharto regime's rural development effort was simply a pragmatic, self-interested counter-revolutionary strategy, it still reflected a history in which the ideal of social justice had played a powerful role, not just for those on the left of the political spectrum, but for the whole of the political elite. In Nigeria, and most other African countries, this has never really been the case. In Kenya, the 'African Socialism' of the Kenyatta era was always more a matter of nationalist rhetoric, and of a bureaucratic instinct for economic intervention, than a matter of genuine commitment to fighting poverty and inequality (Chapter 5). More broadly, it can be said that whereas African nationalisms have tended to take 'bourgeois' forms which focus defensively on issues involving the relationship between national elites and the outside world, South-East Asian nationalisms have taken inclusive forms which focus more on the challenge of improving domestic conditions.

In the case of Indonesia, somewhat ironically, one reason for this was the violent, revolutionary nature of the anti-colonial struggle, which tended to unite all layers of indigenous society, and which through its eventual, unequivocal success rendered international relations less central to nationalist sensibilities than they have been in post-independence Africa. The same cannot be said, however, of Malaysia, where independence was obtained without violence and as part of an essentially counter-revolutionary project in which Malay elites collaborated with the departing colonial power to defeat a communist challenge. Nor can it be said of Thailand, which never came under foreign rule in the first place. Political history, then, cannot entirely explain why development strategies in Africa have been persistently elitist in character, whereas in South-East Asia, at least under the pressure of economic and political crises, they have often become inclusive and relatively equitable. One possible supplementary explanation has to do with the social origins of the responsible decision-makers.

### Social origins of developmental elites

If the Indonesian technocrats deny that their insistence on the primacy of agriculture was politically motivated, they do stress that Suharto gave it very strong personal support, and that this had to do with the president's own rural origins. The technocrats themselves were mostly born and raised in towns, albeit small towns in the hinterland of Java, as sons of teachers and civil servants. Only one prominent technocrat, J. B. Sumarlin, had peasant origins – he was literally born in a paddy field – and ironically Sumarlin was more closely associated with the market liberalization of the 1980s than with the rural development of the 1970s. But Suharto, born into a farming family in a village outside Yogyakarta in 1921, was very consciously a man of the people. The closing sentence of his semi-official biography from 1969 describes him as 'the son of a landless Javanese peasant, who became a General and the Head of State of a proud nation' (Roeder 1969: 189). His later autobiography opens with an emotional account of the ceremony in 1985 at which he was honoured by the international community in recognition of Indonesia's achievement in doubling its rice production since 1969. A footnote describes this as 'one of the most important events of Soeharto's life, in which his early upbringing had an influence on his achievements' (Soeharto 1991: 1).

> You can imagine this moment for a man who, more than 60
> years before was only a small boy, playing in the fields among the
> farmers of the village of Kemusuk, when he walked up to the dais
> and spoke to a hall filled with experts and world dignitaries, as

the leader of a nation that had just solved this enormous problem that concerned the fate of more than 160 million souls. (Ibid.: 4)

Suharto's account of the humbleness of his origins may be somewhat exaggerated: his official father was in fact a minor irrigation official provided with a plot of 'salary land' in lieu of payment for organizing and maintaining the village's system of water distribution, and it has been suggested that the future president was actually the illegitimate child of a trader or civil servant who could better afford to pay for his education (Elson 2001: 4). Nevertheless, he undeniably had a rural upbringing, and this contributed to his later interest in farming and the fate of farmers (Hill 2000b: 133).

> My life among the farmers of Kemusuk during the difficult times of the nineteen-twenties had aroused in me a distinct feeling of sympathy for them. This feeling was nourished not only by my constant contacts with the farmers, but also by the knowledge and experience that I'd gained from the guidance of Pak Prawirowiharjo, the agricultural officer. I often went with my uncle on his inspection rounds and learned from him not only about the theory of agriculture but also about the practical aspects of farming. (Soeharto 1991: 10)

In Malaysia, comparably, Abdul Razak, the driving force behind rural development efforts in the 1960s and 1970s, was the son of a civil servant but had been raised largely by his farming grandparents, whose water buffalo he rode and tended just as Suharto had tended his own grandfather's (Elson 2001: 2; Shaw 1976: 13–14). Razak's biography attributes his concern for the welfare of the rural masses to the fact that 'his early years had been spent working with the ordinary village people in the rice fields' (Shaw 1976: 73).

Widjojo's interest in rural development, on the other hand, did not originate in Suharto's, although it was no doubt among the factors commending Widjojo to Suharto when they first met as teacher and student during a course in economics which Suharto followed at the Staff and Command School of the Indonesian army shortly before he came to power. And if the school inspector's son Widjojo and the farm boy Suharto could show equal concern for the rural poor, a comparative glance at Nigeria confirms that policy preferences do not follow automatically from the class origins of policy-makers. Nigeria's modern political elite, ironically, may well be more rural in its origins than Indonesia's. A regional study from western Nigeria in the 1970s indicated that 56 per cent of politicians, and 59 per cent of civil servants, were the children of farmers (Imoagene 1976: 77, 88). Olusegun Obasanjo, Nigeria's head of state from 1976 to 1979 and again as elected president from 1999 to 2007, was himself a farmer's son, and just as much a village boy as Suharto. Obasanjo's biography, nevertheless, reveals an attitude to rural life palpably different from Suharto's self-conscious nostalgia.

> As the stocky Olusegun grew up, his parents became increasingly concerned about his future. His father wanted his children to escape the drudgery that was peasant farming in Africa. Many Egbas had long realized the increasing relevance of Western education [...]. With it, the toil was less, the financial rewards were more, and opportunities were at the beck and call [...]. On their way home from the farm one day, Obasanjo said to his son: 'Olu, is it this toilsome farming you would want to continue with in life?' [...] 'Would you like to learn a trade?' [...] 'Yes.' 'What trade?' 'Motor mechanic.' [...] 'You would not want to go to school?' his father asked. (Ojo 1997: 35–6)

It is striking that Obasanjo senior held this view despite being by local standards a 'prosperous farmer' with a materially 'contented' family; and that his son, while not entirely devoid of sadness at leaving 'a village he had grown so fond of', appears to concur in viewing his transition from rural to urban life essentially as a successful escape from poverty and drudgery (ibid.: 35, 40). Small wonder, perhaps, that such a man should seek to improve his nation's future, as well as his own, by trying to create avenues of escape from the village, rather than by trying to make village life better and more attractive. Africa, as Wing (1988: 350) points out, offers 'many examples of authoritarian presidents of peasant origin (e.g. Kwame Nkrumah of Ghana, Idi Amin of Uganda and Séko Touré of Guinea) who did not pursue agriculture-oriented policies'. What matters here, evidently, is not rural or urban origins as such, but rather the interpretation and evaluation of those origins.

## Historical origins of the developmental mindset

We have seen that even when African leaders have been of rural origin, they have tended to evaluate the countryside and its ways of life less positively than their South-East Asian counterparts. The perceived social and cultural divide between town and countryside appears wider in Africa, and there is less tendency to admire or idealize village life. Why should this be?

The first point to note here is that historically speaking, the contrast between city and countryside really has been sharper in Africa than in Asia. In South-East Asia there is a long tradition of indigenous urbanism, and colonial rule did not wipe out the old political and cultural links between the towns and their hinterlands. In Africa, by contrast, many of today's cities are colonial foundations which for a long time retained their original character as alien, European enclaves. For Africans of the early twentieth century, to move from the countryside to the city was not just to come closer to the centre of power and wealth; it was to cross a cultural and civilizational divide. In Allison Ayida's biography the city of Lagos, where Ayida attended boarding school in the 1940s, is described as 'the land just next door to England' and the place Nigerians first had to visit if they wished to go 'to the white man's land, to learn the white man's ways, and to be completely transformed into an educated and civilized man' (Kayode and Otobo 2004: 16).

In East Africa, where colonization by Europeans came later than in Nigeria, the antithesis between urban and rural, modern and traditional, and European and African was sharper still. It also coincided with a dramatic religious divide. In colonial Kenya, education for Africans was offered almost exclusively by Christian missionary groups at residential schools where children were fully encapsulated in an alien cultural environment. Kenya's first and second presidents, Kenyatta and Moi, were both first-generation Christian converts who, as boys, deliberately rejected their parents' way of life in favour of the faith and civilization of their European teachers. What the missionaries required of their young converts, as Kenyatta's biographer Murray-Brown (1972: 47) notes, was nothing less than a 'total break with the past'.

For the Kikuyu boys and girls to stand up in church and make their professions of faith was a great leap in the dark. The scowling faces of their fathers and mothers, perhaps framed for an instant in the window or the door, reminded them of the curses of their ancestors. Every day they remained in the dormitory or in the households of the missionaries cut them off from their tribe. Each vow they made committed them more deeply to the missionary view of life and so in the short term – which was all they could envisage – to the colonial system. (Ibid.: 50)

For Moi, too, conversion to Christianity meant that he 'no longer mixed with other villagers as freely or as easily as before'. 'We were not really liked,' recalled one of his school friends. 'All of us, including Moi, had abandoned the traditional life and there was no turning back' (Morton 1998: 37, 39). A frequent concomitant of this alienation from rural society was migration to the new city of Nairobi, founded by the British as a European (and Indian) enclave in a country without an indigenous urban tradition. Kenyatta, notes Murray-Brown (1972: 79), 'had no intention of taking up farming life', having 'left home to escape all that'. At a provincial boarding school in neighbouring Tanzania (Tanganyika) at the same period, the young Julius Nyerere became a devout Christian under the influence of Catholic priests, and for a time considered entering the priesthood himself (Mwakikagile 2002: 86).

One European influence which affected Nyerere at Musoma was that of the Christian Church. [...] He heard the Fathers criticising tribal gods and was convinced by their arguments. He found it good to believe in a single god and a future life. He has retained those beliefs ever since. (Hatch 1976: 8)

All this is not of course to suggest that there was no subsequent attempt, by the first generation of African nationalists, to reappraise their indigenous cultural heritage. But when they did this, they often did so more as outsiders than as insiders: Kenyatta's classic anthropological study of his own Kikuyu people, *Facing Mount Kenya*, was ironically criticized by his teacher Malinowski (1938: xi) for showing 'perhaps a little too much in some passages of European bias'. Nor do I want to suggest that the alienation of African political elites from their rural roots has ever been complete or permanent: Nyerere, after his retirement, moved back to live in his childhood home village of Butiama in northern Tanzania, and anthropologists have noted the continuing tendency of elite Africans who live most of their lives in cities to maintain close ties with rural kin and rural political constituencies (Geschiere and Gugler 1998). Nonetheless the journey back to the village remains essentially a retrogressive one, a return to roots and origins. The countryside represents Africa's past; few African politicians other than Nyerere himself have ever seriously seen it as the logical place to start building a better future – whether for themselves, or for their nation.

More broadly, it is true to say that African attitudes to development have been shaped by experiences, both historical and personal, in which the encounter with the advanced economies of Europe was bound up with a dramatic and comprehensive *transformation*. All areas of life were affected: society and communication, knowledge and belief, material culture, and even eating habits, as urban elites switched from a diet based on indigenous African food crops and maize to one based on imported wheat and rice. One legacy of this transformation has been a collective assumption of what may be called developmental *dualism*: a pervasive conviction that progress can only be achieved by means of a quantum leap from backwardness into modernity.

In South-East Asia, by comparison, the colonial experience was less radically transformative than in Africa, and involved less of a rupture with the past. One major country, Thailand, was not colonized at all, and elsewhere it was only in the Philippines that the religion and language of the colonizing power were widely adopted by its subjects. In Indonesia the leading technocrats were Indonesian-speaking Muslims who, despite their Western education, remained culturally close to the rural masses and were not dismissive – or at least not by African standards – of the abilities of their uneducated compatriots. Widjojo, it has been said, not only trusted in the wisdom of peasant farmers, but also possessed 'deep faith in the culture and history of his country' (Van Gorkom 2007: 184). An important factor here was a widespread perception, even among urban elites, that land, agriculture and rice – the staple and preferred food of both rich and poor – were core elements of national identity.

The soul of Indonesia is its land. Indonesians have been cultivating these lands for millennia. The country's farm communities have not only provided the nation with food and a host of export crops, they have been caretakers of many of the nation's traditions and customs. Above all, however, Indonesia's farms have supplied the people with rice, which since time immemorial, has been the country's prime staple, its 'staff of life'. There have been many periods in Indonesian history when rice harvests were poor. When this happened, the resulting hunger could be calamitous to the hardest hit and destabilizing to the society as a whole. That is why, in 1968, [...] Indonesia's economic policymakers made one of the most important decisons in Indonesia's modern history: to follow a route to economic development based above all on agricultural development. At that time, the typical approach to economic development for a less developed country emphasized exploiting agriculture to make a fast transition to industrialization. For most countries, development planning was essentially synonymous with industrial planning. Of course the government understood that the nation needed to industrialize. However, what was unusual in Indonesia's strategy was that the country gave first priority to agricultural development for its own sake. (Prawiro 1998: 127)

In this way a culturally ingrained association between agriculture and nationalism, combined in the Indonesian case with fear of the political consequences of rice shortages, predisposed South-East Asian elites to believe in development strategies based on the improvement of peasant farming. African elites, meanwhile, looked forward impatiently to a structural transformation of the economy whereby peasant farming would disappear to make way for more modern ways of life.

## Implications for development and development cooperation in Africa

Amid the general optimism surrounding Africa's current economic growth, some commentators argue that the most recent developments in African agriculture have been positive, and that the policy errors of the past with respect to that sector are now in the process of being corrected (Dietz 2011; Nin-Pratt et al. 2012). The relevant statistics, however, are sobering. While agricultural productivity is certainly on the rise, population growth is also rapid, and in 2009 total per capita food production in Africa was still only 12 per cent higher than it was in 1961 (Dietz 2011: 15).

In Maputo in 2003, as noted in Chapter 1, the governments of the African Union did undertake to devote at least 10 per cent of total public spending to 'agricultural and rural development' by 2008. Yet only eight of the fifty-one countries of sub-Saharan Africa (Ghana, Ethiopia, Niger, Mali, Malawi, Burkina Faso, Senegal and Guinea) actually did so (Omilola et al. 2010: 17), and today the situation is not much better. Where the Maputo commitment has been met, moreover, in some cases (notably Malawi) this has been disproportionately due to costly input subsidies – a type of intervention which has certainly played a positive role in Asia, but which cannot substitute for even more badly needed investments in infrastructure and research (Poulton 2012: 8). The 10 per cent target is in any case too low, including as it does all public spending on the vague category of 'rural development' as well as on agriculture itself. In Indonesia during the 1970s the proportion spent annually on agriculture alone ranged from 9 to 15 per cent, with a further 7 to 17 per cent going to transport infrastructure (IMF 2005). Africa, with its less well-developed infrastructure and its more challenging physical conditions for agriculture (especially irrigation), will need to spend more still.

Time and again, as I have tried to show in this book, the divergence in development performance between Africa and South-East Asia has boiled down to a question of intent. If African countries have failed to develop in ways that combine rapid economic growth with mass poverty reduction, this has been in the first place because African leaders have not seriously intended to bring about this kind of pro-poor development. South-East Asian politicians and planners, at least in their best moments, have seen the elimination of poverty as the fundamental aim and essence of development, to be pursued on the largest possible scale, with the greatest urgency, and by all available means. Their African counterparts, even when committed to bringing about development, have been much less directly concerned with the problem of poverty. Their development models, implicitly or explicitly, have focused not pragmatically on mass outreach and rapid impact in the battle against poverty, but on ideas of technological and cultural modernity based on conditions in already rich countries (Chapter 6). These models have led them to adopt elitist policies based on education, industry and urbanization rather than on raising the productivity and profitability of smallholder agriculture, the economic activity on which most of the population of their countries depends. Very schematically, the divergence in prevailing visions of the development process between South-East Asian and African political elites can be summarized as follows (Table 7.1).

TABLE 7.1 Divergent visions of the development process

| South-East Asia | sub-Saharan Africa |
| --- | --- |
| incremental (but potentially rapid) | transformative |
| poor people become richer | poor countries acquire things rich ones have (technologies, industries, goods, rights, institutions) |
| growth | modernization |
| productivity | knowledge |
| inclusive | elitist |
| oriented towards the undesired starting point of development: mass poverty | oriented towards the desired end point of development: industrial or post-industrial modernity |
| concerned with establishing immediate priorities | concerned with making comprehensive plans |

Today as in the past, even members of the African political elite who are themselves of rural origin find it difficult to believe in a strategy that focuses on improving rural life *in situ*, by means of agricultural development, rather than on accelerating the transition to urban modernity of which their own lives have been a microcosm. Yet it remains a fact that in Indonesia and elsewhere in South-East Asia, development of a type which ultimately benefits all sections of the population, including elites and city dwellers, has demonstrably been based on precisely such a pro-poor, pro-rural strategy. Much is potentially to be gained for Africa's poor by drawing this fact emphatically to the attention of Africa's present and future leaders.

Of the three policy priorities which our South-East Asian case studies have indicated are essential preconditions for sustained growth and poverty reduction, two – macroeconomic stability, and economic freedom for farmers and small entrepreneurs – are increasingly being met in Africa. Whether this is mainly due to an indigenous process of learning from past errors, as in the Indonesian case, or whether it is mainly a result of pressure from foreign aid donors and international institutions, is less clear, and if the main causes are external then it is possible that the progress achieved in these policy areas will ultimately prove fragile. What is clear is that the most pressing priority now is the third precondition: pro-poor, pro-rural public spending.

Contrary to a belief common in some quarters, the continuing failure in this respect is not, or at least by no means only, a result of the fact that in the 1980s and 1990s, 'most African countries were subjected to Structural Adjustment Programs (SAP) initiated by the Bretton Woods Institutions' which were 'characterized by the liberalization of domestic markets, imports and exports and the removal of subsidies for agricultural inputs and extension services' (Omilola et al. 2010: 2). Liberalization of domestic markets, if by liberalization is meant the removal of restrictions on the economic freedom of farmers and small entrepreneurs, really was an important element of successful pro-poor development strategies in South-East Asia. In Africa, conversely, the lack of serious, high-level political interest in 'subsidies for agricultural inputs and extension services' dates from well before the 1980s, and in most countries shows little sign of changing under the present, less financially constrained conditions.

How, then, can African policy-makers most effectively be encouraged to give high priority to agricultural and rural development, in accordance with Declaration 7 of the 2003 Maputo assembly of the African Union, and furthermore to ensure that the main and immediate beneficiaries of the resulting public investments are poor peasant farmers rather than large landowners? Clearly, international actors cannot create the kind of revolutionary threat which inspired such policies in some Asian cases, and neither is there much evidence that electoral democracy can generate the same kind of salutary political pressure on African (or indeed Asian) governments (Poulton 2012). Nor is it possible to alter colonial history or the other social factors which have shaped the current attitudes of African leaders and intellectuals to rural and agricultural development. However, the success of international actors and institutions in promoting market reforms and prudent macroeconomic policy in Africa gives grounds for hope that those same actors and institutions can potentially achieve something similar with respect to pro-poor, pro-rural public spending too.

Some encouraging preliminary evidence that this may be possible comes from recent experience in Rwanda. The political economy of Rwanda, where the ruling Rwandan Patriotic Front (RPF) came to power through civil war and following the massacre in 1994 of several hundred thousand members of the country's Tutsi minority, is unusual in the African context and in some ways resembles that of South-East Asia's counter-revolutionary developmental states (Booth and Golooba-Mutebi 2011). The Tutsi were the social and political elite (after Europeans) of colonial Rwanda. The current regime, born in a Tutsi counter-revolution, has strong reasons to prove its legitimacy by showing that despite its still largely Tutsi leadership, it can rule for the benefit of all Rwandans – including those many members of the Hutu majority whose poverty and resentment, combined with ethnic hatred fomented ideologically by the RPF's rivals in the civil war, led to the 1994 genocide.

Despite this promising background, the power of the dualistic assumptions outlined above was such that for many years RPF development policy remained a classic example of urban-industrial bias, and of Africa's elitist obsession with education and technological modernization. As recently as 2009, president Paul Kagame still talked of pioneering a 'short cut' to development, based on information technology, which would bypass peasant agriculture entirely (Van Luyten 2009: 6).

> We understand that achieving prosperity requires a metamorphosis of our economy. We are fundamentally changing our economy to move away from a dependence on agriculture toward a knowledge economy. [...] Rwanda must become a world-class competitor in information and communication technology (ICT), logistics, financial services, and education. (Kagame 2009: 12)

A high-ranking official in Rwanda's Ministry of Agriculture, meanwhile, declared that the priority was not to raise the productivity of small farms, but rather 'to get more people off the land' (Ansoms

2009: 300). While Kagame was interested in Asia's development achievements, his preferred Asian model was not Indonesia – where, ironically, the island of Java offers credible parallels with the fertile but overpopulated rural landscape of Rwanda (Diamond 2006: 311–28) – but rather Singapore, for almost two centuries one of the world's great seaports, and an icon of hypermodernity rather than a practical model of how to develop a poor, landlocked, war-ravaged agrarian country in Africa.

In the last few years, however, there has been a marked change in the Rwandan state's attitude to agricultural and rural development (Booth and Golooba-Mutebi 2012). The Ministry of Agriculture's share of public expenditure rose from 3.5 per cent in 2007 to 7 per cent in 2011, and in 2012 was already expected to reach the Maputo target of 10 per cent. Rapidly increasing emphasis was given not only to export-oriented horticulture, the potential of which had been recognized at an early stage, but also to peasant food crop production (input subsidies, extension services, irrigation) and rural transport infrastructure. The test of a true commitment to pro-poor development, Widjojo (1995: 180) once wrote, 'arrives when the availability of resources is rapidly declining: whether to forgo other claims or to yield to pressures and sacrifice the poverty-reduction programs'. Rwanda seems determined to pass that test: when several major foreign donors suspended aid to the country in late 2012 owing to its alleged military interventions in the Congo, Minister of Finance and Economic Planning John Rwangombwa announced that all development projects in the agricultural and infrastructure sectors would be protected from the inevitable budget cuts (Republic of Rwanda 2013).

In part, this reorientation of official development thinking was an instance of successful learning from experience, in accordance with Sadli's Law. It was triggered by the experience of a serious national food crisis in 2003 and 2004, which in turn served to draw attention to the failure of early growth in the aggregate economy to make a rapid impact on rural income poverty. Another factor, however, was the influence of expert advisers (both foreign and local) who, impressed by a mounting volume of recent academic and professional literature on the importance of agriculture for poverty reduction in Asia and elsewhere (Breisinger and Diao 2008; Cervantes-Godoy and Dewbre 2010; Dorward et al. 2004; Fan 2008; Losch 2012; Mosely 2002; World

Bank 2007), had begun to revise their own views of what it would take to transform Rwanda in accordance with the ambitions of its rulers.

This kind of guided redirection of policy and spending priorities need not be (and was not in Rwanda) a matter of attaching restrictive conditions to foreign aid and loans. Such leverage is in any case less powerful than in the past, now that African governments are no longer in persistent budgetary crisis and the appearance of new sources of finance and investment, notably in Asia itself, have made Africa less dependent on Western aid and international financial institutions. What can perhaps be done instead is to change the mindset of African elites by consistently drawing to their attention the fact that successful development elsewhere in the developing world has been achieved very largely by means of the inclusive, pro-poor, pro-rural strategies documented in the present book. This ideological effort – if it can be called ideological, given that it is based on historical observations rather than arguments from principle – should take precedence over historically much less well-founded admonitions regarding the importance of good governance, democracy, or even free trade.

We have seen how quickly the mindsets of South-East Asian policy-makers were in some respects changed when they grasped certain practical truths regarding what works, and what does not work, in development strategy. The crucial lesson that has not yet been widely understood in Africa is that pro-poor strategies really are the historically proven way not only to relieve rural poverty, but also to initiate processes that can bring prosperity to whole countries, setting them on the surest known path to the kind of industrial and urban modernity which African elites have always admired. It is hard to believe that there are many Africans who, once they appreciate this lesson from developing Asia, will not draw from it practical conclusions regarding what their own governments should do in order to restore the dignity of their countries and their continent.

# REFERENCES

Abdul Razak bin Hussein, Tun Haji (1975) 'New Year message from the Deputy Prime Minister on 26th December, 1959', in *Ucapan-ucapan Tun Haji Abdul Razak bin Hussein 1960*, Kuala Lumpur: Arkib Negara Malaysia, pp. 5–6.

Acemoglu, Daron, Simon Johnson and James A. Robinson (2001) 'The colonial origins of comparative development: an empirical investigation', *American Economic Review*, 91(5): 1369–401.

Africa Confidential (1985) 'Nigeria: the Young Turks?', *Africa Confidential*, 26(18): 1–2, 4 September.

African Centre for Economic Transformation (2014) *2014 African Transformation Report; growth with depth*, Accra: ACET.

Agrawal, Nisha (1995) 'Indonesia; labor market policies and international competitiveness', Policy Research Working Paper 1515, Washington, DC: World Bank.

Ajoku, Kingsley Iheanacho (1992) 'Tradables and nontradables, oil boom, and the Dutch disease: a comparative study of Nigeria and Indonesia', PhD thesis, Howard University, Washington, DC.

Akamatsu, Kaname (1962) 'A historical pattern of economic growth in developing countries', *Journal of Developing Economies*, 1(1): 3–25.

Akinyoade, Akinyinka (2008) 'A comparison of stability and expertise between Nigerian and Indonesian cabinets, 1966–1998', paper prepared for the First Plenary Meeting of Tracking Development, Leiden, 25–28 June.

Akyüz, Yilmaz, Ha-Joon Chang and Richard Kozul-Wright (1999) 'New perspectives on East Asian development', in Yilmaz Akyüz (ed.), *East Asian Development; new perspectives*, London: Frank Cass, pp. 4–36.

Alatas, Syed Hussein (1977) *The Myth of the Lazy Native; a study of the image of the Malays, Filipinos and Javanese from the 16th to the 20th century and its function in the ideology of colonial capitalism*, London: Frank Cass.

Alavi, Rokiah (1996) *Industrialisation in Malaysia; import substitution and infant industry performance*, London: Routledge.

Albert, Isaac Olawale (2005) 'Explaining "godfatherism" in Nigerian politics', *African Sociological Review*, 9(2): 79–105.

Alden, Chris (2007) *China in Africa*, London: Zed Books in association with the International African Institute, Royal African Society, and Social Science Research Council.

Alesina, Alberto and Dani Rodrik (1994) 'Distributive politics and economic growth', *Quarterly Journal of Economics*, 109(2): 465–90.

Amin, Samir (1989) *La faillite du développement en Afrique et dans le tiers-monde; une analyse politique*, Paris: L'Harmattan.

Amsden, Alice (1989) *Asia's Next Giant; South Korea and late industrialization*, Oxford: Oxford University Press.

Andrews, Matt (2008) 'The good governance agenda: beyond indicators without theory', *Oxford Development Studies*, 36(4): 379–407.

Ansoms, An (2009) 'Re-engineering rural

society: the visions and ambitions of the Rwandan elite', *African Affairs*, 108(431): 289–309.

Argwings-Kodhek, Gem, T. S. Jayne, Gerald Nyambane, Tom Awuor and T. Yamano (1998) 'How can micro-level household information make a difference for agricultural policy making? Selected examples from the KAMPAP survey of smallholder agriculture and non farm activities for selected districts in Kenya', Njoro: Kenya Agricultural Marketing and Policy Analysis Project, Tegemeo Institute of Agricultural Policy and Development, Egerton University/ Kenya Agricultural Research Institute/Michigan State University.

Arndt, H. W. (1984) *The Indonesian Economy; collected papers*, Singapore: Chopmen.

Arrighi, Giovanni (1996) 'The rise of East Asia; world systematic and regional aspects', *International Journal of Sociology and Social Policy*, 16(7/8): 6–44.

Aryeetey, Ernest, Julius Court, Machiko Nissanke and Beatrice Weber (2003), *Africa and Asia in the Global Economy*, Tokyo: United Nations University Press.

Asiodu, P. C. (1971) 'Planning for further development in Nigeria', in A. A. Ayida and H. M. A. Onitiri (eds), *Reconstruction and Development in Nigeria; proceedings of a national conference*, Ibadan: Oxford University Press, pp. 185–213.

Aswicahyono, Haryo, M. Chatib Basri and Hal Hill (2000) 'How not to industrialise? Indonesia's automotive industry', *Bulletin of Indonesian Economic Studies*, 36(1): 209–41.

Ayida, Allison A. (1987) *Reflections on Nigerian Development*, Lagos: Malthouse Press.

Bais, Karolien (2008) *Het Nederlandse Afrikabeleid 1998–2006; evaluatie van de bilaterale samenwerking; samenvatting*, The Hague: Inspectie Ontwikkelingssamenwerking en Beleidsevaluatie.

Baneth, Jean (1997) 'The Indonesian exception', in Moh. Arsjad Anwar, Aris Ananta and Ari Kuncoro (eds), *Widjojo Nitisastro 70 tahun; pembangunan nasional: teori, kebijakan, dan pelaksanaan*, vol. 1, Jakarta: Fakultas Ekonomi Universitas Indonesia, pp. 279–313.

Bannerjee, Abhijit V. and Esther Duflo (2011) *Poor Economics; barefoot hedge-fund managers, DIY doctors and the surprising truth about life on less than $1 a day*, London: Penguin.

Bargawi, Omar (2005) 'Cambodia's garment industry – origins and future prospects', ESAU Working Paper 13, London: Overseas Development Institute.

Barker, Randolph, Robert W. Herdt and Beth Rose (1985) *The Rice Economy of Asia*, Washington, DC: Resources for the Future.

Barlow, Colin (1978) *The Natural Rubber Industry; its development, technology, and economy in Malaya*, Kuala Lumpur: Oxford University Press.

Barro, Robert J. (1991) 'Economic growth in a cross section of countries', *Quarterly Journal of Economics*, 106(2): 407–43.

Basri, M. Chatib and Hal Hill (2004) 'Ideas, interests and oil prices: the political economy of trade reform during Soeharto's Indonesia', *The World Economy*, 27(5): 633–55.

Bates, Robert H. (1981) *Markets and States in Tropical Africa; the political basis of agricultural policies*, Berkeley: University of California Press.

— (1983) *Essays on the Political Economy of Rural Africa*, Cambridge: Cambridge University Press.

— (1989) *Beyond the Miracle of the Market; the political economy of agrarian development in Kenya*, Cambridge: Cambridge University Press.

Bayart, Jean-François (1989) *L'État en Afrique; la politique du ventre*, Paris: Fayard.

Bebbington, Anthony and Willy McCourt (eds) (2007) *Development Success; statecraft in the South*, Basingstoke: Palgrave Macmillan.

Beeson, Mark (2000) 'Mahathir and the markets: globalisation and the pursuit of economic autonomy in Malaysia', *Pacific Affairs*, 73(3): 335–51.

Bello, Walden F., Shea Cunningham and Kheng Poh Li (1998) *A Siamese Tragedy; development and disintegration in modern Thailand*, London: Zed Books.

Berendsen, Bernard, Ton Dietz, Henk Schulte Northolt and Roel van der Veen (eds) (2013) *Asian Tigers, African Lions; comparing the development performance of Southeast Asia and Africa*, Leiden: Brill.

Bevan, David L., Paul Collier and Jan Willem Gunning (1999) *The Political Economy of Poverty, Equity, and Growth; Nigeria and Indonesia*, Washington, DC: World Bank/Oxford: Oxford University Press.

Bezemer, Dirk and Derek Headey (2008) 'Agriculture, development, and urban bias', *World Development*, 36(8): 1342–64.

Bienen, Henry S. and Mark Gersovitz (1985) 'Economic stabilization, conditionality and political stability', *International Organization*, 39(4): 729–54.

Birner, Regina and Danielle Resnick (2010) 'The political economy of policies for smallholder agriculture', *World Development*, 38(10): 1442–52.

Blank, Herbert G., Clifford M. Mutero and Hammon Murray-Rust (eds) (2002) *The Changing Face of Irrigation in Kenya; opportunities for anticipating changes in eastern and southern Africa*, Colombo: International Water Management Institute.

Bloom, David E. and Jeffrey D. Sachs (1998) 'Geography, demography, and economic growth in Africa', Brookings Papers on Economic Activity 2, pp. 207–73.

Boeke, J. H. (1953) *Economics and Economic Policy of Dual Societies as Exemplified by Indonesia*, Haarlem: H. D. Tjeenk Willink.

Booth, Anne (1988) *Agricultural Development in Indonesia*, Sydney: Allen and Unwin.

— (1999) 'Initial conditions and miraculous growth: why is South East Asia different from Taiwan and South Korea?', *World Development*, 27(2): 301–21.

— (2007) *Colonial Legacies; economic and social development in East and Southeast Asia*, Honolulu: University of Hawaii Press.

Booth, David (2012) *Development as a Collective Action Problem; addressing the real challenges of African governance*, London: Overseas Development Institute.

Booth, David and Frederick Golooba-Mutebi (2011) 'Developmental patrimonialism? The case of Rwanda', African Power and Politics Programme Working Paper 16, London: Overseas Development Institute.

— (2012) 'Policy for agriculture and horticulture in Rwanda: a different political economy?' Future Agricultures Working Paper 38, Africa Power and Politics Programme, London: Future Agricultures Consortium.

Bosker, E. Maarten and Harry Garretsen (2008) 'Economic geography and economic development in Sub-Saharan Africa', CESifo Working Paper 2490, Munich: Centre for Economic Studies/Ifo Institute.

Bottema, Jan Willem Tako (1995) 'Market formation and agriculture in Indonesia from the mid 19th century to 1990', PhD thesis, Sociale Wetenschappen, Katholieke

Universiteit Nijmegen, Jakarta: Drukkerij Desa Putera.

BPKP (1985) *Norma Pemeriksaan Aparat Pengawasan Fungsional Pemerintah*, Jakarta: Badan Pengawas Keuangan dan Pembangunan, Republik Indonesia (Surat Edaran SE-117/K/1985).

BPS-Statistics Indonesia, Bappenas and UNDP (2004) *National Human Development Report 2004; the economics of democracy: financing human development in Indonesia*, Jakarta: BPS-Statistics Indonesia, Bappenas and UNDP Indonesia.

Braadbaart, Okke (1996) 'Corruption in Indonesian public tendering', in Heleen E. Bakker and Nico G. Schulte Nordholt (eds), *Corruption and Legitimacy*, Amsterdam: Netherlands Universities Institute for Coordination of Research in Social Sciences (SISWO), pp. 95–117.

Bräutigam, Deborah (1995) 'The state as agent: industrial development in Taiwan, 1957–1972', in Howard Stein (ed.), *Asian Industrialization and Africa*, New York: St Martin's Press, pp. 145–81.

— (2003) 'Local entrepreneurship in Southeast Asia and Sub-Saharan Africa: networks and linkages to the global economy', in Ernest Aryeetey, Julius Court, Machiko Nissanke and Beatrice Weber (eds), *Africa and Asia in the Global Economy*, Tokyo: United Nations University Press, pp. 106–27.

— (2009) *The Dragon's Gift; the real story of China in Africa*, Oxford: Oxford University Press.

Bray, Francesca (1986) *The Rice Economies; technology and development in Asian societies*, Oxford: Basil Blackwell.

Breisinger, Clemens and Xinshen Diao (2008) 'Economic transformation in theory and practice: what are the messages for Africa?', ReSAKSS Working Paper 10, Washington, DC: Regional Strategic Analysis and Knowledge Support System, International Food Policy Research Institute.

Bresnan, John (1993) *Managing Indonesia; the modern political economy*, New York: Columbia University Press.

Broad Outlines (1961) *Broad Outlines of the National Overall Development Plan 1961–1969*, Jakarta: National Planning Council, Republic of Indonesia.

Brown, C. P. (1973) 'Rice price stabilization and support in Malaysia', *The Developing Economies*, 11(2): 164–83.

Brunnschweiler, Christa N. and Erwin H. Bulte (2008) 'The resource curse revisited and revised: a tale of paradoxes and red herrings', *Journal of Environmental Economics and Management*, 55(3): 248–64.

Callaghy, Thomas (1987) 'The state as lame Leviathan: the patrimonial administrative state in Africa', in Zaki Ergas (ed.), *The African State in Transition*, London: Macmillan, pp. 87–116.

Campos, Jose Edgardo and Hilton L. Root (1996) *The Key to the Asian Miracle; making shared growth credible*, Washington, DC: Brookings Institution.

Cervantes-Godoy, Dalila and Joe Dewbre (2010) 'Economic importance of agriculture for poverty reduction', OECD Food, Agriculture and Fisheries Working Paper 23, Paris: OECD Publishing.

Chabal, Patrick (2009) *Africa; the politics of suffering and smiling*, London: Zed Books.

Chabal, Patrick and Jean-Pascal Daloz (1999) *Africa Works; disorder as political instrument*, Oxford: James Currey.

Chang, Ha-Joon (2003) 'Trade, industry and technology policies in Northeast Asia', in Machiko Nissanke and Ernest Aryeetey (eds), *Comparative Development Experiences of Sub-Saharan Africa and East Asia*, Aldershot: Ashgate, pp. 243–71.

Chege, Michael (1995) 'Sub-Saharan Africa: underdevelopment's last stand', in Barbara Stallings (ed.), *Global Change, Regional Response; the new international context of development*, Cambridge: Cambridge University Press, pp. 309–48.

Chhibber, Ajay and Chad Leechor (1995) 'From adjustment to growth in Sub-Saharan Africa: the lessons of East Asian experience applied to Ghana', *Journal of African Economies*, 4: 83–114.

Chowdhury, Anis and Iman Sugema (2005) 'How significant and effective has foreign aid to Indonesia been?', *ASEAN Economic Bulletin*, 22(2): 186–216.

Cole, David C. (2007) 'His finest hour: Indonesia from 1966 to 1969', in Moh. Arsjad Anwar, Aris Ananta and Ari Kuncoro (eds), *Tributes for Widjojo Nitisastro by Friends from 27 Foreign Countries*, Jakarta: Kompas, pp. 121–8.

Collier, Paul (1998) 'Comments and discussion' [on David E. Bloom and Jeffrey D. Sachs, 'Geography, demography, and economic growth in Africa'], *Brookings Papers on Economic Activity*, 2: 274–81.

— (2006) 'Is aid oil? An analysis of whether Africa can absorb more aid', *World Development*, 34(9): 1482–97.

— (2007) *The Bottom Billion; why the poorest countries are failing and what we can do about it*, Oxford: Oxford University Press.

Collier, Paul and Stefan Dercon (2006) 'Review article; the complementarities of poverty reduction, equity, and growth: a perspective on the World Development Report 2006', *Economic Development and Cultural Change*, 55: 223–36.

Collier, Paul, and Jan Willem Gunning (2008) 'Sacrificing the future: intertemporal strategies and their implications for growth', in Benno J. Ndulu, Stephen A. O'Connell, Robert H. Bates, Paul Collier and Chukwuma C. Soludo (eds), *The Political Economy of Economic Growth in Africa 1960–2000*, vol. 1, Cambridge: Cambridge University Press, pp. 202–24.

Collier, Paul, Samir Radwan and Samuel Wangwe (1986) *Labour and Poverty in Rural Tanzania; ujamaa and rural development in the United Republic of Tanzania*, Oxford: Clarendon Press.

Collier, Paul, Chukwuma C. Soludo and Catherine Pattillo (eds) (2008) *Economic Policy Options for a Prosperous Nigeria*, Basingstoke: Palgrave Macmillan.

Cooksey, Brian (2003) 'Marketing reform? The rise and fall of agricultural liberalisation in Tanzania', *Development Policy Review*, 21(1): 67–91.

Coulson, Andrew (ed.) (1979) *African Socialism in Practice: The Tanzanian experience*, Nottingham: Spokesman.

Court, David and Dharam Ghai (1974) 'Education, society and development', in David Court and Dharam P. Ghai (eds), *Education, Society and Development; new perspectives from Kenya*, Nairobi: Oxford University Press, pp. 1–26.

Courtenay, Philip (1995) *The Rice Sector of Peninsular Malaysia; a rural paradox*, Sydney: Allen and Unwin.

Crouch, Harold (1996) *Government and Society in Malaysia*, Ithaca, NY: Cornell University Press.

Dang Kim Son and Tran Cong Thang (2008) 'Role of state-owned enterprises in Vietnam's rice markets', in Shahidur Rashid, Ashok Gulati and Ralph Cummings, Jr (eds), *From Parastatals to Private Trade*, Baltimore, MD: Johns Hopkins University Press, pp. 205–21.

Dapice, Daniel O. (2003) *Vietnam's Economy: Success story or weird dualism? A SWOT anaylsis*, prepared for United Nations Development Programme and Prime Minister's Research Commission, Cambridge,

MA: Vietnam Program, Center for Business and Government, Harvard University John F. Kennedy School of Government.

Dasgupta, Dipak (1998) 'Poverty reduction in Indonesia', in Henry S. Rowen (ed.), *Behind East Asian Growth; the political and social foundations of prosperity*, London: Routledge, pp. 209–33.

Datt, Gaurav and Martin Ravallion (2002) 'Is India's economic growth leaving the poor behind?', World Bank Policy Research Working Paper 2846, Washington, DC: World Bank.

Davidson, Basil (1992) *The Black Man's Burden; Africa and the curse of the nation-state*, London: James Currey.

Davis, Diane E. (2004) *Discipline and Development; middle classes and prosperity in East Asia and Latin America*, Cambridge: Cambridge University Press.

De Groote, Hugo, George Owuor, Cheryl Doss, James Ouma, Lutta Muhammad and K. Danda (2005) 'The maize Green Revolution in Kenya revisited', *Journal of Agricultural and Development Economics*, 2(1): 32–49.

De Pourtales, Helie (2007) 'May others follow his example', in Moh. Arsjad Anwar, Aris Ananta and Ari Kuncoro (eds), *Tributes for Widjojo Nitisastro by Friends from 27 Foreign Countries*, Jakarta: Kompas, pp. 287–8.

De Silva, K. Migara O. (1996) 'The political economy of macroeconomic change: case studies of Nigeria and Indonesia', PhD thesis, Washington University, St Louis, MO.

De Soto, Hernando (2000) *The Mystery of Capital; why capitalism triumphs in the West and fails everywhere else*, London: Black Swan.

Deguen, Daniel M. (2007) 'His role in restoring the creditworthiness of Indonesia', in Moh. Arsjad Anwar, Aris Ananta and Ari Kuncoro (eds), *Tributes for Widjojo Nitisastro by*

*Friends from 27 Foreign Countries*, Jakarta: Kompas, pp. 143–5.

Deininger, Klaus (2003) *Land Policies for Growth and Poverty Reduction*, Washington, DC: World Bank.

Devan Nair, C. V. (ed.) (1976) *Socialism that Works ... the Singapore Way*, Singapore: Federal Publications.

Development Plan (1964) *Development Plan for the period from 1st July, 1964, to 30th June, 1970*, Nairobi: Republic of Kenya.

— (1966) *Development Plan 1966–70*, Nairobi: Republic of Kenya.

— (1969) *Development Plan for the period 1970 to 1974*, Nairobi: Republic of Kenya.

— (1974) *Development Plan for the period 1974 to 1978*, Nairobi: Republic of Kenya.

— (1979) *Development Plan for the period 1979 to 1983*, Nairobi: Republic of Kenya.

— (1984) *Development Plan for the period 1984 to 1988*, Nairobi: Republic of Kenya.

Development Programme (1957) *The Development Programme 1957/60*, Sessional Paper no. 77 of 1956/57, Nairobi: Kenya Colony and Protectorate.

— (1960) *The Development Programme 1960/63*, Sessional Paper no. 4 of 1959/60, Nairobi: Kenya Colony and Protectorate.

Diamond, Jared (2006) *Collapse; how societies choose to fail or survive*, London: Penguin.

Dibie, Robert (1998) 'Cross-national economic development in Indonesia and Nigeria', *Scandinavian Journal of Development Alternatives and Area Studies*, 17(1): 65–85.

Dick, Howard (1985) 'Survey of recent developments', *Bulletin of Indonesian Economic Studies*, 21(3): 1–23.

Dieleman, Marleen (2007) *The Rhythm of Strategy; a corporate biography of the Salim Group of Indonesia*, Monographs 1, ICAS Publications Series, Amsterdam: Amsterdam University Press.

Dietz, Ton (2011) 'Silverlining Africa; from images of doom and gloom to glimmers of hope, from places to avoid to places to enjoy', professorial inaugural address, Leiden University and African Studies Centre, 14 January.

Dixon, Chris (1999) *The Thai Economy; uneven development and internationalisation*, London: Routledge.

Djankov, Simeon, Jose G. Montalvo and Marta Reynal-Querol (2008) 'The curse of aid', *Journal of Economic Growth*, 13(3): 169–94.

Djurfeldt, Göran and Magnus Jirström (2005) 'The puzzle of the policy shift – the early Green Revolution in India, Indonesia and the Philippines', in Göran Djurfeldt, Hans Holmén, Magnus Jirström and Rolf Larsson (eds), *The African Food Crisis; lessons from the Asian Green Revolution*, Wallingford: CABI Publishing, pp. 43–63.

Djurfeldt, Goran, Hans Holmén, Magnus Jirström and Rolf Larsson (2005a) *The African Food Crisis; lessons from the Asian Green Revolution*, Wallingford: CABI Publishing.

Djurfeldt, Göran, Hans Holmén, Magnus Jirström and Rolf Larsson (2005b) 'African food crisis – the relevance of Asian experiences', in Göran Djurfeldt, Hans Holmén, Magnus Jirström and Rolf Larsson (eds), *The African Food Crisis; lessons from the Asian Green Revolution*, Wallingford: CABI Publishing, pp. 1–8.

Doner, Richard F. (2009) *The Politics of Uneven Development; Thailand's economic growth in comparative perspective*, Cambridge: Cambridge University Press.

Doner, Richard F. and Ansil Ramsay (2000) 'Rent-seeking and economic development in Thailand', in

Mushtaq H. Khan and Jomo Kwame Sundaram (eds), *Rents, Rent-seeking and Economic Development; theory and evidence in Asia*, Cambridge: Cambridge University Press, pp. 145–81.

Doner, Richard F., Bryan K. Ritchie and Dan Slater (2005) 'Systemic vulnerability and the origins of developmental states: Northeast and Southeast Asia in comparative perspective', *International Organization*, 59(2): 327–61.

Dorward, Andrew, Jonathan Kydd, Jamie Morrison and Ian Urey (2004) 'A policy agenda for pro-poor agricultural growth', *World Development*, 32(1): 73–89.

Drabble, John H. (2000) *An Economic History of Malaysia, c. 1800–1990; the transition to modern economic growth*, Basingstoke: Macmillan.

Draft Development Plan (1950) *Draft Development Plan of the Federation of Malaya*, Kuala Lumpur: Government Press.

Easterly, William (2002) *The Elusive Quest for Growth; economists' adventures and misadventures in the tropics*, Cambridge, MA: MIT Press.

— (2006) *The White Man's Burden; why the West's efforts to aid the rest have done so much ill and so little good*, Oxford: Oxford University Press.

Easterly, William and Ross Levine (1995) 'Africa's growth tragedy; a retrospective 1960–89', Policy Research Working Paper 1503, Washington, DC: World Bank.

— (1997) 'Africa's growth tragedy: policies and ethnic divisions', *Quarterly Journal of Economics*, 112(4): 1203–50.

— (1998) 'Troubles with the neighbours: Africa's problem, Africa's opportunity', *Journal of African Economies*, 7(1): 120–42.

Edwards, Chris (1995) 'East Asia and industrial policy in Malaysia: lessons for Africa?', in Howard Stein (ed.), *Asian Industrialization and Africa; studies in policy alternatives to structural adjustment*, Basingstoke: Macmillan, pp. 239–56.

Elbadawi, Ibrahim A., Benno J. Ndulu and Njuguna S. Ndung'u (2003) 'Macroeconomic performance in Sub-Saharan Africa in a comparative setting', in Machiko Nissanke and Ernest Aryeetey (eds), *Comparative Development Experiences of Sub-Saharan Africa and East Asia*, Aldershot: Ashgate, pp. 72–112.

Ellis, Frank (1983) 'Agricultural marketing and peasant–state transfers in Tanzania', *Journal of Peasant Studies*, 10(4): 214–42.

Ellsworth, Paul T. et al. (1959) *A Public Development Program for Thailand; report of a mission organized by the International Bank for Reconstruction and Development (The World Bank) at the request of the Government of Thailand*, Baltimore, MD: Johns Hopkins University Press.

Elson, R. E. (2001) *Suharto; a political biography*, Cambridge: Cambridge University Press.

Ergas, Zaki R. (1982) 'Kenya's Special Rural Development Program (SRDP): was it really a failure?', *Journal of Developing Areas*, 17(1): 51–66.

Eriksson Skoog, Gun (2000) *The Soft Budget Constraint; the Emergence, Persistence and Logic of an Institution*, Boston, MA: Kluwer Academic.

Eshiwani, G. S. (1990) 'Implementing educational policies in Kenya', World Bank Discussion Papers, Africa Technical Department Series, 85, Washington, DC: World Bank.

Evaluation of the First Six-Year Plan (1967) *Evaluation of the First Six-Year Plan 1961–1966*, Bangkok: National Economic Development Board, Office of the Prime Minister, Government of Thailand.

Evans, Peter (1999) 'Transferable lessons? Re-examining the institutional prerequisites of East Asian economic policies', in Yilmaz Akyüz (ed.), *East Asian Development; new perspectives*, London: Frank Cass, pp. 66–86.

Faaland, Just (1990) *Growth and Ethnic Inequality; Malaysia's New Economic Policy*, London: Hurst.

Falae, Olu (2004) *The Way Forward for Nigeria: The economy and polity*, Akure: Flocel Publishers.

Falcon, Walter P. (2007) 'The key role he played in achieving food security and poverty alleviation in Indonesia', in Moh. Arsjad Anwar, Aris Ananta and Ari Kuncoro (eds), *Tributes for Widjojo Nitisastro by Friends from 27 Foreign Countries*, Jakarta: Kompas, pp. 25–31.

Fan, Shenggen (ed.) (2008) *Public Expenditures, Growth, and Poverty; lessons from developing countries*, Baltimore, MD: Johns Hopkins University Press in cooperation with the International Food Policy Research Institute.

Fan, Shenggen, Bingxin Yu and Anuja Saurkar (2008) 'Public spending in developing countries: trends, determination, and impact', in Shenggen Fan (ed.), *Public Expenditures, Growth, and Poverty; lessons from developing countries*, Baltimore, MD: Johns Hopkins University Press in cooperation with the International Food Policy Research Institute, pp. 20–55.

Fatton, Robert (1992) *Predatory Rule; state and civil society in Africa*. Boulder, CO: Lynne Rienner.

Felker, Greg and K. S. Jomo (2007) 'Technology policy in Malaysia', in K. S. Jomo (ed.), *Malaysian Industrial Policy*, Singapore: NUS Press, pp. 128–56.

Fifth Malaysia Plan (1986) *Fifth Malaysia Plan 1986–1990*, Kuala Lumpur: National Printing Department.

First Five-Year Development Plan (1969) *The First Five-Year Development Plan (1969/70–1973/74)*, vol. 1, Jakarta:

Department of Information, Republic of Indonesia.

First Malaysia Plan (1965) *First Malaysia Plan 1966–1970*, Kuala Lumpur: Jabatan Chetak Kerajaan.

Five-Year Plan (1964) *Five-Year Plan for Economic and Social Development, 1st July, 1964–30th June, 1969*, Dar es Salaam: Republic of Tanzania.

Forrest, Tom (1993) *Politics and Economic Development in Nigeria*, Boulder, CO: Westview Press.

Fourth Malaysia Plan (1981) *Fourth Malaysia Plan 1981–1985*, Kuala Lumpur: National Printing Department.

Fourth National Development Plan (1981) *Fourth National Development Plan 1981–85*, Lagos: Federal Republic of Nigeria.

Fox, James J. (1991) 'Managing the ecology of rice production in Indonesia', in Joan Hardjono (ed.), *Indonesia; resources, ecology, and environment*, Singapore: Oxford University Press, pp. 61–84.

Francks, Penelope (1984) *Technology and Agricultural Development in Pre-war Japan*, New Haven, CT: Yale University Press.

Frank, André Gunder (1978) *Dependent Accumulation and Underdevelopment*, London: Macmillan.

— (1998) *ReOrient; global economy in the Asian age*, Berkeley: University of California Press.

Fuady, Ahmad Helmy (2012) 'Elites and economic policies in Indonesia and Nigeria, 1966–1998', PhD thesis, University of Amsterdam.

Furnivall, J. S. (1939) *Netherlands India; a study of plural economy*, Cambridge: Cambridge University Press.

Gallup, John Luke, Jeffrey D. Sachs and Andrew D. Mellinger (1998) 'Geography and economic development', NBER Working Paper 6849, Cambridge: MA: National Bureau of Economic Research.

Geertz, Clifford (1963) *Agricultural Involution; the process of ecological change in Indonesia*, Berkeley: University of California Press.

General Statistical Office (2000) *Statistical Data of Vietnam; agriculture, forestry and fishery 1975–2000*, Hanoi: Statistical Publishing House.

Gennaioli, Nicola and Ilia Rainer (2007) 'The modern impact of precolonial centralization in Africa', *Journal of Economic Growth*, 12: 185–234.

Geschiere, Peter and Josef Gugler (1998) 'The urban–rural connection: changing issues of belonging and identification', *Africa; Journal of the International African Institute*, 68(3): 309–19.

Giddens, Anthony (1976) *New Rules of Sociological Method: A positive critique of interpretative sociologies*, London: Hutchinson.

Goldstein, Andrea (2002) 'The political economy of high-tech industries in developing countries: aerospace in Brazil, Indonesia and South Africa', *Cambridge Journal of Economics*, 26(4): 521–38.

Goujon, Michael (2006) 'Fighting inflation in a dollarized economy: the case of Vietnam', *Journal of Comparative Economics*, 34(3): 564–81.

Gourou, Pierre (1947) *Les Pays tropicaux; principes d'une géographie humaine et économique*, Paris: Presses Universitaires de France.

Hanatani, Atsushi (2008) 'Asian experiences of economic development and their implications for Africa', in IFIC/JICA, *Role of government in promoting sustained and accelerated growth in Africa and lessons from Asian experiences; JICA/JBIC international workshop report 'Asian Experiences of Economic Development and Their Policy Implications for Africa', February 6, 2008, Tokyo*, Tokyo: Institute for International Cooperation/Japan International Cooperation Agency, pp. 3–6.

Handley, Paul M. (2006) *The King Never Smiles; a biography of Thailand's Bhumibol Adulyadej*, New Haven, CT: Yale University Press.

Harahap, Rudy M. (1999) 'Strategies for preventing corruption in Asia', Asia Pacific School of Economics and Management Working Paper GOV99-3, Canberra: Asia Pacific Press at the Australian National University.

Hardin, Garrett (1968) 'The tragedy of the commons', *Science*, 162: 1243–8.

Harrold, Peter, Malathi Jayawickrama and Deepak Bhattasali (1996) 'Practical lessons for Africa from East Asia in industrial and trade policies', World Bank Discussion Paper 310, Washington, DC: World Bank.

Harun Zain (2008) 'True patriot of national development (honest and unpretentious reflections from an old friend)', in Moh. Arsjad Anwar, Aris Ananta and Ari Kuncoro (eds), *Testimonials of Friends about Widjojo Nitisastro*, Jakarta: Kompas.

Hassan, Rashid M. and Daniel D. Karanja (1997) 'Increasing maize production in Kenya: technology, institutions, and policy', in Derek Byerlee and Carl K. Eicher (eds), *Africa's Emerging Maize Revolution*, Boulder, CO: Lynne Rienner, pp. 81–93.

Hatch, John (1976) *Two African Statesmen; Kaunda of Zambia and Nyerere of Tanzania*, London: Secker and Warburg.

Hayami, Yujiro (2001) 'Ecology, history, and development: a perspective from rural Southeast Asia', *World Bank Research Observer*, 16(2): 169–98.

Hayton, Bill (2010) *Vietnam; rising dragon*, New Haven, CT: Yale University Press.

Hazlewood, Arthur (1979) *The Economy of Kenya; the Kenyatta era*, Oxford: Oxford University Press.

Henley, David (2010) 'Microfinance in Indonesia; evolution and revolution, 1900–2000', in Aditya Goenka and David Henley (eds), *Southeast Asia's Credit Revolution; from moneylenders to microfinance*, London: Routledge, pp. 173–89.

— (2012) 'Agrarian roots of industrial growth: rural development in Southeast Asia and Sub-Saharan Africa', *Development Policy Review*, 30(S1): 25–47.

Henley, David and Aditya Goenka (2010) 'Introduction; from moneylenders to microfinance in Southeast Asia', in Aditya Goenka and David Henley (eds), *Southeast Asia's Credit Revolution; from moneylenders to microfinance*, London: Routledge, pp. 1–17.

Henley, David, Riwanto Tirtosudarmo and Ahmad Helmy Fuady (2012) 'Flawed vision: Nigerian development policy in the Indonesian mirror, 1965–90', *Development Policy Review*, 30(S1): 49–71.

Heyer, Judith (1966) 'Kenya's cautious development plan', *East Africa Journal*, 3(5): 3–8.

— (1976) 'Achievements, problems and prospects in the agricultural sector', in Judith Heyer, J. K. Maitha and W. M. Senga (eds), *Agricultural Development in Kenya; an economic assessment*, Nairobi: Oxford University Press, pp. 1–31.

Higgins, Benjamin (1968) *Economic Development; problems, principles, and policies*, 2nd edn, New York: W. W. Norton.

Hill, Hal (1996a) *The Indonesian Economy since 1966; Southeast Asia's emerging giant*, Cambridge: Cambridge University Press.

— (1996b) 'Indonesia's industrial policy and performance: "orthodoxy" vindicated', *Economic Development and Cultural Change*, 45(1): 147–74.

— (1997) 'Towards a political economy explanation of rapid growth in ASEAN; a survey and analysis', *ASEAN Economic Bulletin*, 14(2): 131–49.

— (2000a) 'Export success against the odds: a Vietnamese case study', *World Development*, 28(2): 283–300.

— (2000b) *The Indonesian Economy*, 2nd edn, Cambridge: Cambridge University Press.

Hill, Hal and Thee Kian Wie (2008) 'Moh. Sadli (1922–2008), economist, minister and public intellectual', *Bulletin of Indonesian Economic Studies*, 44(1): 151–6.

Hofstede, Geert and Michael Harris Bond (1988) 'The Confucius connection: from cultural roots to economic growth', *Organizational Dynamics*, 16(4): 5–21.

Holmén, Hans (2005) 'Spurts in production – Africa's limping Green Revolution', in Göran Djurfeldt, Hans Holmén, Magnus Jirström and Rolf Larsson (eds), *The African Food Crisis; lessons from the Asian Green Revolution*, Wallingford: CABI Publishing, pp. 65–85.

Hope, Nicholas C. (2007) 'In terms of the practice of political economy, he has no peer in the period since the Second World War', in Moh. Arsjad Anwar, Aris Ananta and Ari Kuncoro (eds), *Tributes for Widjojo Nitisastro by Friends from 27 Foreign Countries*, Jakarta: Kompas, pp. 225–33.

Husain, Ishrat (1991) 'How did the Asian countries avoid the debt crisis?', World Bank Policy, Research, and External Affairs Working Paper WPS 785, Washington, DC: International Economics Department, World Bank.

Hyden, Goran (1980) *Beyond Ujamaa in Tanzania; underdevelopment and an uncaptured peasantry*, Berkeley: University of California Press.

— (1983) *No Shortcuts to Progress; African development management in perspective*, London: Heinemann.

Ikiara, Gerrishon K. (1998) 'Rising to the challenge: the private sector response in Kenya', in Pekka Seppälä (ed.), *Liberalized and Neglected? Food marketing policies in Eastern Africa*, World Development Studies 12, Helsinki: United Nations University World Institute for Development Economics Research (UNU/WIDER), pp. 94–118.

ILO (International Labour Office) (1972) *Employment, Incomes and Equality; a strategy for increasing productive employment in Kenya*, Geneva: ILO.

Ilorah, Richard (2006) 'Measuring producer benefits of price stabilization in the Nigerian primary sector: history revisited', *African Development Review*, 18: 30–41.

IMF (International Monetary Fund) (2005) *Historical Government Finance Statistics (1972–1989 in GFSM 1986 format)*, Washington, DC: International Monetary Fund Statistics Department (data CD).

Imoagene, Oshomha (1976) *Social Mobility in Emergent Society; a study of the new elite in western Nigeria*, Changing African Family Project Series, Monograph 2, Canberra: Department of Demography, Australian National University.

Ingram, James C. (1971) *Economic Change in Thailand 1850–1970*, 2nd edn, Stanford, CA: Stanford University Press.

Irvin, George (1995) 'Vietnam: assessing the achievements of *doi moi*', *Journal of Development Studies*, 31(5): 725–50.

Jaspersen, Frederick Z., Anthony H. Aylward and A. David Knox (2000) 'Risk and private investment: Africa compared with other developing areas', in Paul Collier and Catherine Pattillo (eds), *Reducing the Risk of Investment in Africa*, Basingstoke: Macmillan, pp. 71–95.

Jayasankaran, S. (1993) 'Made-in-Malaysia: the Proton project', in K. S. Jomo (ed.), *Industrialising Malaysia; policy, performance, prospects*, London: Routledge, pp. 272–85.

Jayne, Thomas S., Robert J. Myers and James Nyoro (2008) 'The effects of

NCPB marketing policies on maize market prices in Kenya', *Agricultural Economics*, 38(3): 313–25.

Jenkins, Glenn P. and Andrew Lai (1989) *Trade, Exchange Rate, and Agricultural Pricing Policies in Malaysia*, Washington, DC: World Bank.

Jesudason, James V. (1989) *Ethnicity and the Economy; the state, Chinese business, and multinationals in Malaysia*, Singapore: Oxford University Press.

Johnson, Simon, Jonathan D. Ostry and Arvind Subramaniam (2007) 'The prospects for sustained growth in Africa: benchmarking the constraints', IMF Working Paper 07/52, Washington, DC: International Monetary Fund.

Jomo, K. S. (1997) *Southeast Asia's Misunderstood Miracle*, Boulder, CO: Westview Press.

Jomo, K. S. and Michael Rock (2003) 'Resource exports and resource processing for export in Southeast Asia', in Ernest Aryeetey, Julius Court, Machiko Nissanke and Beatrice Weber (eds), *Africa and Asia in the Global Economy*, Tokyo: United Nations University Press, pp. 128–74.

Jones, Catherine (1993) 'The Pacific challenge; Confucian welfare states', in Catherine Jones (ed.), *New Perspectives on the Welfare State in Europe*, London: Routledge, pp. 198–217.

Kagame, Paul (2009) 'The backbone of a new Rwanda', in Michael Fairbanks, Malik Fal, Marcela Escobari-Rose and Elizabeth Hooper (eds), *In the River They Swim; essays from around the world on enterprise solutions to poverty*, West Conshohocken, PA: Templeton Press, pp. 11–14.

Kaji, Gautam (2007) 'His role, the World Bank and Indonesia's development: a study in partnership', in Moh. Arsjad Anwar, Aris Ananta and Ari Kuncoro (eds), *Tributes for Widjojo Nitisastro by Friends from 27 Foreign Countries*, Jakarta: Kompas, pp. 245–50.

Kang, Kenneth and Vijaya Ramachandran (1999) 'Economic transformation in Korea: rapid growth without an agricultural revolution?', *Economic Development and Cultural Change*, 47(4): 783–801.

Karshenas, Massoud (1995) *Industrialization and Agricultural Surplus; a comparative study of economic development in Asia*, Oxford: Oxford University Press.

— (1998) *Capital Accumulation and Agricultural Surplus in Sub-Saharan Africa and Asia*, Geneva: United Nations Conference on Trade and Development (UNCTAD/GDS/MDPB/Misc.1).

— (2001) 'Agriculture and economic development in Sub-Saharan Africa and Asia', *Cambridge Journal of Economics*, 25(3): 315–42.

Kayode, Femi and Dafe Otobo (eds) (2004) *Allison Akene Ayida; Nigeria's quintessential public servant*, Lagos: Malthouse Press.

Kelsall, Tim (2013) *Business, Politics and the State in Africa; challenging the orthodoxies on growth and transformation*, London: Zed Books.

Kenya Vision (2007) *Kenya Vision 2030; a competitive and prosperous Kenya*, Nairobi: Government of the Republic of Kenya.

Kerkvliet, Benedict J. Tria (2005) *The Power of Everyday Politics; how Vietnamese peasants transformed national policy*, Singapore: ISEAS Publications.

Keyfitz, Nathan (2007) 'I will always be proud of having his friendship', in Moh. Arsjad Anwar, Aris Ananta and Ari Kuncoro (eds), *Tributes for Widjojo Nitisastro by Friends from 27 Foreign Countries*, Jakarta: Kompas, pp. 33–8.

Khan, Mushtaq H. (2007) 'Governance, economic growth and development since the 1960s', DESA Working Paper 54, New York: United Nations Department of Economic and Social Affairs.

Khan, Mushtaq H. and K. S. Jomo (eds) (2000) *Rents, Rent-seeking and Economic Development; theory and evidence in Asia*, Cambridge: Cambridge University Press.

Kilama, Blandina (2013) 'The diverging South; comparing the cashew sectors of Tanzania and Vietnam', PhD thesis, Leiden University.

Kimura, Fukunari (2004) 'New development strategies under globalization: foreign direct investment and international commercial policy in Southeast Asia', in Akira Kohsaka (ed.), *New Development Strategies; beyond the Washington Consensus*, Basingstoke: Palgrave Macmillan, pp. 115–33.

Kinuthia, Bethuel Kinyanjui (2010) 'Poverty reduction in Malaysia', *Journal of Poverty Alleviation and International Development*, 1(1): 55–79.

— (2013) 'Reversed fortunes in the south; a comparison of the role of FDI in industrial development in Kenya and Malaysia', PhD thesis, Leiden University.

Kono Yasuyuki (2001) 'Canal development and intensification of rice cultivation in the Mekong Delta: a case study in Cantho province, Vietnam', *Southeast Asian Studies*, 39(1): 70–85.

Kramnick, Isaac and Barry Sheerman (1993) *Harold Laski; a life on the Left*, London: Hamish Hamilton.

Krugman, Paul (1991) *Geography and Trade*, Cambridge, MA: MIT Press.

Kuznets, Simon (1955) 'Economic growth and income inequality', *American Economic Review*, 45(1): 1–28.

Lawrence, Peter and Colin Thirtle (eds) (2001) *Africa and Asia in Comparative Economic Perspective*, Basingstoke: Palgrave.

Leavey, Edmond H. et al. (1963) *The Economic Development of Kenya; report of a mission organized by the International Bank for Reconstruction and Development at the request of the governments of Kenya and the United Kingdom*, Baltimore, MD: Johns Hopkins University Press.

Lee, E. (1976) 'Rural poverty in West Malaysia, 1957 to 1970', World Employment Programme Research, Working Paper WEP 10-6/WP 2, Geneva: International Labour Office.

Leliveld, André and Han ten Brummelhuis (2013) 'Agricultural policies and performance in an African and an Asian poor agrarian society: Uganda and Cambodia compared', in Bernard Berendsen, Ton Dietz, Henk Schulte Northolt and Roel van der Veen (eds), *Asian Tigers, African Lions; comparing the development performance of Southeast Asia and Africa*, Leiden: Brill, pp. 417–52.

Leo, Christopher (1978) 'The failure of the "progressive farmer" in Kenya's Million-Acre Settlement Scheme', *Journal of Modern African Studies*, 16(4): 619–38.

Leonard, David K. (1991) *African Successes; four public managers of Kenyan rural development*, Berkeley: University of California Press.

Lewis, Peter M. (2007) *Growing Apart; oil, politics, and economic change in Indonesia and Nigeria*, Ann Arbor: University of Michigan Press.

Lewis, W. Arthur (1954) 'Economic development with unlimited supplies of labour', *Manchester School of Economic and Social Studies*, 22(2): 139–91.

— (1980) 'Autobiographical note', *Social and Economic Studies* (University of the West Indies, Kingston), 29(4): 1–4.

Leys, Colin (1975) *Underdevelopment in Kenya; the political economy of neo-colonialism, 1964–1971*, London: Heinemann.

Lim Chong-Yah (1967) *Economic Development of Modern Malaya*, Kuala Lumpur: Oxford University Press.

Lindauer, David L. and Michael Roemer

(eds) (1994) *Asia and Africa; legacies and opportunities in development*, California: Institute for Contemporary Studies Press.

Lipton, Michael (1977) *Why Poor People Stay Poor; a study of urban bias in world development*, London: Temple Smith.

Losch, Bruno (2012) *Agriculture: The key to the employment challenge*, Development Strategies Perspective 19, October, Paris: CIRAD Agricultural Research for Development.

Macintyre, Andrew (2000) 'Funny money: fiscal policy, rent-seeking and economic performance in Indonesia', in Mushtaq H. Khan and Jomo Kwame Sundaram (eds), *Rents, Rent-seeking and Economic Development; theory and evidence in Asia*, Cambridge: Cambridge University Press, pp. 248–73.

— (2001) 'Investment, property rights, and corruption in Indonesia', in J. Edgardo Campos (ed.), *Corruption; the boom and bust of East Asia*, Quezon City: Ateneo de Manila University Press, pp. 25–44.

Mahbubani, Kishore (1998) *Can Asians Think?*, Singapore: Times Books International.

Maier, Karl (2000) *This House Has Fallen; midnight in Nigeria*, New York: Public Affairs.

Malinowski, B. (1938) 'Introduction', in Jomo Kenyatta, *Facing Mount Kenya; the tribal life of the Gikuyu*, London: Secker and Warburg, pp. vii–xiv.

Mamdani, Mahmood (1996) *Citizen and Subject; contemporary Africa and the legacy of late colonialism*, London: James Currey.

Manning, Chris (1998) *Indonesian Labour in Transition; an East Asian success story?*, Cambridge: Cambridge University Press.

Masselman, George (1963) *The Cradle of Colonialism*, New Haven, CT: Yale University Press.

Masters, Edward (2007) 'Holding a unique team in the world which has completely turned around the economy of the fourth most populous nation', in Moh. Arsjad Anwar, Aris Ananta and Ari Kuncoro (eds), *Tributes for Widjojo Nitisastro by Friends from 27 Foreign Countries*, Jakarta: Kompas, pp. 67–9.

Mazumdar, Dipak (1993) 'Labor markets and adjustment in open Asian economies: the Republic of Korea and Malaysia', *World Bank Economic Review*, 7(3): 349–80.

McCawley, Peter (2007) 'One of the most effective anti-poverty programs ever implemented in any country in the world', in Moh. Arsjad Anwar, Aris Ananta and Ari Kuncoro (eds), *Tributes for Widjojo Nitisastro by Friends from 27 Foreign Countries*, Jakarta: Kompas, pp. 89–97.

McKendrik, David (1992) 'Obstacles to "catch-up": the case of the Indonesian aircraft industry', *Bulletin of Indonesian Economic Studies*, 28(1): 39–66.

McKinsey Global Institute (2010) *Lions on the Move: The progress and potential of African economies*, McKinsey Global Institute.

McLeod, Ross H. (2000) 'Soeharto's Indonesia: a better class of corruption', *Agenda; a Journal of Policy Analysis and Reform*, 7(2): 99–112.

McNeil, Mary and Carmen Malena (eds) (2010) *Demanding Good Governance; lessons from social accountability initiatives in Africa*, Washington, DC: World Bank.

McNicoll, Geoffrey (2011) 'Achievers and laggards in demographic transition: a comparision of Indonesia and Nigeria', *Population and Development Review*, 37(supplement): 191–214.

Mellor, John W. (ed.) (1995) *Agriculture on the Road to Industrialization*, Baltimore, MD: Johns Hopkins University Press.

Meredith, Martin (2005) *The State of Africa; a history of fifty years of independence*, London: Free Press.

Mkandawire, Thandika (2001) 'Thinking about developmental states in Africa', *Cambridge Journal of Economics*, 25: 289–313.

Montalvo, Jose G. and Marta Reynal-Querol (2005) 'Ethnic diversity and economic development', *Journal of Development Economics*, 76: 293–323.

Morfit, Michael (1986) 'Strengthening the capacities of local government: policies and constraints', in Colin MacAndrews (ed.), *Central Government and Local Development in Indonesia*, Singapore: Oxford University Press, pp. 56–76.

Morrissey, Oliver (2001) 'Lessons for Africa from East Asian economic policy', in Peter Lawrence and Colin Thirtle (eds), *Africa and Asia in Comparative Economic Perspective*, Basingstoke: Palgrave, pp. 34–48.

Morton, Andrew (1998) *Moi; the making of an African statesman*, London: Michael O'Mara Books.

Mosely, Paul (2002) 'The African green revolution as a pro-poor policy instrument', *Journal of International Development*, 14(6): 695–724.

Moynihan, Martin J. (1964) 'Ops. Room technique', *Public Administration*, 42(4): 391–414.

Moyo, Dambisa (2009) *Dead Aid; why aid is not working and how there is a better way for Africa*, New York: Farrar, Straus and Giroux.

Murray-Brown, Jeremy (1972) *Kenyatta*, London: George Allen and Unwin.

Muscat, Robert J. (1994) *The Fifth Tiger; a study of Thai development policy*, New York: United Nations University Press.

Mwabu, Germano and Eric Thorbecke (2004) 'Rural development, growth and poverty in Africa', *Journal of African Economies*, 13, AERC Supplement 1: i16–i65.

Mwakikagile, Godfrey (2002) *Nyerere and Africa: End of an era; biography of Julius Kambarage Nyerere (1922–1999), president of Tanzania*, Atlanta, GA: Protea Publishing.

Mwase, Nkunde and Benno J. Ndulu (2008) 'Tanzania: explaining four decades of episodic growth', in Benno J. Ndulu, Stephen A. O'Connell, Robert H. Bates, Paul Collier and Chukwuma C. Soludo (eds), *The Political Economy of Economic Growth in Africa 1960–2000*, vol. 2: *Country Case Studies*, Cambridge: Cambridge University Press, pp. 426–70.

Myrdal, Gunnar (1968) *Asian Drama; an inquiry into the poverty of nations*, New York: Twentieth Century Fund/Random House.

Nabli, Mustapha Kamel (2008) *Breaking the Barriers to Higher Economic Growth; better governance and deeper reforms in the Middle East and North Africa*, Washington, DC: World Bank.

Nai Peng Tey (2007) 'The family planning program in peninsular Malaysia', in Warren C. Robinson and John A. Ross (eds), *The Global Family Planning Revolution; three decades of population policies and programs*, Washington, DC: World Bank, pp. 257–76.

National Development Plan 1962–68 (1962) *National Development Plan 1962–68*, Lagos: Federal Ministry of Economic Development, Federation of Nigeria.

National Irrigation and Drainage Policy (2009) *National Irrigation and Drainage Policy*, Nairobi: Ministry of Water and Irrigation, Republic of Kenya.

NBS (2012) *Nigeria Poverty Profile 2010*, Abuja: National Bureau of Statistics.

Ndulu, Benno J., Lopamudra Chakraborti, Lebohang Lijane, Vijaya Ramachandran and Jerome Wolgin (2007) *Challenges of African Growth: Opportunities, constraints and strategic directions*, Washington, DC: World Bank.

Ndulu, Benno J., Stephen A. O'Connell, Robert H. Bates, Paul Collier, Chukwuma C. Soludo, Jean-Paul Azam, Augustin K. Fosu, Jan Willem Gunning and Dominique Njinkeu (eds) (2008) *The Political Economy of Economic Growth in Africa, 1960–2000*, 2 vols, Cambridge: Cambridge University Press.

NEEDS (2004) *National Economic Empowerment and Development Strategy; NEEDS*, Abuja: National Planning Commission, Federal Republic of Nigeria.

Nelson, Richard R. (1956) 'A theory of the low-level equilibrium trap in underdeveloped economies', *American Economic Review*, 46: 894–908.

NEPAD (New Partnership for Africa's Development) (2010) 'Implementing CAADP for Africa's food security needs: a progress report on selected activities', New Partnership for Africa's Development (African Union) briefing paper, July.

Ness, Gayl D. (1967) *Bureaucracy and Rural Development in Malaysia; a study of complex organisations in stimulating economic development in new states*, Berkeley: University of California Press.

Nguyen Do Anh Tuan (2006) *Agricultural Surplus and Industrialization in Vietnam since the Country's Reunification*, PhD thesis, Institute of Social Studies, The Hague, Maastricht: Shaker Publishing.

Nguyen Hoa and Ulrike Grote (2004) 'Agricultural policies in Vietnam: producer support estimates, 1986–2002', ZEF Discussion Papers on Development Policy 93, Bonn: Zentrum für Entwicklungsforschung, Universität Bonn.

Nguyen Thang, Le Dang Trung, Vu Hoang Dat and Nguyen Thu Phuong (2006) 'Poverty, poverty reduction and poverty dynamics in Vietnam', background paper for the Chronic Poverty Report 2008–09, Manchester: Chronic Poverty Research Centre.

Nin-Pratt, Alejandro, Michael Johnson and Bingxin Yu (2012) 'Improved performance of agriculture in Sub-Saharan Africa: taking off or bouncing back?', IFPRI Discussion Paper 01224, Washington, DC: International Food Policy Research Institute.

Nissanke, Machiko and Ernest Aryeetey (eds) (2003a) *Comparative Development Experiences of Sub-Saharan Africa and East Asia; an institutional approach*, Aldershot: Ashgate.

— (2003b) 'Comparative institutional analysis: Sub-Saharan Africa and East Asia', in Machiko Nissanke and Ernest Aryeetey (eds), *Comparative Development Experiences of Sub-Saharan Africa and East Asia*, Aldershot: Ashgate, pp. 30–70.

North, Douglass C. (1990) *Institutions, Institutional Change and Economic Performance*, Cambridge: Cambridge University Press.

Nottidge, C. P. R. and J. R. Goldsack (1966) *The Million-Acre Settlement Scheme 1962–1966*, Nairobi: Department of Settlement, Republic of Kenya.

Nyagetera, Bartholomew M. (2001) 'Malaysian economic development: some lessons from Tanzania', *Utafiti; Journal of the Faculty of Arts and Social Sciences, University of Dar es Salaam* (new series), 4: 1–30.

Nyerere, Julius K. (1979) 'The Arusha Declaration ten years after', in Andrew Coulson (ed.), *African Socialism in Practice; the Tanzanian experience*, Nottingham: Spokesman, pp. 43–71.

O'Brien, F. S. and Terry C. I. Ryan (2001) 'Kenya', in Shantayanan Devarajan, David R. Dollar and Torgny Holmgren (eds), *Aid and Reform in Africa; lessons from ten case studies*, Washington, DC: World Bank, pp. 469–532.

OECD (Organisation for Economic Co-operation and Development) (2011) *African Economic Outlook 2011; special theme: Africa and its emerging partners*, Paris: OECD Publishing.

Ojo, Onukaba Adinoyi (1997) *In the Eyes of Time; a biography of Olusegun Obasanjo (former Nigerian leader and one of Africa's most revered statesmen)*, New York: Africana Legacy Press.

Okolie, Andrew C. (1995) 'Oil rents, international loans and agrarian policies in Nigeria, 1970–1992', *Review of African Political Economy*, 64: 199–212.

Olaopa, Tunji (1997) *A Prophet is with Honour: The life and times of Oletunji Aboyade*, Ibadan: Fountain Publications.

Olomola, Ade S. (1995) 'Sources of growth and performance trends in Nigeria's agriculture, 1960–1992', in Anthony E. Ikpi and Joseph K. Olayemi (eds), *Sustainable Agriculture and Economic Development in Nigeria*, Arlington, VA: Winrock International Institute for Agricultural Development, pp. 97–101.

Olson, Mancur (2000) *Power and Prosperity; outgrowing communist and capitalist dictatorships*, New York: Basic Books.

Oluoch-Kosura, Willis and Joseph T. Karugia (2005) 'Why the early promise for rapid increases in maize productivity in Kenya was not sustained: lessons for sustainable investment in agriculture', in Göran Djurfeldt, Hans Holmén, Magnus Jirström and Rolf Larsson (eds), *The African Food Crisis; lessons from the Asian Green Revolution*, Wallingford: CABI Publishing, pp. 181–96.

Omilola, Babatunde, Mbaye Yade, Joseph Karugia and Pius Chilonda (2010) 'Monitoring and assessing targets of the Comprehensive Africa Agriculture Development Programme (CAADP) and the Millennium Development Goals (MDG) in Africa', ReSAKSS Working Paper 31, Washington, DC: Regional Strategic Analysis and Knowledge Support System, International Food Policy Research Institute.

Onyeiwu, Steve and Hemanta Shrestha (2004) 'Determinants of foreign direct investment in Africa', *Journal of Developing Societies*, 20(1/2): 89–106.

Orubu, Christopher O. (1995) 'Anti-inflation policy in Nigeria: pre- and post-adjustment', *Nigerian Journal of Economic and Social Studies*, 38(2): 111–28.

Osaghae, Eghosa E., Victor A. Isumonah and Isaac O. Albert (1998) *Liberalization Policies and the Changing Structures of Legitimacy in Nigeria*, Ibadan: NISER.

Oshima, Harry T. (1987) *Economic Growth in Monsoon Asia; a comparative survey*, Tokyo: University of Tokyo Press.

Othman, Aris bin (1984) 'Growth, equality and poverty in Malaysia, 1957–80', PhD thesis, Boston University (reproduced by University Microfilms International, Ann Arbor, Michigan, 1986).

Otsuka, Keijiro and Kaliappa P. Kalirajan (2006) 'Rice Green Revolution in Asia and its transferability to Africa: an introduction', *The Developing Economies*, 44(2): 107–22.

Ouédraogo, Alpha and Dominique Gentil (eds) (2008) *La Microfinance en Afrique de l'Ouest; histoires et innovations*, Paris: Karthala.

Parkinson, Brien K. (1967) 'Non-economic factors in the economic retardation of the rural Malays', *Modern Asian Studies*, 1(1): 31–46.

Peacock, Frank (1981) 'Rural poverty and development in West Malaysia (1957–70)', *Journal of Developing Areas*, 15(4): 639–54.

People's Plan for Progress (1969) *The*

*People's Plan for Progress; a popular version of the Second Five Year Plan for Economic and Social Development, 1969–1974*, Dar es Salaam: Republic of Tanzania.

Phang, Sock-Yong (2007) 'The Singapore model of housing and the welfare state', in Richard Groves, Alan Murie and Christopher Watson (eds), *Housing and the New Welfare State; perspectives from East Asia and Europe*, Aldershot: Ashgate, pp. 15–44.

Phongpaichit, Pasuk and Chris Baker (2009) *Thaksin*, 2nd edn, Chiang Mai: Silkworm.

Pick's Currency Yearbook (1955–79) *Pick's Currency Yearbook*, New York: Pick Publishing Corporation.

Pingali, Prabhu L. and Vo-Tong Xuan (1992) 'Vietnam: decollectivization and rice productivity growth', *Economic Development and Cultural Change*, 40(4): 697–718.

Pinto, Brian (1987) 'Nigeria during and after the oil boom: a policy comparison with Indonesia', *World Bank Economic Review*, 1: 419–45.

Plan of Development (1956) *A Plan of Development for Malaya 1956–60*, Kuala Lumpur: Economic Secretariat, Federation of Malaya.

Platteau, Jean-Philippe (2000) *Institutions, Social Norms, and Economic Development*, Amsterdam: Harwood Academic.

Pletcher, James (1989) 'Rice and padi market management in West Malaysia, 1957–1986', *Journal of Developing Areas*, 23(3): 363–84.

— (1991) 'Regulation with growth: the political economy of palm oil in Malaysia', *World Development*, 19(6): 623–36.

Posner, Daniel N. (2004) 'Measuring ethnic fractionalization in Africa', *American Journal of Political Science*, 48(4): 849–63.

Poulton, Colin (2012) 'Democratisation and the political economy of agricultural policy in Africa', Future Agricultures Working Paper 43, Africa Power and Politics Programme, London: Future Agricultures Consortium.

Prawiro, Radius (1998) *Indonesia's Struggle for Economic Development; pragmatism in action*, Kuala Lumpur: Oxford University Press.

Preston, David A. (1989) 'Too busy to farm: under-utilisation of farm land in Central Java', *Journal of Development Studies*, 26(1): 43–57.

Radelet, Steven (2010) *Emerging Africa; how 17 countries are leading the way*, Washington, DC: Center for Global Development.

Rajah Rasiah (1993) 'Free Trade Zones and industrial development in Malaysia', in K. S. Jomo (ed.), *Industrialising Malaysia; policy, performance, prospects*, London: Routledge, pp. 118–46.

Ramli Mohamed (1988) 'The New Economic Policy and the Muda irrigation scheme: research agenda for Kampung Kubang Jawi', *Southeast Asian Studies*, 26(2): 205–17.

Ravallion, Martin and Shaohua Chen (2007) 'China's (uneven) progress against poverty', *Journal of Development Economics*, 82: 1–42.

Redding, S. Gordon (1993) *The Spirit of Chinese Capitalism*, Berlin: Walter de Gruyter.

Reeve, David (1985) *Golkar of Indonesia; an alternative to the party system*, Oxford: Oxford University Press.

Reno, William (1995) *Corruption and State Politics in Sierra Leone*, Cambridge: Cambridge University Press.

Report of the Maize Commission (1966) *Report of the Maize Commission of Inquiry, June 1966*, Nairobi: Republic of Kenya.

Republic of Rwanda (2013) 'Rwanda's parliament approves revised budget for fiscal year 2012/13', www.gov.rw/Rwanda-s-Parliament-Approves-Revised-Budget-for-fiscal-year-2012-

13?lang=en, accessed 14 February
2013.

ReSAKSS (Regional Strategic Analysis
and Knowledge Support System)
(2011) *Monitoring African agricul-
tural development processes and
performance: a comparative analysis*,
Regional Strategic Analysis and
Knowledge Support System, Africa
Wide Annual Trends and Outlook
Report 2010, Washington, DC:
International Food Policy Research
Institute.

Resosudarmo, Budy P. and Ari Kuncoro
(2006) 'The political economy of
Indonesian economic reforms:
1983–2000', *Oxford Development
Studies*, 34(3): 341–55.

Rieffel, Alexis (1969) 'The Bimas program
for self-sufficiency in rice production', *Indonesia*, 8: 103–33.

Rigg, Jonathan (2001) *More than the Soil;
rural change in Southeast Asia*, Harlow:
Pearson Education/Prentice Hall.

— (2003) *Southeast Asia; the human
landscape of modernization and development*, 2nd edn, London: Routledge.

Rimmer, Douglas (1985) 'The overvalued
currency and over-administered
economy of Nigeria', *African Affairs*,
84(336): 435–46.

Roberts, John and Sonja Fagernäs (2004)
'Why is Bangladesh outperforming
Kenya? A comparative study of
growth and its causes since the 1960s',
ESAU Working Paper 5, London: Eco-
nomics and Statistics Analysis Unit,
Overseas Development Institute.

Robertson, A. F. (1975) 'A new kind of
Malaysian? A sociological view of
the Federal Land Development
Authority', *Journal of Administration
Overseas*, 14(1): 30–8.

Robinson, James A., Ragnar Torvik and
Thierry Verdier (2006) 'Political
foundations of the resource curse',
*Journal of Development Economics*,
79(2): 447–68.

Robinson, Marguerite S. (2001) *The

Microfinance Revolution; sustainable
finance for the poor*, Washington, DC:
World Bank.

— (2002) *The Microfinance Revolution*,
vol. 2: *Lessons from Indonesia*, Washington, DC: World Bank.

Robison, Richard and Vedi R. Hadiz
(2004) *Reorganising Power in Indonesia; the politics of oligarchy in an
age of markets*, London: Routledge.

Rock, Michael T. (1995) 'Thai industrial
policy: how irrelevant was it to export success?', *Journal of International
Development*, 7(5): 745–57.

— (1999) 'Reassessing the effectiveness
of industrial policy in Indonesia: can
the neoliberals be wrong?', *World
Development*, 27(4): 691–704.

— (2002) 'Exploring the impact of
selective interventions in agriculture
on the growth of manufactures in
Indonesia, Malaysia, and Thailand',
*Journal of International Development*,
14(4): 485–510.

Rodrik, Dani (2003) 'Introduction', in
Dani Rodrik (ed.), *In Search of Prosperity; analytic narratives of economic
growth*, Princeton, NJ: Princeton
University Press, pp. 1–19.

— (2007) *One Economics, Many
Recipes; globalization, institutions,
and economic growth*, Princeton, NJ:
Princeton University Press.

— (2008) 'Second-best institutions',
*American Economic Review*, 98(2):
100–4.

Rodrik, Dani, Arvind Subramaniam and
Francesco Trebbi (2004) 'Institutions
rule: the primacy of institutions
over geography and integration in
economic development', *Journal of
Economic Growth*, 9(2): 131–65.

Roeder, O. G. (1969) *The Smiling General;
President Soeharto of Indonesia*,
Jakarta: Gunung Agung.

Roemer, Michael (1994) 'Industrial
strategies: outward bound', in David
L. Lindauer and Michael Roemer
(eds), *Asia and Africa; legacies and

opportunities in development, San Francisco, CA: Institute for Contemporary Studies Press, pp. 233–68.

Rosovsky, Henry (2007) 'I marvel at his accomplishments and salute a model economist: an example to all developing countries', in Moh. Arsjad Anwar, Aris Ananta and Ari Kuncoro (eds), *Tributes for Widjojo Nitisastro by Friends from 27 Foreign Countries*, Jakarta: Kompas, pp. 39–42.

Rosser, Andrew (2007) 'Escaping the re-source curse: the case of Indonesia', *Journal of Contemporary Asia*, 37(1): 38–58.

Rostow, W. W. (1960) *The Stages of Economic Growth; a non-communist manifesto*, Cambridge: Cambridge University Press.

Rudner, Martin (1994) *Malaysian Development; a retrospective*, Ottawa: Carleton University Press.

Sachs, Jeffrey D. (2000) 'Tropical underdevelopment', CID Working Paper 57, Cambridge, MA: Center for International Development at Harvard University.

Sadli, Mohammad (1960) 'Structural and operational aspects of public (especially industrial) enterprises in Indonesia', *Ekonomi dan Keuangan Indonesia*, 8(5/6): 227–53.

— (1993) 'Recollections of my career', *Bulletin of Indonesian Economic Studies*, 29(1): 35–51.

— (1997) 'Technocratic decision making in economic policy', in Moh. Arsjad Anwar, Aris Ananta and Ari Kuncoro (eds), *Widjojo Nitisastro 70 tahun; pembangunan nasional: teori, kebijakan, dan pelaksanaan*, vol. 1, Jakarta: Fakultas Ekonomi Universitas Indonesia, pp. 241–52.

Sahasakul, Chaipat, Nattapong Thongpakde and Keokam Kraisoraphung (1991) 'Thailand', in Paul Mosley, Jane Harrigan and John Toye (eds), *Aid and Power; the World Bank and policy-based lending*, vol. 2, London: Routledge, pp. 72–149.

Sala-i-Martin, Xavier and Maxim Pinkovskiy (2010) 'African poverty is falling ... much faster than you think!', NBER Working Paper 15775, Cambridge, MA: National Bureau of Economic Research.

Salim, Emil (1997) 'Recollections of my career', *Bulletin of Indonesian Economic Studies*, 33(1): 45–74.

— (2011) 'Foreword', in Emil Salim (ed.), *The Indonesian Development Experience; a collection of writings and speeches of Widjojo Nitisastro*, Singapore: ISEAS Publishing.

Schein, Edgar H. (1996) *Strategic Pragmatism; the culture of Singapore's Economic Development Board*, Cambridge, MA: MIT Press.

Scherr, Sara J. (1989) 'Agriculture in an export boom economy: a comparative analysis of policy and performance in Indonesia, Mexico and Nigeria', *World Development*, 17(4): 543–60.

Schmit, Leonardus Theodorus (1991) *Rural Credit between Subsidy and Market; adjustment of the village units of Bank Rakyat Indonesia in sociological perspective*, Leiden Development Studies, 11, Leiden: Vakgroep Culturele Antropologie en Sociologie der Niet-Westerse Samenlevingen, Rijksuniversiteit Leiden.

Schultz, T. Paul (2001) 'The fertility transition: economic explanations', Center Discussion Paper 833, New Haven, CT: Economic Growth Center, Yale University.

Schweizer, Thomas (1989) 'Economic individualism and the community spirit: divergent orientation patterns of Javanese villagers in rice production and the ritual sphere', *Modern Asian Studies*, 23(2): 277–312.

Scott, James C. (1972) 'Patron–client politics and political change in

Southeast Asia', *American Political Science Review*, 66(1): 91–113.

— (1985) *Weapons of the Weak; everyday forms of peasant resistance*, New Haven, CT: Yale University Press.

— (1998) *Seeing like a State; how certain schemes to improve the human condition have failed*, New Haven, CT: Yale University Press.

Second Five-Year Development Plan (1974) *The Second Five-Year Development Plan (1974/75–1978/79)*, vol. 1, Jakarta: Department of Information, Republic of Indonesia.

Second Five-Year Plan (1961) *Second Five-Year Plan 1961–1965*, Kuala Lumpur: Government Press, Federation of Malaya.

Second Five-Year Plan (1969) *Second Five-Year Plan for economic and social development, 1st July, 1969–30th June, 1974*, Dar es Salaam: United Republic of Tanzania.

Second Malaysia Plan (1971) *Second Malaysia Plan 1971–1975*, Kuala Lumpur: Government Press.

Second National Development Plan (1970) *Second National Development Plan 1970–74; programme of post-war reconstruction and development*, Lagos: Federal Republic of Nigeria.

Second National Economic and Social Development Plan (1967) *Second National Economic and Social Development Plan (1967–71)*, Bangkok: National Economic Development Board, Office of the Prime Minister, Government of Thailand.

Sen, Amartya K. (1977) 'Rational fools: a critique of the behavioral foundations of economic theory', *Philosophy and Public Affairs*, 6(4): 317–44.

Shamsul Bahrin, Tunku and P. D. A. Perera (1977) *FELDA 21 Years of Land Development*, Kuala Lumpur: FELDA.

Shaw, William (1976) *Tun Razak; his life and times*, London: Longman.

Shigetomi, Shinichi (2004) 'Four decades of development in Thailand's rural

sector and the role of government', in Takamasa Akiyama and Donald F. Larson (eds), *Rural Development and Agricultural Growth in Indonesia, the Philippines and Thailand*, Canberra: Asia Pacific Press, pp. 294–379.

Siamwalla, Ammar, Suthad Setboonsarng and Direk Patamasiriwat (1993) 'Agriculture', in Peter G. Warr (ed.), *The Thai Economy in Transition*, Cambridge: Cambridge University Press, pp. 81–117.

Siber, Kemal (2007) 'Indonesia's economic crisis management 1966–1969', in Moh. Arsjad Anwar, Aris Ananta and Ari Kuncoro (eds), *Tributes for Widjojo Nitisastro by Friends from 27 Foreign Countries*, Jakarta: Kompas, pp. 99–119.

Simatupang, Batara (1996) 'Economic transformation and liberalization in Indonesia', in Alex E. Fernández Jilberto and André Mommen (eds), *Liberalization in the Developing World; institutional and economic changes in Latin America, Africa and Asia*, London: Routledge, pp. 51–71.

Siriprachai, Somboon (2007) 'Thailand', in Anis Chowdhuri and Iyanatul Islam (eds), *Handbook on the Northeast and Southeast Asian Economies*, Cheltenham: Edward Elgar, pp. 129–48.

Sivalingam, G. (1993) *Malaysia's Agricultural Transformation*, Petaling Jaya: Pelanduk.

Slater, Dan (2010) *Ordering Power; contentious politics and authoritarian leviathans in Southeast Asia*, Cambridge: Cambridge University Press.

Snodgrass, Donald (1980) *Inequality and Economic Development in Malaysia*, Kuala Lumpur: Oxford University Press.

Soeharto (1991) *My Thoughts, Words and Deeds; an autobiography as told to G. Dwipayana and Ramadhan K. H.*, Jakarta: Citra Lamtoro Gung Persada.

Soludo, Charles Chukwuma (2003) 'Export-oriented industrialisation and foreign direct investment in Africa', in Ernest Aryeetey, Julius Court, Machiko Nissanke and Beatrice Weber (eds), *Africa and Asia in the Global Economy*, Tokyo: United Nations University Press, pp. 246–81.

Stein, Howard (ed.) (1995a) *Asian Industrialization and Africa; studies in policy alternatives to structural adjustment*, New York: St Martin's Press.

— (1995b) 'Policy alternatives to structural adjustment in Africa: an introduction', in Howard Stein (ed.) *Asian industrialization and Africa; studies in policy alternatives to structural adjustment*, New York: St Martin's Press, pp. 1–30.

— (2008) *Beyond the World Bank Agenda; an institutional approach to development*, Chicago, IL: University of Chicago Press.

Stiglitz, Joseph (2005) 'Finance for development', in Melvin Ayogu and Don Ross (eds), *Development Dilemmas; the methods and political ethics of growth policy*, Abingdon: Routledge, pp. 15–29.

Stiglitz, Joseph E., José Antonio Ocampo, Shari Spiegel, Ricardo Ffrench-Davis and Deepak Nayyar (2006) *Stability with Growth; macroeconomics, liberalization, and development*, Oxford: Oxford University Press.

Stubbs, Richard (2005) *Rethinking Asia's Economic Miracle*, Basingstoke: Palgrave Macmillan.

Suberu, Rotimi T. (2008) 'The Supreme Court and federalism in Nigeria', *Journal of Modern African Studies*, 46(3): 451–85.

— (2009) 'Federalism in Africa: the Nigerian experience in comparative perspective', *Ethnopolitics*, 18(1): 67–86.

Sugema, Iman and Anis Chowdhury (2007) 'Has aid made the government of Indonesia lazy?', *Asia-Pacific Development Journal*, 14(1): 105–24.

Sumitro Djojohadikusumo (1986) 'Recollections of my career', *Bulletin of Indonesian Economic Studies*, 22(3): 27–39.

Sutton, Keith (1989) 'Malaysia's FELDA land settlement model in time and space', *Geoforum*, 20(3): 339–54.

Suwannathat-Pian, Kobkua (1995) *Thailand's Durable Premier; Phibun through three decades, 1932–1957*, Kuala Lumpur: Oxford University Press.

Swamy, Gurushri (1994) 'Kenya; structural adjustment in the 1980s', Policy Research Working Paper 1238, Washington, DC: World Bank.

Swynnerton, R. J. M. (1954) *A Plan to Intensify the Development of African Agriculture in Kenya*, Nairobi: Colony and Protectorate of Kenya.

Tanzanian Economic Trends (1991) 'Trends and cycles in Gross Domestic Product in Tanzania', *Tanzanian Economic Trends; a Quarterly Review of the Economy*, 4(1): 46–87.

Thee Kian Wie (2001) 'In memoriam: Professor Sumitro Djojohadikusumo, 1917–2001', *Bulletin of Indonesian Economic Studies*, 37(2): 173–81.

— (2003) 'Introduction', in Thee Kian Wie (ed.), *Recollections; the Indonesian economy, 1950s–1990s*, Canberra: Research School of Pacific and Asian Studies, Australian National University, pp. 2–43.

— (2012) *Indonesia's Economy since Independence*, Singapore: Institute of Southeast Asian Studies.

Therkildsen, Ole (2011) 'Policy making and implementation in agriculture: Tanzania's push for irrigated rice', DIIS Working Paper 2011:26, Copenhagen: Danish Institute for Development Studies.

Third Five-Year Development Plan (1979) *The Third Five-Year Development Plan 1979–1984 (summary)*, Jakarta: Department of Information, Republic of Indonesia.

Third Malaysia Plan (1976) *Third Malaysia Plan 1976–1980*, Kuala Lumpur: Government Press.

Third National Development Plan (1975) *Third National Development Plan 1975–80*, vol. 1, Lagos: Central Planning Office, Federal Ministry of Economic Development.

Thompson, Nicholas and Scott Thompson (2000) *The Baobab and the Mango Tree; lessons about development; African and Asian contrasts*, Bangkok: White Lotus.

Thorbecke, Erik (1998) 'The institutional foundations of macroeconomic stability: Indonesia versus Nigeria', in Yujiro Hayami and Masahiko Aoki (eds), *The Institutional Foundations of East Asian Economic Development: Proceedings of the IEA conference held in Tokyo, Japan*, Basingstoke: Macmillan, pp. 106–39.

Timmer, C. Peter (1993) 'Rural bias in the East and South-east Asian rice economy: Indonesia in comparative perspective', *Journal of Development Studies*, 29(4): 149–76.

— (1997) 'Building efficiency in agricultural marketing: the long-run role of Bulog in the Indonesian food economy', *Journal of International Development*, 9(1): 133–45.

— (2004) 'The road to pro-poor growth: the Indonesian experience in regional perspective', *Bulletin of Indonesian Economic Studies*, 40(2): 177–207.

— (2005) *Operationalizing Pro-poor Growth; country study for the World Bank; Indonesia*, siteresources.worldbank.org/INTPGI/Resources/342674-1115051237044/oppgindonesiaMay2005.pdf.

— (2007) 'How Indonesia connected the poor to rapid economic growth', in Timothy Besley and Louise J. Cord (eds), *Delivering on the Promise of Pro-poor Growth; insights and lessons from country experiences*, Washing-ton, DC: World Bank (with Palgrave Macmillan), pp. 29–57.

Tin Maung Maung Than (2007) *State Dominance in Myanmar; the political economy of industrialization*, Singapore: Institute of Southeast Asian Studies.

Tolbert, Stokes (2007) '"Never, never, never, never, never give up". The economic team never did', in Moh. Arsjad Anwar, Aris Ananta and Ari Kuncoro (eds), *Tributes for Widjojo Nitisastro by Friends from 27 Foreign Countries*, Jakarta: Kompas, pp. 235–41.

Towards a Better Future (1966) *Towards a Better Future for Our People*, Nairobi: Ministry of Economic Planning and Development, Republic of Kenya.

Towse, Adrian, Anne Mills and Viroj Tangcharoensathien (2004) 'Learning from Thailand's health reforms', *British Medical Journal*, 328: 103–5.

Tran Thi Que (1998) *Vietnam's Agriculture; the challenges and achievements*, Singapore: Institute of Southeast Asian Studies.

Transformation Agenda (2011) *The Transformation Agenda 2011–2015; summary of Federal Government's key priority policies, programmes and projects*, Abuja: National Planning Commission, Federal Republic of Nigeria.

UN (United Nations) (2011) *The Millennium Development Goals Report 2011*, New York: United Nations.

UN Economic Commission for Africa (2011) *Economic Report on Africa 2011; governing development in Africa – the role of the state in economic transformation*, Addis Ababa: UN Economic Commission for Africa.

— (2014) *Economic Report on Africa 2014; dynamic industrial policy in Africa*, Addis Ababa: UN Economic Commission for Africa.

Un Leang (2012) 'A comparative study of education and development in post-conflict Cambodia and Uganda', PhD thesis, University of Amsterdam.

Unger, Danny (1998) *Building Social Capital in Thailand; fibres, finance and infrastructure*, Cambridge: Cambridge University Press.

UNHSP (2005) *Toward the Poverty Eradication Goal; the structure and infrastructure of the microfinance and microcredit industry in eastern Africa*, Nairobi: United Nations Human Settlements Programme.

Van Arkadie, Brian and Do Duc Dinh (2004) 'Economic reform in Tanzania and Vietnam: a comparative commentary', Working Paper 706, Ann Arbor, MI: William Davidson Institute.

Van de Walle, Nicolas (2001) *African Economies and the Politics of Permanent Crisis, 1979–1999*, Cambridge: Cambridge University Press.

Van der Eng, Pierre (1996) *Agricultural Growth in Indonesia; productivity change and policy impact since 1880*, Basingstoke: Macmillan.

— (2002) 'Indonesia's growth performance in the twentieth century', in Angus Maddison, D. S. Prasada Rao and William F. Shepherd (eds), *The Asian Economies in the Twentieth Century*, Cheltenham: Edward Elgar, pp. 143–79.

Van der Veen, Roel (2004) *What Went Wrong with Africa; a contemporary history*, Amsterdam: KIT Publishers.

— (2010) *Waarom Azië rijk en machtig wordt*, Amsterdam: KIT Publishers.

Van Dijk, Meine Pieter (ed.) (2009) *The New Presence of China in Africa*, Amsterdam: Amsterdam University Press.

Van Donge, Jan Kees (2012) 'Governance and access to finance for development: an explanation of divergent development trajectories in Kenya and Malaysia', *Commonwealth and Comparative Politics*, 50(1): 53–74.

Van Donge, Jan Kees, David Henley and Peter Lewis (2012) 'Tracking development in Southeast Asia and Sub-Saharan Africa: the primacy of policy', *Development Policy Review*, 30(S1): 5–24.

Van Gorkom, L. H. J. B. (2007) 'An example for North and South', in Moh. Arsjad Anwar, Aris Ananta and Ari Kuncoro (eds), *Tributes for Widjojo Nitisastro by Friends from 27 Foreign Countries*, Jakarta: Kompas, pp. 177–84.

Van Luyten, Marcia (2009) 'Hulp geeft je geen zelfrespect' [interview with Paul Kagame], *NRC Weekblad & Wetenschap*, 18–24 July, pp. 6–9.

Vasoo, S. and James Lee (2001) 'Singapore: social development, housing and the Central Provident Fund', *International Journal of Social Welfare*, 10(4): 276–83.

Vatikiotis, Michael R. J. (1993) *Indonesian Politics under Suharto; order, development, and pressure for change*, London: Routledge.

Vincent, Jeffrey R., and Rozali Mohamed Ali (2005) *Managing Natural Wealth; environment and development in Malaysia*, Washington, DC/Singapore: Resources for the Future/Institute of Southeast Asian Studies.

Vlasblom, Dirk (2013) *The Richer Harvest; economic development in Africa and Southeast Asia compared; the 'Tracking Development' study 2006–2011*, Leiden: Afrika Studiecentrum.

Von der Mehden, Fred R. with Al Troner (2007) *Petronas: A national oil company with an international vision*, Houston, TX: James A. Baker III Institute for Public Policy, Rice University.

Von Freyhold, Michaela (1979) *Ujamaa Villages in Tanzania; analysis of a social experiment*, New York: Monthly Review Press.

Von Haugwitz, Hans-Wilhelm and Hermann Thorwart (1972) *Some Experiences with Smallholder Settlement in Kenya 1963/64 to 1966/67*, Afrika-Studien 72, Ifo-Institut für

Wirtschafsforschung München, Munich: Weltforum Verlag.

Wade, Robert (1990) *Governing the Market; economic theory and the role of government in East Asian industrialization*, Princeton, NJ: Princeton University Press.

Wade, Robert and Frank Veneroso (1998) 'The Asian crisis: the high debt model versus the Wall Street–Treasury–IMF complex', *New Left Review*, 228: 1–22.

Wallerstein, Immanuel (1986) *Africa and the Modern World*, Trenton, NJ: Africa World Press.

Wangia, Caleb, Sabina Wangia and Hugo de Groote (2004) 'Review of maize marketing in Kenya: implementation and impact of liberalisation, 1989–1999', in D. K. Friesen and A. F. E. Palmer (eds), *Integrated Approaches to Higher Maize Productivity in the New Millennium; proceedings of the 7th Eastern and Southern Africa Regional Maize Conference, Nairobi, Kenya, 11–15 February 2002*, Mexico City: International Maize and Wheat Improvement Center (CIMMYT), pp. 10–20.

Warr, Peter G. (1993) 'The Thai economy', in Peter G. Warr (ed.), *The Thai Economy in Transition*, Cambridge: Cambridge University Press, pp. 1–80.

— (2005) 'Industrialization, trade policy and poverty reduction: evidence from Asia', in Sisira Jayasuriya (ed.), *Trade Theory, Analytical Models and Development; essays in honour of Peter Lloyd*, vol. 2, Cheltenham: Edward Elgar, pp. 239–58.

Wasserman, Gary (1973) 'Continuity and counter-insurgency: the role of land reform in decolonizing Kenya, 1962–70', *Canadian Journal of African Studies*, 7(1): 133–48.

Watkins, Kevin (1998) *Economic Growth with Equity; lessons from East Asia*, Oxford: Oxfam Publications.

Weber, Max (1951 [1915]) *The Religion of China; Confucianism and Taoism*, trans. Hans H. Gerth, Glencoe, NY: Free Press.

Wedeman, Andrew (2002) 'Development and corruption: the East Asian paradox', in Edmund Terence Gomez (ed.), *Political Business in East Asia*, London: Routledge, pp. 34–61.

Widjojo Nitisastro (1960) 'The relevance of growth models for less developed economies', *Ekonomi dan Keuangan Indonesia*, 8(11/12): 499–513.

— (1970) *Population Trends in Indonesia*, Ithaca, NY: Cornell University Press.

— (1995) 'Reduction of poverty: the Indonesian experience', in James M. Boughton and K. Sarwar Lateef (eds), *Fifty Years after Bretton Woods; the future of the IMF and the World Bank; proceedings of a conference held in Madrid, Spain, September 29–30, 1994*, Washington, DC: International Monetary Fund, pp. 176–82.

— (2010) *Pengalaman pembangunan Indonesia; kumpulan tulisan dan uraian*, ed. Emil Salim, Jakarta: Kompas.

— (2011) *The Indonesian Development Experience; a collection of writings and speeches of Widjojo Nitisastro*, ed. Emil Salim, Singapore: ISEAS Publishing.

Williams, Gavin (1985) 'Marketing without and with marketing boards: the origins of state marketing boards in Nigeria', *Review of African Political Economy*, 12(34): 4–15.

Wing Thye Woo (1988) 'Devaluation and domestic politics in developing countries: Indonesia in 1978', *Journal of Public Policy*, 8(3/4): 335–52.

Wolf, Diane Lauren (1992) *Factory Daughters; gender, household dynamics, and rural industrialization in Java*, Berkeley: University of California Press.

Wolff, Peter (1999) *Vietnam; the incomplete transformation*, German Development Institute Book Series, 12, London: Frank Cass.

Wong, Diana (1987) *Peasants in the Making; Malaysia's Green Revolution*,

Singapore: Institute of Southeast
Asian Studies.

Wood, Adrian and Jörg Mayer (2001)
'Africa's export structure in comparative perspective', *Cambridge Journal
of Economics*, 25(3): 369–94.

World Bank (1975) *Malaysia; Loan 434-
MA: Muda Irrigation Project; Comple-
tion report; June 15, 1975*, Washington,
DC: World Bank.

— (1989) *Africa from Crisis to Sustainable
Growth*, Washington, DC: World Bank.

— (1993) *The East Asian Miracle;
economic growth and public policy*,
Oxford: Oxford University Press.

— (2005) *World Development Report
2006; equity and development*,
Oxford: Oxford University Press.

— (2007) *World Development Report
2008; agriculture for development*,
Washington, DC: World Bank.

— (2010) *Africa Development Indicators
2010; silent and lethal – how quiet corruption undermines Africa's development efforts*, Washington, DC: World
Bank.

World Currency Yearbook (1984–93)
*World Currency Yearbook*, Brooklyn,
NY: International Currency Analysis,
Inc.

Wyatt, David K. (2003) *Thailand; a short
history*, 2nd edn, New Haven, CT:
Yale University Press.

Yaïche, Hichem Ben (2011) 'The
Malaysian experience', *New African*
(London), April, pp. 24–6.

You, Lingzhi, Claudia Ringler, Gerald
Nelson, Ulrike Wood-Sichra, Richard
Robertson, Stanley Wood, Zhe Guo,
Tingju Zhu and Yan Sun (2010) 'What
is the irrigation potential for Africa?
A combined biophysical and socio-
economic approach', IFPRI Discussion
Paper 00993, Washington, DC:
International Food Policy Research
Institute.

Young, Kenneth B., Eric J. Wailes, Gail L.
Cramer and Nguyen Tri Khiem (2002)
*Vietnam's Rice Economy: Develop-
ments and prospects*, Research Report
968, Fayetteville, AR: Arkansas
Agricultural Experiment Station.

# INDEX